Additional Praise for <u>Clients for Life</u>

"In a world defined by electronic interfaces—where relationships are often reduced to the click of a mouse—honest face-to-face advice, counsel, and guidance are more crucial than ever to help one navigate the seas of change. For those professionals wanting to make the leap from simple vendor to trusted adviser, Sheth and Sobel provide a necessary guide. It's mandatory reading for management consultants, financial advisers, public relations pros—for any professional who wants to make it successfully in today's advice industry."

> —**Ray Smith,** *former Chairman and CEO, Bell Atlantic*

"This book has moved the discussion of the value of professional advisers up to a new level. It is alive with cases, wisdom, and excellent advice." **—Sir Brian Pitman,** *Chairman, Lloyds TSB Group*

"The ideas in this book represent the best thinking I have ever seen on how professionals can make the transition to a consultative, analytical sales approach and develop long-term client relationships. It goes far beyond effectiveness with clients, perfectly describing the attributes of mentorship required to develop new leaders—and for this alone it is worth reading. It will be an important book for all of Lanier's worldwide representatives."

> —**Wesley E. Cantrell,** *Chairman and CEO, Lanier Worldwide*

"I didn't just read *Clients for Life*—I devoured it! Sheth and Sobel have produced a beautiful jewel. A step-by-step guide on how to serve a client effectively, this book is power-packed with information I can put to immediate use. It's replete with actual life stories, anecdotes that make the case, and quotations that are relevant and penetrating. It's profound, wonderfully readable, and just plain fun. I'm going to get a copy for every one of the consultants in my firm."

> —**Jerold Panas,** *Executive Partner, Jerold Panas, Linzy and Partners, and author of* Finders Keepers and Boardroom Verities

"Distilling the immeasurable concept of a 'good adviser' into a book which is both instructive and readable is a task thought beyond even as talented a duo as Sheth and Sobel. They have succeeded brilliantly and enjoyably, and many—especially those whose profession the book examines so perceptively—will benefit from reading *Clients for Life*."

—**Sir Win Bischoff,** *Chairman, Schroders plc*

"In our new economy, enduring client relationships are more important than ever. Sheth and Sobel have masterfully articulated the personal and intellectual qualities that professionals must develop in order to cultivate these broad-based, high-impact relationships. Rich with examples, useful ideas, and fresh thinking, *Clients for Life* is an insightful, pioneering book that should be read by anyone whose livelihood depends on effectiveness with clients."

—**James Kelly,** *founder of the MAC Group, former Chairman of Gemini Consulting, and coauthor of* Transforming the Organization

"The successful services-based company is client-centered and able to develop long-lasting client relationships characterized by richness, intimacy, and breadth. *Clients for Life* sets out a clear path to achieve all of this. Sheth and Sobel provide significant strategies for nurturing customer transactions into enduring, value-added relationships. Full of wisdom, practical ideas, and vivid examples that bring it all down to earth, it's both thought-provoking and enjoyable to read."

—**Carlos Palomares,** *Chairman, Citibank International*

"In the age of Web speed, Sheth and Sobel have highlighted something timeless—relationships based on integrity, insight, and genuine added value. They've written a unique guide to thriving in the new economy." —**Jim Robbins,** *President and CEO, Cox Communications*

CLIENTS
FOR
LIFE

*Evolving from an Expert for Hire
to an Extraordinary Advisor*

JAGDISH SHETH
and
ANDREW SOBEL

A FIRESIDE BOOK
PUBLISHED BY SIMON & SCHUSTER
NEW YORK   LONDON   TORONTO   SYDNEY

FIRESEIDE
Rockefeller Center
1230 Avenue of the Americas
New York, NY 10020

First Fireside Edition 2002
FIRESIDE and colophon are
registered trademarks of Simon & Schuster, Inc.
For information about special discounts for bulk purchases,
please contact Simon & Schuster Special Sales:
1-800-456-6798 or business@simonandschuster.com
Designed by Edith Fowler
Manufactured in the United States of America

20 19 18 17 16 15 14 13

The Library of Congress has cataloged
the Simon & Schuster edition as follows:

Sheth, Jagdish N.
    Clients for life : how great professionals develop
breakthrough relationships / Jagdish Sheth and
Andrew Sobel.
       p.   cm.
    1. Business consultants.   I. Sobel, Andrew
II. Title.

HD69.C6 S525   2000
001'.068—dc21   00-033906

ISBN 0-684-87029-0
       0-684-87030-4 (Pbk)

CLIENTS
FOR
LIFE

To my wife, Madhu Sheth, who has been a great adviser to me.

JAGDISH SHETH

To Mary Jane, Christopher, Elizabeth, and Emma: you taught me the importance of unconditional love. To my parents, Raymond Sobel and Alma Watson Sobel: you gave me a passion for learning.

ANDREW SOBEL

CONTENTS

INTRODUCTION

WE WOULD ALL LIKE to have loyal clients who come back to us year after year. Clients who treat us as valued professionals and seek our advice on their most important issues and problems. Clients who don't shop around each time they think about buying our services, who come back because they will always get fresh perspectives, insights, and ideas from us and because they trust us. Clients who will enthusiastically recommend us to others even if we aren't serving them at that moment.

Reflect for a moment on your own client relationships. If you're like most professionals, you may have a few loyal clients, such as the ones we've just described, who have drawn you into their inner circle of advisers. They consult you on a broad range of issues and wouldn't dream of using a competitor to provide your service.

Others, though, are just buying your expertise—they use you because you have specific knowledge and skills that you deliver at a competitive price. The next time around, however, these same clients may very well turn to someone else. They view you as a commodity.

Somewhere in the middle are those bread-and-butter clients who keep asking you back, year after year, but never seem to let you get very close to them. You may have worked for them for years, but your influence and the scope of your work is limited; and although they feel *some* loyalty to you, it's not enough to prevent them from switching to someone else if they see a major economic benefit.

Do you wish you had more clients who would draw you

into their inner circle? Do you sometimes feel you're treated like a vendor instead of a respected professional? Would you like to compete less on price and more on the *value* you can add? Is it getting harder to differentiate yourself from other professionals in your field, be they other management consultants, lawyers, or accountants?

If you answered yes to some or all of these questions, we wouldn't be surprised. The fact is, most professionals are on a journey—defined by the role they play with their clients—and few have finished it. When it begins, you're an expert for hire who offers information and expertise to your clients on a transaction basis. Further along, you may earn the right to be a steady supplier, and you'll be asked back repeatedly. When you've reached the final and most rewarding stage, you'll become a trusted adviser who consistently develops collaborative relationships with your clients and provides insight rather than just information. At this stage you will have *breakthrough* relationships. Because of the broad, influential role that you play and the unusual degree of trust that you develop, these relationships will be of a significantly higher order than the run-of-the-mill associations that so many professionals have with their clients.

This developmental journey—from expert for hire to trusted adviser—is the focus of *Clients for Life*. From extensive research, we have developed a client-validated model for success—a roadmap of the specific characteristics that underlie extraordinary performance with clients—that will help you establish and sustain more of these enduring, advisory relationships.

FORGET CONVENTIONAL WISDOM

The abiding client relationships we're talking about not only bring us immense personal and professional satisfaction, but in fact they make our careers. Unfortunately, the conventional wisdom about how to develop them and achieve professional success is woefully inadequate. "Do good work, act with integrity, and the rest will follow" has been the time-honored prescription for individuals who sell and deliver services. "Find an area to specialize in, focus on it, and make your name there" could be added to the nostrum.

Clients today are highly sophisticated, educated, and informed buyers who select professionals from increasingly competitive and mature service industries. In a world of continual corporate cost-cutting and almost unlimited information, institutional buyers have less loyalty to suppliers than ever before. Studies have shown, for example, that over 50 percent of executives who switch providers say they were "satisfied" with them before switching.[1] And though specialization is important to a point, the corporate leaders we have interviewed say that most of the highly specialized professionals they deal with are incapable of advising them on broader business issues. You have to do far more, in other words, than "satisfy" your clients and do a "good job" if you want to create long-term loyalty and enter into the collaborative relationships that allow you to have a major impact on your clients and their decisions.

WHY DO SOME PROFESSIONALS COMMAND ENDURING CLIENT LOYALTY?

The genesis of this book lay in a simple observation: the telephones of some professionals we knew never stopped ringing—clients called them, rather than vice versa. At the same time, we saw others treated like vendors by their clients: these professionals were constantly challenged on price, and they often struggled to get new business through laborious RFPs (requests for proposal) that eliminate practically all human contact during the client's decision-making process.

Was the difference just that the former worked harder, were smarter, and did higher-quality work? These were the obvious reasons, and while certainly relevant, they did not provide anything near a satisfactory explanation for the intense client loyalty we observed. After all, we also knew many smart, hard-working professionals who were *not* able to develop so many loyal clients. Clearly, these qualities were necessary but not sufficient.

We set out, then, to comprehensively research and answer a series of fundamental questions: Why do some professionals manage to develop long-term relationships and become trusted business advisers to their clients while others get called in on a one-off basis like commodities? What qualities do leaders look for in the professionals—in fields as diverse as law, consulting, finance, and technology—whom they bring into their inner circle? How do clients define value?

Our starting point was our own fifty years of combined experience in advising senior managers in many organizations around the world. We went well beyond our own personal experience, however, and spoke at length with the present and past leaders of dozens of major corporations, such as Kodak, BellSouth, Cox Communications, Motorola, American Express, Citibank, Eli Lilly, and General Electric, listening as these chief executives shared their *lifetimes* of experience in buying services and seeking advice from professionals. These interviews were eye-opening, and they debunked many of the widely held notions about why clients value certain professionals over others. We were struck by the dissatisfaction many clients expressed about the outside professionals they engaged and by the difficulty they experienced in finding truly objective individuals to help them resolve their most important issues.

We then extensively interviewed a number of well-known advisers who counsel and consult to leading executives and politicians, as well as many less-known but high-performing professionals who face the same day-to-day challenges that we all do in trying to build client relationships. We studied some of the greatest advisers in history, such as Aristotle, Thomas More, J. P. Morgan, George Marshall, David Ogilvy, and Henry Kissinger, individuals you'll meet later on in the book.

The result is that we have identified the *essence* of what it takes to become an extraordinary professional and consistently provide value to clients. In the pages that follow, we illustrate, step-by-step, how you can develop the attributes and attitudes that will enable you to develop your own breakthrough client relationships.

Our title, *Clients for Life*, has several distinct meanings. The first is literal: this book is about how to develop lifetime clients—or at least long-term ones—when such a relationship is mutually beneficial for the client and the professional.

Second, the title is figurative because in some cases a continual relationship may not be practical, realistic, or even desired. A client, for example, may need the ongoing services of an accountant every year for many years, whereas he might call in a management consultant or executive recruiter only once every four or five years. A few professionals may also choose a transactional model of serving clients, where they work on specific issues rather than on a retainer basis (the law firm Wachtell, Lipton, Rosen & Katz, for example, successfully adopted this approach in the early 1970s). Even a transactional strategy, however, will succeed or fail based on having repeat clients.

Clients, thus, can be *attitudinally* loyal for life—they remember us for having done an outstanding job, they call us back if they ever need our particular service again, and they enthusiastically recommend us to others.

CLIENTS FOR LIFE: WHO CAN BENEFIT?

This book is intended for professionals who serve clients. We define a *professional* as someone who practices an occupation requiring a high degree of education and training, and who has clients rather than customers. This definition includes not just service professionals, but also technology consultants and sales executives who sell a complex product. It does not include teachers or musicians, for example, because they don't have individual or organizational clients the way consultants and accountants do, although this is not to say these and other types of professionals can't profit from reading our book.

The professionals we have studied and use as exemplars are drawn from a variety of fields, including consulting, law, accounting, advertising, finance, medicine, sales, and the military. Although each profession has specific skills and knowledge that its practitioners must master—consumer behavior for an advertiser, financial reporting requirements if you're an accountant, contract law if you're a lawyer, and so on—we have found that achieving client leadership is premised on a set of common factors that *transcend* individual professional requirements.

All types of professionals—and their clients—can benefit from long-term relationships. These relationships give you the opportunity to engage in extensive client learning, which greatly increases your ability to offer tailored solutions, develop new ideas, and provide germane insights rather than generic platitudes. They are also the proving grounds where you can expand your service offering and therefore your professional experience—a loyal client who trusts you will try you out in areas that a new client wouldn't let you touch. Finally, the positive financial impact of having even just a few lifelong advisory relationships, if they are managed profitably, can be enormous.

The distinction between a client and a customer is more than semantic. Customers, for example, buy a product or service with well-defined characteristics that match their needs, with little or no negotiation and discussion between buyer and seller; the professional's relationship with a client, in contrast, has a consultative aspect to it—there is give-and-take to clarify needs, identify problems, and recommend solutions. While there doesn't have to be a personal relationship between a customer and the seller of the product or service, with a client there is typically a close, personal relationship with a high degree of trust. And finally, a professional offers a client an authoritative body of knowledge and expertise. So while the customer can have it his way at Burger King, a client taking tax advice *can't* always have it his way (unless he wants to get into trouble with the IRS).

Our focus on clients, therefore, is a deliberate one. If you have customers, your relationships will tend to be narrow in scope, whereas if you serve clients, you have the opportunity to develop the collaborative, broad-gauge relationships that are the focal point of this book.

Although there has been much research and writing on the subject of customer loyalty and retention, a different approach is required for sophisticated clients who buy complex products and services. For example, although we may believe that the customer is always right—a standard prescription for managing customers—we sometimes have to tell our clients how they are wrong and why we disagree with them.

WHAT KIND OF PROFESSIONAL ARE YOU?

There are three types of professionals who will especially benefit from this book. The first group includes service professionals—lawyers, management and technology consultants, accountants, corporate bankers, financial advisers, executive recruiters, advertising executives, and so on. These individuals are in an ideal position to become broad-based business advisers to their clients: their services are of high strategic importance to their clients, and they are intimately involved in the sale and delivery of the service. If you are one of these professionals, all of the material in this book should speak directly to you.

The second group consists of sales executives who want to be considered *business consultants* rather than simply salespeople. If you sell a complex product or service that is critical to your client's business, such as telecommunications systems, computer equipment, power plants, or mission-critical software, your client will have a significant need for advice and consultation, and the opportunity exists for you to become an *adviser* to him rather than just a salesperson. By applying the concepts in this book, you can truly distinguish yourself in the sales world.

Finally, professionals who are staff or functional managers within corporations can also profit from the concepts in this book. Human resources or finance specialists who report to line executives, for example, face the same challenges that outside professionals do in creating value, and they are held back by similar barriers. The frameworks in chapters 3 through 6 in particular, covering topics such as becoming a deep generalist and cultivating big-picture thinking skills, will help you to think and act less like an employee and more like a client-focused, independent professional who continually builds personal intellectual capital.

In chapter 1 we look at some extraordinary professionals who have consistently engaged clients for life, identify how they add value, and discuss the barriers that prevent other professionals from achieving the same level of success. Chapters 2 through 8 describe the seven core attributes of great client advisers—the ingredients for success with clients—and provide specific suggestions for how you can cultivate these qualities. Chapter 9 outlines the major pitfalls that professionals can fall into as they develop and manage client relationships, and it describes some particular types of clients that need to be either avoided or carefully managed. Chapter 10, "The Soul of the Great Professional," captures the intangible but fundamental outlooks characteristic of great professionals and illustrates the importance of seizing *breakthrough* opportunities in your client relationships.

Throughout the chapters, we have used famous historical advisers as well as highly accomplished contemporary professionals to illustrate the journey from *expert for hire* to *trusted adviser.* By the end of this book, you should have a firmer understanding of what made each successful, and how you can develop more of your own enduring advisory relationships.

ONE

WHAT CLIENTS WANT
From Knowledge Worker to Wisdom Worker

The great professional helps you eliminate issues that are not a problem, and then he focuses you in on the really critical dimensions of the situation. You are permitted to be a bit confused and general. And at the right moment, the good ones ask the right questions. It's an iterative process; you don't want someone peddling a solution, who comes with an agenda—which many do. The good adviser excels at the integration process, but he doesn't necessarily arrive at the solution for you. He knows my industry, but is broader than that. Finally, he can bring you comfort as well. Empathy, not sympathy.

RAY SMITH, *former chairman and CEO, Bell Atlantic*

IN JANUARY OF 1941, President Franklin D. Roosevelt invited Wendell Willkie, who had lost his own bid for the presidency the year before, to visit him at the White House. Sitting in front of the fireplace in the Oval Office, Willkie steered the topic of conversation to Harry Hopkins, who was Roosevelt's most trusted adviser. Hopkins had been instrumental in helping Roosevelt clarify and achieve his objectives as president, undertaking sensitive diplomatic missions to meet Churchill and Stalin and providing sage counsel during times of crisis. Self-effacing, incorruptible, and enormously capable, Hopkins nonetheless drew fierce criticism because of his intimate relationship with Roosevelt. "Why," asked 21

Willkie, "do you keep Hopkins so close to you? You surely must realize that people distrust him and resent his influence."

Roosevelt stared directly at Willkie and replied, "Someday you may well be sitting here where I am now as president of the United States. And when you are, you'll be looking at that door over there and knowing that practically everybody who walks through it wants something out of you. You'll learn what a lonely job this is and discover the need for somebody like Harry Hopkins who asks for nothing except to serve you." [1]

The extraordinary advisers among today's professionals—those individuals who develop *breakthrough* client relationships—share many characteristics with Harry Hopkins, and they are as valued by their clients as Hopkins was by Roosevelt. Let's begin by looking at two in particular, James Kelly and Nancy Peretsman.

James Kelly: The Ultimate Corporate Troubleshooter

Management consultant James Kelly always seems to work a bit of magic with his top management clients. Having founded and led a major international consulting firm, Kelly now advises a small group of senior executives on issues ranging from corporate strategy to leadership and organization design, frequently shuttling between Europe and the United States. He combines deep expertise about corporate strategy development with a remarkable breadth of knowledge of other functional areas, such as finance, marketing, and operations, and then layers in empathetic listening, well-developed powers of intellectual synthesis, and keen judgment.

Win Bischoff, chief executive of the leading British merchant bank Schroders, has used Kelly as his adviser for eighteen years. As an investment banker and a company CEO, Bischoff is himself a master of the advice business, and a very discerning client. Talking about Kelly, he says, "What sets him apart is his genuine, deeply felt conviction; his bedside manner—important here in Europe—which is relaxed and non-threatening; his empathy and listening skills; and the fact that he's able to see the big picture very clearly. Sometimes he offers specific ideas or solutions, but on other occasions he helps us arrive at them ourselves." Bischoff's praise is not surprising: over the years Kelly has pushed Schroders in some controversial directions—encouraging it to stay out of the equity brokerage business in the United Kingdom, for example—that turned out to be dead right for this highly successful merchant bank.

Sir Brian Pitman, chairman of Lloyds TSB Group and another client of Kelly's, echoes Bischoff's praise: "Back in the mid-1980s, Kelly and his team confronted us with an insight that proved catalytic—that our cost of equity was higher than we thought, and we weren't earning it. This was well before 'shareholder value' became a buzzword or 'economic value added' was in vogue. He helped set us on a path to maximize shareholder value, and our market capitalization today places Lloyds TSB among the top five banks in the world."

Kelly hasn't always inhabited the heights of the boardroom, however. He vividly recalls selling accounting systems door-to-door in Harvard Square in the early 1960s, during his first few years working as a consultant for Dick Vancil, the head of Harvard Business School's accounting department. Some formative and humbling experiences—for example, starting a European business from scratch—helped him to evolve from a business *expert* to a business *adviser* by developing his empathy, knowledge breadth, and judgment skills.

Nancy Peretsman: A Relationship Banker Conquers the Internet

It's no accident that Nancy Peretsman, an investment banker who heads the media group for Allen & Company, was the financial adviser on $77 billion in mostly Internet-related deals during the first half of 1999 alone. In an industry where client loyalties can shift frequently and unpredictably, Peretsman commands an exceptionally loyal client base that she has developed during her twenty-year career.

A large part of her success is her ability to see the big picture. While other bankers are driving headlong into the next deal without pause, she takes time to reflect on the long-term direction of the media industry and the opportunities that may present themselves. "I operate in a somewhat old-fashioned way with my clients," Peretsman tells us. "I try to give them a world view about what's happening in and around their industries, and of the role that they might play."

Despite being a star in a galaxy known for big egos, and having been recently named one of the ten most powerful women in American business, Peretsman is remarkably down-to-earth. Instead of exercising her hard-earned right to lord over teams of associates working twenty-hour days, she still routinely rolls up her sleeves and dives into the day-to-day work of merger transactions. As we'll see later on, this has some unusual benefits for her clients.

While working in the United Kingdom on the financing of new cable companies in the late 1980s, Peretsman saw how they were planning to combine video and telephone services and thought this idea would make sense in the United States. Most of the early deals involving cable and telephone companies that she tried to market in this country failed, however, because the idea was just a bit ahead of its time (not anymore—AT&T spent over $100 billion in 1999 to buy cable companies); but her clients have remembered her prescience at this and other moments, such as when she put her own money on the line to help finance Priceline.com, the now highly valued Internet company that lets you name your own price for airline tickets and hotels. Priceline's founder and chairman Jay Walker has said that "Nancy is the confidante of about twenty moguls . . . she is the last generation of investment bankers whose power is their long-term relationships."[2]

James Kelly and Nancy Peretsman work in different fields, but each of them is an extraordinary adviser to clients, and each commands enormous client loyalty. They didn't start out their careers as great advisers; in fact, both of them can cite early difficulties in learning how to develop the long-term, broad-based relationships that they both now enjoy. But they learned from their experiences, and they developed and grew. In addition to their special areas of expertise, they've developed strong powers of synthesis and keen judgment. Like the other great client advisers we'll meet in this book, they are insatiable learners. They know how to listen. They balance selflessness with objectivity and independence. They have deeply felt convictions born of a well-developed value system. And they are able to build trust through their impeccable integrity and discretion. The result? Clients come back to them again and again.

PROFESSIONAL SERVICES AND ADVICE: A $500 BILLION INDUSTRY

Behind every great leader—in fact, behind most successful individuals—you'll probably find at least one great adviser. Alexander the Great's tutor and counselor was Aristotle, ancient Greece's famed philosopher and scientist. France's King Louis XIII chose as his chief adviser Cardinal Richelieu, who became the architect of modern state government; and President Franklin D. Roosevelt had the services of the trustworthy Harry Hopkins as well as the great General George Marshall. References to famous advisers in history and literature are contained in words like "éminence grise," "mentor," and "Machiavellian"[3] which are now fixtures in our modern vocabulary.

Today, a group of over five million service professionals in a variety of fields, such as management consulting, law, banking, advertising, finance, and accounting, have largely replaced the clergymen and philosophers who once advised society's leaders. Collectively, these professionals comprise what is in fact one of the largest industries in the world with over $500 billion in annual revenue.[4] If we include all professionals who develop client relationships, such as salespeople, the total number of individuals who manage and advise clients in the United States is close to 15 million.

Virtually all of the large service firms endeavor to develop advisory or consultative relationships with their clients, emulating those very few—McKinsey in consulting, for example, or Goldman Sachs in investment banking—that have a history and culture of building deep relationships. Stockbrokers are now "financial advisers"; accounting and consulting firms aspire to advise senior management, not just undertake reengineering projects; software programmers are referred to as "consultants"; and companies like Reuters don't just sell databases but want to be your "information adviser." Often, however, the words "adviser" and "consultant" lack substance and have a hollow ring to them.

Ironically, just at a time when the professions are experiencing their greatest growth in history, just as so many are striving to become trusted advisers, many clients are in fact *dissatisfied* with the quality of the advice they receive and the attitude of those who give it. It's getting harder and harder for them to find professionals like James Kelly and Nancy Peretsman.

But why? What holds professionals back from an undeniably attractive role that is highly valued by clients?

BARRIERS TO DEVELOPING
BREAKTHROUGH RELATIONSHIPS

Three barriers stand in the way of becoming a business adviser to your clients, and of experiencing the client loyalty and professional fulfillment that accompany this role:

1. *Most professional service firms demand specialization.* If you work for a large consulting or accounting firm, you might become a reengineering expert for the chemical industry or an auditor for automotive companies. This is fine for starters, but the problem is that the more expert

you become in the niche where your company has placed you, the more "valuable"—at least in the short term—your firm thinks you are. This becomes a disincentive to providing you with other experiences.

While there is great benefit in developing a deep expertise, this specialization will eventually become a liability if you want to play a broader-gauge role with clients. Some firms recognize this issue and try to address it by systematically diversifying the experience of their junior staff, but many do not. (This push for specialization, by the way, is pervasive not just in the business world but in medicine, academia, science, and other fields.) In addition, while large firms provide tremendous opportunities and training for young professionals, they also have financial and growth goals that must be met (many are now publicly held companies). Sometimes, these short-term pressures override the long-term process necessary to build deep, trusted client relationships.

2. *Expertise is becoming automated and reduced to a commodity.* Ironically, while service professionals have been major beneficiaries of the late twentieth-century information economy, there are now signs that many types of expertise are losing value. Just as the industrial revolution replaced skilled craftsmen with low-wage factory workers during the early nineteenth century, the "expertise" sold by professionals is becoming easily replicable, more widely available, and increasingly cheaper in our Internet-speed, technology-driven economy. Already, the average incomes of some classes of professionals—doctors, for example—are starting to decline.[5]

Several forces combine to diminish the value of expertise:

- *The supply of service professionals is growing significantly.* The historically rigid controls on the supply of graduates have been relaxed, and many individuals with lesser certifications (e.g., paralegals, physicians' assis-

tants) are doing the work formerly entrusted to de-
greed professionals such as lawyers or doctors.

- *Price-based competition has become a permanent feature of
  the market for professional services.* In the corporate
  world, most major contracts for professional services
  are now competitively bid, and the competition (for
  management consulting and advertising services, for
  example) can be ferocious.
- *The Internet and expert software now provide unparalleled access to all kinds of expertise, at far lower prices than ever before.*
  Market research reports that used to cost thousands of
  dollars or that investment banks provided only to their
  big-spending corporate clients can now be obtained
  free over the Internet. Increasingly, professionals are
  paying to have their "expertise" put in front of clients. A
  new Web site for CEOs, which already has the participa-
  tion of big names such as Michael Dell of Dell Computer Corporation, is charging professional firms
  $50,000 for the *privilege* of putting their articles or re-
  search up on the site.

  In other areas, Web-based sales automation is reducing the need for expensive sales forces; and millions of consumers use inexpensive software like
  Turbotax to do their taxes and even write wills, thus
  avoiding tax advisers and lawyers.
- *Labor mobility among knowledge workers is increasing.* U.S.
  firms, for example, are tapping into pools of English-
  speaking talent in countries such as India, South
  Africa, and Australia. Law school graduates are cross-
  ing over into adjacent fields, such as consulting and
  investment banking.

The effects of these trends are readily apparent. In
fields as diverse as law, accounting, consulting, and technology services there is significant consolidation occurring, with new mergers being announced almost
monthly. What used to be the "Big 8" accounting firms
are now the "Big 5." Law firms, which historically en-

joyed long-term retainer relationships with their clients, are being asked to bid competitively for work; some even went out of business altogether in the 1990s, and we are now beginning to see a growth in mergers as law firms consolidate. Consulting firms are being asked by major corporations to submit breakdowns of their cost structure, their partner-to-associate ratios, and their billing schedules so that the profitability of their projects can be managed and reduced. Many companies are now conducting frequent, tough reviews of their advertising agencies, forcing incumbents to continually justify their relationship.

These and other signs of intense competition and industry maturation are now widespread. High-end services, such as merger and acquisition advisory work, may never become commodities. But just as we can now put a vacation out to bid on the Internet to see which airline wants to sell us a ticket at the best price, we believe the day is not far away when this will be done for *services* as well. Imagine asking doctors to "bid" to conduct a routine surgical procedure or inviting lawyers to compete for your estate planning business.

3. *Many professionals are held back by stereotypes about what clients want them to be and how they should behave.* Here are typical statements we have heard from these professionals:

- "My job is to provide answers."
- "I need to become as expert as possible in one specific subject area within my field and then to make my name in it."
- "When I meet prospective clients, I need to demonstrate my expertise. After all, that's what they're buying from me."
- "If I work in a new industry or function, I will be ignorant of basic concepts. I will add little value, and clients will reject me."

- "This is a professional, business relationship. The personal side is separate. Furthermore, my loyalty is to the greater goals of the institution, not to the individual."
- "Clients will take advantage of you. You have to stick up for your own interests."

There is *some* validity to all these statements. They are incomplete, however. In contrast, consider these comments from clients who have spent a lifetime using professionals:

- "The really good professionals ask great questions. Often, they enable solutions rather than supply them."
- "The best business advisers have a good understanding of my industry, but also breadth. Some of the best insights I have gotten have come from professionals who bring analogies from other fields."
- "Good professionals are great listeners. They hear what you mean, not necessarily what you say."
- "It's very tough finding 'honest brokers' who are unbiased and not pushing their own agenda with you. Everyone walks in here wanting something."
- "Investment bankers cannot be true advisers. They are too focused on the deals."
- "Our consultants always end the session with a half-hour presentation on 'next steps,' the execution of which cannot, of course, be accomplished without the consultants. What I really value instead are working sessions which advance our thinking."
- "Our lawyers focus on every detail with equal emphasis. That's OK to a point, but they rarely pull back and help us see the big picture."

Many professionals, in short, focus on providing answers, being perceived as "experts," doing great analysis, and specializing more and more during their careers. Clients, in contrast, seek professionals who can ask the right questions, provide knowledge breadth as well as depth, demonstrate big-picture thinking as well as analysis, and listen rather than just tell.

Professor J. Brian Quinn of Dartmouth's Amos Tuck School of Business, who has spent nearly forty years advising business and political leaders, including several U.S. presidents, puts his own slant on the issue of stereotypes: "I used to believe that solving the problem was paramount. In reality, when the good advisers deliver their recommendations, most of them have already been implemented. I realize now that the process of problem solving is more important than the solution."

Clients do value professionals who can play a broad advisory role. Theodore Sorensen, in his book *The Kennedy Legacy,* reports that just a few days before his inauguration, John F. Kennedy was presented with a list of 250 items requiring a decision from him. He apparently blurted out, "Now I know why Ike had Sherman Adams!" (Adams was President Eisenhower's trusted adviser). The fact is, clients at any level, whether they are presidents of nations or corporate managers, appreciate someone who can help them put their issues in perspective, solve problems, and make better, faster decisions.

Experts versus Advisers

Many of the clients we interviewed for this book made pointed references to the distinctions they saw between experts and advisers: "With an adviser, trust is critical. Of course, if you just need an expert, you don't have to trust him" was a typical comment. Our research, in fact, has suggested that experts and advisers are different in many important ways as outlined in the following table.

Professionals who are client advisers, in short, behave very differently than experts, and consequently they develop client relationships that are broader, deeper, and richer. Part

Experts versus Advisers	
Experts	**Advisers**
Have depth	Have depth *and* breadth
Tell	Listen
Provide answers	Ask great questions
Develop professional trust	Develop professional *and* personal trust
Control	Collaborate
Supply expertise	Supply insight
Analyze	Synthesize

of the difference lies in their skill and knowledge base: they are wide-ranging exploratory learners and big-picture thinkers. Part is due to attitude: they collaborate rather than control.

Let's be clear that there is an important distinction between expert and expertise. Both experts and great advisers have deep expertise, which they continually develop throughout their careers. But business advisers build an additional set of skills that leverage their specialized knowledge and enable them to be highly effective with clients.

Eric Silverman, for example, counsels business leaders on legal issues but does it in the context of their total business; he's an expert who has developed into a trusted adviser. With a law degree from Georgetown University, Silverman joined Milbank, Tweed, a large New York law firm, in 1981, taking an interest in a new area for the firm: financing energy projects. He sought out the only partner—indeed the only other lawyer at Milbank—who was doing work in this area. The two of them slowly began building up a business.

At first, he spent several years grinding out the contractual documents necessary to execute these large project financings. But because there were only two of them in the practice, Silverman quickly began to take on client management responsibilities. He actively studied the business issues inherent in these multibillion-dollar, global energy projects. His knowledge base grew well beyond the contractual issues, which is what he and his firm were ostensibly hired for. He became an expert in the companies themselves, in their strategies and their organizational structures, and in the energy markets where they conducted their operations.

Silverman's clients, typically treasurers, chief counsels, or chief financial officers, began to seek him out as a source of broad-based business advice. The other lawyers they dealt with wanted to talk about the barriers, the 200 legal points that had to be reviewed before anything could proceed. Silverman talked about the possibilities and alternatives, not the limitations. "I'm more of a constructive facilitator for these huge projects," he says modestly. "I try to get the parties to work together, to keep the big picture in front of us . . . some of the other attorneys who are involved get very focused on the minutiae." Today, Silverman heads Milbank's Global Project Finance group. With fifteen partners and eighty associates, it contributes one quarter of the firm's total revenues!

Compare Eric Silverman's story with the following statement we heard from a consultant at a leading management consulting firm. Keep in mind that this is a smart, engaging individual who is some eight years into his consulting career:

> I specialize in the pharmaceutical industry. I know exactly how product management should be organized in a drug company. I can go into any drug company, anywhere in the world, and immediately tell them how they should organize product management. It's basically the same everywhere.

This person has in-depth expertise that is invaluable to his firm. He is highly paid. But his career, and his professional and personal satisfaction, will run dry if he continues to dip ever deeper into his current well—product management practices in drug companies—and fails to add breadth to his depth.

Adversity Is Part of the Plan

Although we often feel our careers should proceed from one success to the next, the development of these qualities is actually facilitated by struggles and setbacks. James Kelly survived several devastating experiences that nearly bankrupted his firm, the MAC Group; both Nancy Peretsman and Eric Silverman went through painful, dry patches where they couldn't interest their clients in any of their ideas.

Many of the famous historical advisers we'll examine also struggled. George Marshall, who became one of the towering figures of the twentieth century with the Marshall Plan after World War II, almost had to beg his way into officer training school. During the 1920s he spent many discouraging years in dead-end positions in an underfunded, ignored U.S. Army. Harry Hopkins suffered from a debilitating and ultimately fatal illness, yet as we'll see in chapter 8, he actually drew strength from his misfortune.

Learning from your struggles and taking active control of your own development will put you on the path to becoming an integrated, fulfilled professional who offers far more than just expertise to clients. You can evolve from a knowledge worker, an expert for hire, to a *wisdom worker*, a trusted adviser.

Think back for a moment to the analogy of the craftsman and the factory worker. When craftsmen were reduced to commodities and their work automated during the industrial revolution, it was the artists among them—those individuals whose work transcended mere skill at working iron or wood—who continued to thrive. Similarly, in the twenty-first century the knowledge workers who excel will be those who transcend simple expertise and are able to provide insights to their clients in the context of a collaborative, learning relationship.

INSIGHT × COLLABORATIVE RELATIONSHIP = CLIENT VALUE

How do trusted advisers create value? Value is a complex concept that can mean different things to different clients, depending on their needs at a given point in time. Generally, however, value is created by solving problems, helping your clients achieve business and personal objectives, getting critical work done, and enabling your clients to feel good about themselves as people and professionals as you complete your assignment.

We have found that when leaders talk about great professionals who actually achieve these goals, they emphasize in particular the nature of the insight those professionals can offer and the quality of the relationship they share with them. The journey to becoming a great adviser, in fact, can be tracked and measured along these dimensions. Do you offer expertise and information, or can you deliver real insight? Do you work on the basis of performing tasks or transactions, or are you capable of developing deep, long-lasting, and collaborative relationships? The accompanying illustration sets out these key dimensions and depicts the three stages of client relationships that we described in the Introduction.

Everyone begins his or her career in the lower-left box— as an expert for hire who works on transactions (at the very start, you are not even an expert yet, you offer expertise for hire). Becoming a steady supplier usually happens naturally over time as you develop your client base. The real breakthrough occurs when you move beyond the steady supplier role—many people never do—and become a trusted adviser. At this stage you've put yourself in what we call the "client value zone." The closer you can get to this position, the more personally and professionally rewarding your work will be and the more effective you will become with your clients.

Clients define insight broadly; it doesn't have to be a radical new idea or inspiration. Professionals who are insightful, clients tell us, do some or all of the following things:

Moving into the Client Value Zone

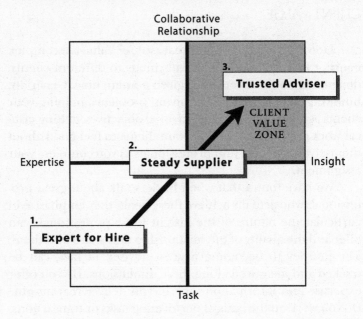

- They add significant new perspectives to the problem or issue at hand.
- They help to focus the discussion on the most critical, relevant issues.
- They provide specific ideas and solutions.
- Sometimes, clients feel their advisers are insightful when, through artful questioning, listening, and discussion, they enable clients to arrive at their own solutions.

Remember that advisers who provide insight also bring to bear some kind of deep expertise, which is still very important in this game. Strong, consistently demonstrated professional competence in your specialty is both the ticket for admission and an ongoing requirement; we don't want to downplay it.

Clients define their relationship with trusted advisers using words like "trust," "shared values," "integrity," "chemistry," and so forth; it's far more than golf and lunch. Fundamentally, a relationship enables you to learn about your client. Through the relationship, you end up knowing more about your client—about his needs, preferences, and habits—than anyone else, and your ability to provide insights rather than just information or generic recommendations increases significantly. This creates a powerful entry barrier for competing professionals who may want your client's business.

Building a relationship takes time. In the words of Jim Robbins, CEO of Cox Communications, "Nobody calls you up on the telephone and says, 'Hey, I'm your adviser.' No way! You have to build trust and establish that there are shared values." Echoing this from the adviser's perspective, the former chairman of an old-line U.K. merchant bank once said, "One of the facets of the art is that if you do not get on with the people you are trying to advise, then you find yourselves out the door."[6]

The collaboration that develops between you and your client also amplifies your own expertise. Rather than just imparting information or knowledge—a one-way street—you collaboratively develop solutions. Your knowledge and experience play off against your client's knowledge and experience in a constructive, creative fashion. Ultimately, the deeper the relationship, the more insight you're able to bring to the table, and this in turn reinforces your value.

THE INGREDIENTS
FOR BREAKTHROUGH RELATIONSHIPS

There are seven key attributes that, when blended together in the right quantities and in the right manner, facilitate the development of insight and the formation of deep, trusting relationships. These characteristics are a blend of innate talent, acquired skill, and attitude, and it's pointless to try to determine exactly which is which. That's why we use the more general term "attribute" to describe them. Empathy, for example, is definitely something you develop at a young age (a "talent"), yet we know that people can improve their empathetic ability late in life. Native ability certainly counts, but hard work and openness to change can improve any of these qualities, an assertion borne out by the experiences of the many great professionals we've studied.

There is a natural, logical progression to the development of these attributes and to the order in which they usually come into play in building an advisory relationship. The two foundational attributes for any professional who aspires to serve clients are *selfless independence* and *empathy*. Great advisers have an attitude of complete financial, intellectual, and emotional independence. They balance this independence, however, with selflessness—they are dedicated, loyal, and focus on their client's agenda, not their own. It is a fine line to draw: on the one hand, being responsive to a client's needs and problems and, on the other, maintaining objectivity and honesty at all times. This selfless independence illustrates why clients are different from customers.

The second attribute, empathy, is what opens the door to learning. Empathy fuels your ability to discern a client's emotions and thoughts, and to appreciate the context within which that client operates. It enables you to diagnose what the problem really is and later underpins a learning relationship with your client. Dr. Michael Gormley, a London-based physician and renowned diagnostician who treats several members of the British royal family, provides an apt medical metaphor when he tells us, "You can't just chop the patient up into little pieces and then examine each one of them under the microscope. You have to understand the whole context of his daily life."

The next three attributes concern your ability to think and reason. You simply have to have something valuable to say before you can develop the long-term professional relationship. A passion for learning drives the professional to develop a core expertise and then to become a *deep generalist* by continually broadening her knowledge. *Synthesis* is the ability to see the big picture, to draw out the themes and patterns inherent in masses of data and information. It includes related skills, such as critical thinking and problem solving. The ability to synthesize sets the business adviser apart from the subject matter expert who relies mainly on analysis. *Judgment* is often—but not always—the culmination of a particular engagement or advice session, drawing on all the learning and synthesis you have undertaken.

Conviction and *integrity* constitute two important character attributes that are common to all of the extraordinary professionals we have studied. When credibility of content has been established, trust can follow, and the depth of a client's trust in you will be very much governed by his assessment of your character.

Conviction comes into play as the adviser begins to offer opinions, recommendations, and judgments in earnest. Conviction, however, does not exist in a vacuum; it is based on a set of compelling, explicit personal beliefs and values. Properly harnessed, it is a powerful force that can motivate and energize both professional and client.

The attribute of integrity comprises a constellation of skills and behaviors that build trust, including discretion, consistency, reliability, and the ability to discern right from wrong. Without this trust, it is unlikely you will develop a collaborative relationship. Your client will always keep you at arm's length and treat you like a supplier.

There are other qualities, of course—motivation, optimism, tenacity, determination, analytical skills, and so on—that are valuable for professionals and indeed necessary to be a successful expert. The seven we have identified, however, are the ones that truly stand out and make a difference in a professional's effectiveness. They enable you to go beyond expertise and become a broad-based adviser. These are the qualities that foster the development of the insights and relationships that lead to consistent *value creation* for clients, and they are the characteristics that great advisers themselves have intuitively developed. If you want, in short, to become an extraordinary professional who commands unwavering client loyalty, you need especially to develop and strengthen these attributes.

Becoming an Integrated Professional

These attributes build on and interact with each other to create a whole that is greater than the sum of the parts. Casual observers might call an individual who has successfully integrated them a "seasoned professional" or someone who really "has a head on her shoulders." Drawing on his thirty-eight years as a successful client adviser, James Kelly articulates this state of integration and its benefits:

> I have come to accept that I am constantly learning, and will never, ever know it all. I've learned to become an intense observer of people—I know that situations are never quite what they seem at first. I accept that sometimes I'm wrong, but that's the cost of intellectual boldness, of daring to be right. I have a constant sense of being surrounded by expert resources that I can call on—they're everywhere. When you get your ego out of it and allow yourself to relax and observe, you really do get into the flow of events and ideas. I'm working for my clients, but I'm also feeling quite independent from them—I'm driven not because I'm being paid but by a desire to help my clients, to learn, to satisfy a higher purpose. The ideas and solutions come quite freely in this state.
>
> This happened just last week—I was the last speaker at a three-day conference for a group of top executives. When I was younger, I would have prepared a canned speech days in advance. This time I listened intensely for the first two days. I observed the participants carefully. I opened up my mind to the variety of ideas that were being presented and discussed—even though I didn't like some of them. On the third morning, I got up early

---

Characteristics of a Successful Client Adviser

- ✔ Clients often ask you for advice, both on subjects directly within your field of expertise and in peripheral areas that happen to be of concern.

- ✔ Most of your client relationships are long-term ones. The vast majority of your clients would enthusiastically recommend you to someone else.

- ✔ There is strong mutual trust, on a professional *and* a personal level, between you and your clients.

- ✔ You collaborate extensively with your clients to define the product or service you deliver to them and match it to their needs.

- ✔ You frequently approach your clients with unsolicited ideas and suggestions.

- ✔ Your clients believe you consistently deliver value in excess of your fees. They rarely if ever shop around to see if they can get the kind of services you offer more cheaply elsewhere.

---

and took out a pen and paper. The themes began to flow—it was immediately clear to me what I would say in order to pull together the entire conference.

THESE BUILDING-BLOCK attributes are fundamental and straightforward. The reality, however, is that most professionals don't practice or actively develop them. Or they delude themselves into thinking that they have already mastered them. Often, what they think passes for insight is, to their clients, merely expertise. They forget that this year's insight has a very limited shelf life and can quickly revert to simple expertise—debt underwriting and reengineering consulting used to be value-added services, for example. Now they are virtual commodities.

C. K. Prahalad, the noted academic, strategist, and top-management adviser, tells us, "To keep yourself fresh as an adviser, you must constantly push yourself into new areas and unfamiliar territory. You have to get out of your comfort zone." By getting out of your comfort zone you will expand it, greatly increasing your versatility and effectiveness with clients.

TWO

SELFLESS INDEPENDENCE
Balancing Detachment and Dedication

In the ideal, a professional adviser should be independently wealthy. He would then be objective, independent, and less likely to be pushing his own agenda.

CHUCK LILLIS, *CEO, MediaOne*

THE PRISONER, condemned to death, was awakened by his guards at 5:00 A.M. and informed that he would be beheaded rather than hanged, drawn, and quartered. The cell, located high in the Tower of London, was pitch-black—when his books and papers had been confiscated a week earlier, he covered the narrow windows with strips of cloth. He spent his last days in constant prayer and meditation.

A large crowd gathered outside the Tower, and people jostled each other for the best view as the gaunt, unshaven, long-haired man was brought to the block. "Pray for me on earth as I will pray for you in heaven," he told the crowd. The executioner raised his ax and beheaded him with a single stroke.

So ended the life of Thomas More, former lord chancellor of England, chief adviser to King Henry VIII, and the most brilliant legal mind of his age. More, who had risen to become the most powerful man in the country after the king, fell from royal favor when he refused to endorse Henry's di-

43

vorce from Catherine of Aragon and his break with the Catholic Church. More found these actions, which were contrary to his fundamental beliefs and principles, repugnant. Despite his dedication to his client, he refused to give up his independence as an adviser, even if it cost him his life.

Thomas More was born in the heart of London in 1478. He trained as a lawyer, and after rising steadily through the ranks of the English legal system, he was appointed in 1515 to the king's council, which resolved major legal disputes over property and title. More could not be tempted by the bribes and inducements that influenced other officials of his day. His reputation for intellectual acumen, Solomon-like judgment, and unimpeachable integrity was no doubt one of the first things that attracted King Henry VIII to him when he was looking for an adviser.

Although More was unquestionably gifted with a razor-sharp mind, there were two important aspects to his character—qualities he consciously cultivated—that made him more than just a talented lawyer. First, he had an abiding faith. More believed deeply in God and the tenets of the Catholic Church, and he actively practiced Biblical virtues. In his early twenties, he lived for four years as a boarder at Charterhouse, a monastery in central London. He gave generously to charity and later as lord chancellor regularly attended his small local church in Chelsea, singing in the choir and, on several occasions, keeping King Henry waiting until Mass was over.

The second great love of More's life, after God, was learning. He used to say, "Live as if you are to die tomorrow, study as if you were to live forever." [1] More, who spoke and read Greek, Latin, and French, was constantly reading, studying, and increasing his knowledge. He had four daughters and established a home school for them at his manor house in Chelsea, complete with skilled tutors and a curriculum that he had personally designed. At this time in history few women received any kind of formal education. They were kept at home and trained in domestic duties until they were ready to be married off. More, however, "was the first Englishman seriously to consider the education of women, whom he considered not a jot less intelligent or scholarly than men."[2]

The beginning of More's demise came when his client, King Henry, fixed his wandering eyes on Anne Boleyn. After eighteen years of marriage to Catherine of Aragon, who could give him no male heir, King Henry decided to divorce her. When the pope proved uncooperative, Henry put in motion a series of parliamentary acts that undermined the authority of the Catholic Church and established his preeminence in religious as well as secular affairs.

One of his first steps was to dismiss Cardinal Wolsey as his lord chancellor and replace him with Thomas More, the first layman in one hundred years to occupy this powerful post. The parallels with modern advising are striking here. Just as a corporate CEO may fire his existing professional adviser (say, his accountant or consultant) and hire another in order to get a more sympathetic opinion, Henry exchanged Wolsey for More. Although Wolsey had cooperated with Henry in his efforts to get a divorce, perhaps the king felt that because Wolsey was a Catholic prelate he might hesitate further down the road as the confrontation with the pope grew more bitter.

Why did Henry choose More, however, who he knew had a staunchly independent character? And why did More accept, knowing the king would pressure him to publicly support his divorce? More had been a close adviser to Henry for over ten years, and the fact is that Henry trusted him and assumed he could eventually persuade him to his point of view. More, on his part, really couldn't refuse the promotion to lord chancellor. In sixteenth-century England, when the king offered you the top job in the country, you didn't tell him, "No thanks." More also believed that serving the king was a divine duty. He must have known that he would cross swords with Henry in a battle of wills that, perhaps naively, he thought he might win by appealing to Henry's strong religious convictions.

Once Henry began passing laws that undermined the ecclesiastical authorities in England, More, after three years on the job, resigned his post as lord chancellor. Subsequently, he enraged the king in three acts of defiance: first, he did not attend the coronation of Henry's new queen, Anne Boleyn; second, he refused to write, at Henry's request, a treatise justifying the divorce from Catherine of Aragon; and third, he refused to sign the "oath of succession," a statement recognizing the act of Parliament, which legitimized Henry's divorce. At this point he was accused of treachery and imprisoned. More never once spoke out *against* the king, however. Instead, he spoke out *for* his belief in God and his adherence to Catholic doctrine.

CREATING A FOUNDATION
FOR YOUR RELATIONSHIPS

Great professionals maintain a delicate balance between dedication to their clients and detachment from them, exercising what we call *selfless independence*. It is a foundational attribute for anyone who aspires to become a trusted adviser to clients. Without selfless independence, you lack substance as a client adviser—you're just another expert for hire. With it, you are able to inspire both respect and loyalty from your clients.

Thomas More is a heroic example of selfless independence: he was completely devoted to King Henry, yet there were some things he just wouldn't do—in this case, condone Henry's seizure of power that once defined the separation of church and state. More's devotion to his client embodied many elements of selflessness: he believed his job was to serve the king in whatever way possible; his focus was on the king's agenda, not his own; and he was entirely self-effacing. More's independence, on the other hand, was rooted in his deeply held beliefs and values. This belief system, combined with the fact that he had become quite wealthy in the course of his legal career, provided More with intellectual, emotional, and financial independence from his client. All of these factors fueled a powerful self-confidence that enabled More to maintain a persona that was distinct from the king's.

Fortunately, modern professionals don't have to die in the exercise of their independence, although they do have to be prepared to suffer short-term financial losses and temporary career setbacks.

Clients put a high value on a professional's dedication to their cause. The number one complaint we hear from executives is that many of the professionals they employ focus too much on their own objectives and needs. The following comment is typical: "You get into a discussion with them, and they have their own agenda, their own solution. They're distracted by their own issues and cannot adequately focus on yours." Another client told us, "The higher up you go in the organization, the harder it is to find professional advisers who will really put your agenda first, who truly have your interests at heart. You tend to become more and more isolated because everyone is working an agenda with you. Their ambitions get in the way."

The other side of this equation is independence. One client stated to us, "I divide the advisers I use into two groups: those who will do anything I say, and those who are independent." Selflessness, unaccompanied by independence, makes you a lackey—you become willing to do whatever the client asks and agree with whatever he says. The great client advisers do everything in their power to make their clients successful, but they also speak their minds and won't compromise their integrity and beliefs. They know where to draw the line.

Many clients feel, and often with good reason, that it is increasingly difficult to find independent sources of advice and information. Consider, for example, the recommendations of stock analysts at banks and brokerage firms. Fund managers and individual investors have traditionally relied on the in-depth research and advice of these analysts to guide their choice of stocks. In 1983, 24.5 percent of the recommendations were "buys" and 26.8 percent were "sells." Today, however, only 1.4 percent of all analysts' recommendations—less than one in seventy—are "sells."[3] Unfortunately, the pressure on analysts not to make sell recommendations to their clients is enormous. If their own bank underwrites the stock in the first place or does investment banking business with the client's company, there is internal pressure to support the stock with favorable reports. Analysts' own clients put pressure on them as well: if an analyst says unfavorable things about a company, he risks the wrath of its senior management and may get unofficially blackballed and cut off from important future information. The result of this lack of independence is unreliable advice. In the end, both client and professional suffer.

This problem is not unique to the banking and brokerage industries. To preserve the impartiality of advice, federal regulations in the United States govern many aspects of professional practice. Accountants cannot have close ties with the companies they audit, for example, and physicians are restricted in their ability to refer patients to testing laboratories in which they have a financial interest. The best answer for the individual professional, of course, is self-regulation: you need to develop your own reputation for absolute independence and impartiality.

Harvard Law School professor Alan Dershowitz, who has represented more than his share of high-profile individuals, including Claus von Bülow and Mike Tyson, is a fierce advocate for his clients. He also has a well-articulated philosophy about independence and the need to be perceived by one's client as an equal. He tells us quite bluntly, "The professional who is truly independent from his client is something you rarely see nowadays. My focus is on winning the case, not trying to keep the client. Some advisers surround their clients, telling them exactly what they want to hear—I just won't do that. I told Leona Helmsley, for example, that if she continued to be mean and cruel toward her employees, they would of course continue to turn against her. She fired me." (Helmsley, a famous hotel heiress who was notoriously tough on her staff, was charged with tax evasion and other crimes and eventually served time in jail.) He adds, "Many lawyers also get financially intertwined with their clients. I once had a well-known financier as a client, and all his other advisers would ask him for investment tips. I refuse to take that kind of advice from a client—it compromises you."

INDEPENDENCE: YOUR GREATEST ALLY

Out of our national political scene, with all its traditional deal making and dissembling, the name of a leader occasionally surfaces whose integrity and independence are absolute. These rare individuals rise head and shoulders above everyone else. Figures such as Senator George Mitchell, who negotiated the Irish peace settlement, and Senator Warren Rudman, who was one of the early leaders in the movement to establish a balanced federal budget in the United States, come to mind. Colin Powell, chairman of the Joint Chiefs of Staff during the Gulf War, is another name that resonates in this regard. Regardless of our political persuasions, we respect these figures because they won't allow themselves to be influenced—their opinions cannot be bought, like those of some paid expert witnesses at court trials. The names of these individuals conjure up images of fairness, honesty, equanimity, and rock-solid independence.

Most clients have a similar respect for the professionals who stick to their guns and say what they really believe. Sometimes corporate executives can't get a straight answer from their own organizations; their own staff may not be objective about an issue that has a major impact on people's jobs and livelihoods. If you develop a reputation for independence of thought and intellectual honesty, it will put you into a relatively small pantheon of professionals who, in the eyes of clients, are irreplaceable. One executive put it this way: "The professional whose opinions I truly value gives it to me straight, with no bull. This kind of honesty is invaluable."

Does everyone want such honesty? The managing partner of one large professional service firm commented to us that "all executives say they want the straight story, but in reality, only about half do. The other half get angry and defensive." This is an important issue for professionals: how to reconcile the need for honesty and directness with a client's natural defensiveness. Clients fall along a wide spectrum in this regard: some are extremely open to criticism and bad news, whereas others really don't want to hear it (in chapter 9 we'll explore some of the factors that condition a client's "bandwidth for bad news"). We know a few client advisers who are always blunt, direct, and never pull their punches. They tend to drop their opinions on a take-it-or-leave-it basis, however, and are often unwilling to work with clients to win them over. They get along well with some clients, who like that style, and not at all with others, who think that they are too outspoken and close-minded. The other extreme, as we've pointed out, is the yes-man.

Our own view is that many clients need convincing, and this can be a long process. If you turn them off too quickly, you lose your chance to influence them. It's a bit like U.S. foreign policy, which usually favors engagement with nations whose domestic policies we don't like, based on the premise that we'll be better able to effect positive change if we work with them than if we shut them off.

Sir John Harvey-Jones, the former CEO of the British chemical giant ICI and something of a tough-talking management authority, worked as a consultant to the heads of a number of European companies after his retirement from corporate life. His engaging but blunt style was so captivating that the BBC created a TV series, *Troubleshooter*, based on his consultations. Each episode revealed a similar pattern: Harvey-Jones, with his uncanny managerial instinct, would immediately identify a major flaw in his client's strategic direction. Each time, the CEO would push back and tell him that he really didn't understand the company. Over time, though, most of the clients slowly relented as they saw the truth in Harvey-Jones's words. When he told Apricot Computer, a once-successful maker of non-IBM compatible PCs, to get out of manufacturing and focus on software and services, the reaction was anger and stony disbelief. "They're try-ing to push water uphill," he told the show's viewers. Despite the initial resistance, however, Apricot eventually sold its hardware division and was soon back in the black for the first time in years. People change slowly.

Anger and defensiveness are, then, typical reactions to news we don't want to hear. After reflecting on what you have to say, your client may eventually come to accept your per-spective. In any event, it's your responsibility to be objective and straightforward; if the client reacts poorly, you've still done your job. Ultimately, you'll probably choose not to work with clients who aren't really interested in points of view that contradict their own.

Three Types of Independence

There are three distinct types of independence that great professionals exercise:

- *Intellectual independence*. Many professionals forget that one of the reasons they are being employed is to pro-vide independent perspectives. They want to be sup-portive of a client at every stage of the relationship, and sometimes this desire compromises intellectual integrity. If you're just starting the engagement, you may be afraid that you'll alienate your client by being too contradictory, and if you're in the midst of a long-term relationship, your personal friendship can also get in the way. Great advisers always find an appropri-ate way to say what they think. This is harder than it sounds—some clients don't take bad news gracefully and blame the messenger.
- *Emotional independence*. Every professional knows that working with clients can be an emotional roller coaster. Staying calm and centered while the client or the organization is "hitting the walls" can be difficult. Furthermore, since your livelihood or promotion

prospects often hinge on the outcome of your work, you may start to hang on every nuance of mood or emotion that your client expresses.

One client, referring to our own roles as advisers, said, "You [as professionals] have a very difficult job. You have to always remain calm and levelheaded, even when the clients you're working with are being emotional and irrational. You have to be involved, yet detached at the same time." Strong professionals develop levels of self-esteem and self-confidence that enable them to be independent of the good (or bad) opinions of others, including their clients (qualities not to be confused, by the way, with the virtues of listening and responsiveness).

- *Financial independence.* Advisers have to cultivate a mindset of independent wealth. The best advisers are highly paid, but they act as though they are not being paid and don't really need the money. If you are feeling financially needy and allow this need to intrude on your intellectual and emotional independence, you're lost. An anonymous adviser once counseled, "Never act hungry—it makes people want to stop on the street and kick you."

Former Harvard Business School professor and consultant Dick Vancil used to say, "I've probably turned away more relationships than most people actually have in a lifetime!" He wasn't bragging in the least. Vancil believed deeply in the importance of independence to a professional adviser, and he would never accept a consulting engagement if he sensed that the client would attempt to compromise his integrity.

Some clients, of course, don't like a completely independent professional. Robert Maxwell, the British media tycoon who apparently committed suicide in the face of an incipient financial scandal within his company, was notorious for having his own way with his advisers. When Lord Kearton, a highly respected company CEO, was questioned about the advice he had once given Maxwell, he said, "If you want to advise Maxwell and you want him to respect you, you must *not* accept any payment. As soon as he pays you he thinks he owns you."

The Importance of Saying No

Indeed, sometimes it's necessary to make short-term financial or career sacrifices in order to remain independent. Andrea de Cholnoky, for example, is an extraordinary client adviser who coheads the financial institutions practice at the executive search firm of Spencer Stuart. In the executive recruitment business, Spencer Stuart stands out as a firm that is very focused on developing deep, long-term client relationships. "Early in my career," de Cholnoky tells us, "I worked as an investment banker at Goldman Sachs. There, I learned an important lesson: the best way to preserve your own integrity is to make sure the clients you work for have integrity themselves. Goldman Sachs, right up to the managing partners, was very concerned about the character of the people they did business with."

Like many great professionals, de Cholnoky has the intellectual and emotional independence to turn down clients. She says, "You have to provide advice and direction based on what you know is true, and these have to be rooted in an independent perspective—otherwise you don't provide value. Sometimes, a client has completely unrealistic expectations about the kind of person that can be attracted to a certain position. Or they don't put the value on human capital that we feel it deserves—I have, on several occasions, turned down these kinds of engagements. This always hurts in the short run. But I have to be able to look at myself in the mirror each day and be happy about what I've done. And in any event, over the long-term you earn back whatever you've lost because you become a better professional and you're more effective with your other clients."

SELFLESSNESS: FOCUSING ON YOUR CLIENT

Independence has to be tempered with an attitude of selflessness. Selflessness does not mean complete subjugation to the client or martyrdom to client service, which is ultimately a losing proposition for both parties. Rather, it is a *mindset* in which the adviser, while preserving integrity, concentrates on serving the client and meeting her needs. This mindset has to be active throughout all day-to-day activities, manifesting itself in effective, empathetic listening during meetings, responding rapidly to client requests, and developing proposals that truly reflect the client's agenda rather than the adviser's sales quota for that quarter.

Selflessness has many dimensions to it:

- *A focus on your client's agenda rather than your own.* When you walk into a meeting, you should be thinking about the client's needs at that moment, not your own; about how your services can help achieve *his* objectives rather than how much you can sell.

- *An understanding that you are there to serve and to support your client's needs.* If you don't have this fundamental outlook, you're probably in the wrong field. You have to have a genuine concern for your client and the issues he faces.

- *A willingness to share or even relinquish control in the relationship.* Remember that experts wish to control, whereas advisers are comfortable sharing control as equals. Each client will have a preferred pace, style, or approach, and you have to be willing to accommodate it. There is a limit, of course, to how far you can go: it happens occasionally, for example, that a client wishes to have work completed in less time than the professional believes is possible. You may have to refuse the assignment, at least as the client has designed it.

- *A conviction that your responsibility as an adviser is to supply the right questions; your client has most of the right answers.* Too many professionals have convinced themselves that their raison d'être is constantly to provide *answers*. We are reminded of Picasso's quip about computers: "Computers are useless. They can only give you answers." Sometimes, providing a specific solution or idea is how you add value. Often, however, you have to help your client find the answer herself.

- *Respect for clients.* A partner at a large consulting firm once told a journalist, "We don't learn anything from our clients; we learn from each other." In a demonstration of arrogance raised to the nth degree, many professionals become scornful of their clients, labeling them as stupid and ignorant.
- *Self-effacement.* The message here is simple: although it's essential to periodically let your clients know what you've done for them, never try to steal their glory. The best advisers slip unnoticed into the background and allow their clients to bask in the applause and accolades. The less *public* credit you try to take, the more *private* credit your client will give you.
- *The ability to see your client's needs—undistorted—just as they are.* Preparing for a career in psychotherapy, a therapist seeks to identify and isolate his own neuroses or psychological issues that might affect the treatment of patients. Not to recognize these deep-seated emotions and feelings is to run the risk of misinterpreting the patient's own symptoms. Similarly, the serious professional adviser puts aside personal objectives and needs in order to concentrate on the client's concerns. Orit Gadiesh, CEO of consultants Bain & Company, sums it up by saying, "It's all about the *client*, not the adviser."

The Archetypal Adviser

An enigmatic, legendary figure who epitomized selfless independence was Merlin, one of King Arthur's chief advisers. Although some historians believe Merlin was a real person, it's unclear whether he was one individual, a composite of several people, or simply a figure out of folklore. In any event, he has become an archetype in our culture for the sage, devoted adviser who is also completely independent (the books, movies, and merchandise spin-offs based on Merlin are endless—the *Star Wars* films, for example, make heavy use of the Merlin character in the form of Obi Wan Kanobi, the Jedi knight played originally by Alec Guinness).

Merlin maintained a tireless devotion to his "client" Arthur, but at the same time put limits on the relationship in order to preserve his independence. Invariably, if Arthur was having difficulty during a battle, the image of a red dragon— Merlin's symbol—would be spotted over the battlefield, signifying his imminent arrival at Arthur's side. As soon as a battle was won, however, Merlin would disappear back into the woods, leaving Arthur to take all the credit. He lived in his own fortress on the coast of Wales rather than with Arthur at his castle, and he never—or so it seems—got compensated by Arthur, providing instead for his own livelihood. As devoted as he was to his royal clients (and he had several), Merlin's determination to keep Wales and the English north country free from the Saxon invaders inspired everything he did. He had a strong belief system, in other words, that underpinned his independence and superseded his allegiance to any one individual.

CULTIVATING SELFLESS INDEPENDENCE

One of the most important things a professional can do to cultivate *selfless independence* is to develop and articulate her own beliefs and values, a process we describe in detail in chapter 7. These fuel your conviction, which is necessary for the *independence* part of the equation. There are, in addition, some other practices that will help:

Be clear about your ethical principles. Know in advance what you are and are not willing to do. Some things should be obvious: lying, violating professional ethics, infringing on people's rights, and committing illegal acts, are clearly out of bounds for any professional who has integrity. Violating your own personal and professional principles should also be off-limits. For example, if you believe in excellence, and always performing to the best of your ability, then turning in substandard work to a client should be inconceivable. If fairness is one of your tenets, then you would never send a bill to a client that either under- or overcharges him for a particular service.

Many of us, like Thomas More, wouldn't endorse a client's point of view that we disagreed with. Some areas are gray, however, and require careful reflection and self-examination. For example, what if a client asked you to "edit" a report you wrote, so that it could be distributed to a wider audience in his organization? No problem, you say. What if the material he wanted edited contained some of your strongest findings and recommendations? Perhaps you're still not bothered. Going further, what if your client wanted you to skew and actively misrepresent data you had collected? We can suggest different options for dealing with cases like this. For example, you could refuse to edit the report, or you could sit down with your client to discuss the basis for his fears about informing and empowering his organization.

In truth, however, no one can tell you how to handle every situation where you have to trade off client service with professional independence. A few professions (law and accounting, for example) do provide some ethical and legal guidance for maintaining client independence and impartiality. Being clear in advance about your basic principles as an individual, however, is critical.

Develop a mindset of independent wealth. This is one of the most valuable things you can do to strengthen your effectiveness with clients. An attitude of "independent wealth" doesn't mean you have a disregard for money or that you ignore the fundamental economics of your business and the need to make profits. Rather, it means you do the right thing without regard to the monetary outcome. Here are some examples of how your behavior and outlook might reflect a mindset of independent wealth:

- When you propose additional work to a client, it is because you absolutely believe it's the right thing for the client's business and you are the best person to perform the work. You never sell your services just to increase your bonus or because you'll look good to your colleagues. You are (within limits of course) able to divorce your thinking and actions from their financial impact.
- You don't take on clients or specific assignments that either compromise your integrity or to which you can't add value. You also won't accept an engagement when you know you are overstretched and can't deliver a quality job. You are willing to say no and turn work down.
- You avoid personal financial involvement with your clients. If a client invests in your business ventures—or vice versa—you consciously give up the *client* part of the relationship, and the client becomes instead a business partner.
- You don't always demand an immediate, commensurate, short-term reward from your clients in exchange for something extra that you do for them. Rather, you put it in the context of the overall relationship. When expended for the right clients, you know that extra effort now will pay dividends later.

If you think and act in this way—if you prudently manage the overall profitability of your relationships at a high level, but on a day-to-day basis always do what you honestly believe is the right thing—your clients will recognize it, and their trust in you will increase dramatically. Ironically, this attitude of independent wealth, which embraces a certain disregard for money when making decisions about clients, will enable you to accumulate far more wealth than if you zealously count every penny and undertake assignments you don't want just for the income. This is because it will help you cultivate an abundance mentality—something we'll come to in the final chapter—and professionals who have an abundance mentality are far more attractive to clients than professionals who project scarcity.

Take a hard look at your client list. Some clients won't be right for you, either on the basis of personal incompatibility or lack of fit with your firm's target client profile. The former is something you'll discover early on in the relationship; the latter you have to define for your own particular business. Saying *no* is a powerful way to focus your practice and ensure you're spending time with motivated clients who appreciate you. For a large corporation, turning down business opportunities that aren't appropriate is a major part of strategy. The same is true for professionals, who need periodically to say no to client engagements that aren't fun, aren't learning experiences, and don't allow you to truly add value and do a great job. In his *reinventing work* series, Tom Peters offers some good advice about client selection: "I simply don't want clients who are going to be satisfied with 'acceptable' work. Invest—heavily!—in terribly 'cool' clients who will test you. And help you grow." Peters suggests rating all of your clients, regularly, on a scale of 1 to 10, where 1 equals "Dull as dishwater" and 10 equals "Provokes me and stretches me continually . . . love to be around 'em."[4] If you do this, examine closely the clients you assigned a 1, 2, or 3. Do you really want to work with them?

Constantly reflect on your client's needs and how to fulfill them. Many professionals have a reactive attitude toward their clients: only when the client has a specific request that he is clearly willing to pay for do they spring into action. Instead, you need to constantly observe, ask, and probe to identify how you can add value.

Some years ago, for example, a partner from a management consulting firm was working with a senior executive at a major automaker. One day the executive was deep in thought during a luncheon engagement, and the consultant asked what was on his mind. "I wonder," he replied, "how many combinations of options we provide in our typical car." Unasked, this partner turned his attention to researching the question, and after a great deal of work discovered that the company made available combinations of options that numbered in the tens of thousands. Furthermore, he developed a list of ideas that might be used to simplify the current system. The executive was astounded by this excess and initiated procedures to shrink the number in favor of predetermined "packages" of options on the company's vehicles.

Many professionals, in contrast, might not have acted on the client's question or even elicited it in the first place. "That's out of project scope" or, more bluntly, "We weren't hired to do that" are the oft-heard phrases used by professionals when a client asks for something that's not in the original proposal or agreement. In this case, the consultant could never have followed up on his client's almost unspoken agenda without a client-centered attitude. Certainly, it was in his interest to develop new avenues of work, but there was no guarantee whatsoever that this additional analysis would be rewarded.

Be prepared to help your client with any of his needs. The first step to satisfying your clients is to do an outstanding job on the specific task or project you've been asked to complete. Great professionals who are advisers go beyond this, however, and assist their clients in additional ways. This may include giving an opinion about a personnel issue, or advising your client on how to get an idea successfully endorsed by the organization.

In one case, a corporation's outside attorney helped the CEO identify, and provided introductions to, several specialized financial institutions that could help the CEO complete a leveraged buyout of one of the company's divisions. In a different sphere, a European client complained to the consultant working on a project for him that he was worried sick about his eighteen-year-old daughter, who was spending the summer thousands of miles away in New York City. The con-

Do You Practice Selfless Independence?

✔ You don't hold back your opinions—if you have a point of view on an issue of importance to your clients, you find a way to communicate it.

✔ You know where you will draw the line with clients—you're clear about the things you just won't do or put up with.

✔ You have, on occasion, turned down assignments or terminated a client relationship.

✔ Regardless of your financial situation, you feel as if you are affluent.

✔ You often surprise your clients with ideas and suggestions that they didn't ask for.

✔ You look at all of the current events around you through the lens of your client engagements, trying to discern what the implications might be for your clients.

✔ You ensure that your client—and not you—takes full public credit for victories, even if you had a key role in them.

sultant happened to be from New York, and she quickly arranged for some friends and family to meet the client's daughter and ensure that the young woman was settled in. In both cases, the advisers made suggestions beyond the definition of the project at hand. There was perceived value added as well as gratitude on the part of the client.

The point is not to become a dog walker for your client—the classic fear of private bankers whose wealthy clients demand total service—but rather to constantly tune into ways you can help and serve. King Henry VIII, for example, once consulted Thomas More on the proper education of Henry's bastard son!

• • •

SELFLESS INDEPENDENCE defines a state of balance between two extremes: the disconnected, aloof priest of advice and the unctuous yes-man. If you're completely independent but lack a client-centric view of the world, you'll probably attract clients for one-shot consultations but no more. The opposite is also dangerous—you don't want to be lumped in with those professionals who, as one client remarked, "will do exactly what you say." Dedicate yourself to your clients, but never allow anxiety about losing their business to blunt your honesty and independence.

THREE

HIDDEN CUES
Becoming Empathetic

To choose a finalist for the project, we had a "beauty contest" where several firms came and discussed their approach. The partner who presented for one of them was incredibly bright, but my executives just looked at each other and said, "There's no way this guy can be our adviser. He completely lacks empathy."

WIN BISCHOFF, *chairman and CEO, Schroders*

"**M**ISS BELL," the housekeeper announced, "the palace has called. The king would like to see you this evening." Gertrude Bell looked up from her writing desk and set down the small paper fan that was her only defense against the sweltering Baghdad heat. "I'll change immediately. We'll leave in half an hour," she replied. King Faisal, the first ruler of modern Iraq, son of the guardian of Mecca, and a direct descendant of the prophet Mohammed, had been appointed ruler of Mesopotamia, now Iraq, only a few weeks earlier on August 23, 1921. Bell, who had been the principal architect of the British government's reconstitution of Iraq after World War I, had been one of Faisal's key advisers in the two years leading up to his British-backed coronation as king. Now he began to rely more than ever on her clear advice and sound, objective judgment.

After dinner, Faisal invited Bell into the garden at the 63

center of his palace. Resplendent in his white robes, the stocky, handsome king took a sip of thick, black Turkish coffee and began confiding his deepest fears and doubts. He addressed her as *Khatun,* meaning Important Lady, or one who keeps an open eye and ear for the benefit of the state. Speaking in Arabic, a language that Bell mastered years earlier during her long sojourns in the deserts of the Middle East, he asked her advice on a variety of topics. How could he best win the loyalty of the disparate tribes within Iraq's new borders? Could Bell suggest how to establish the kinds of personal relationships he needed with the Bedouin leaders? How should he deal with his new British masters?

Bell listened intently, watching his body language, his eyes. Faisal trusted her totally. He knew that no other man or woman in all the Middle East, including the famous T. E. Lawrence, understood the pulse of the country, and the sentiments of the various leaders, as Bell did. He felt that she had only his interests at heart and that she would be totally objective in her opinions and advice. Most important, he sensed that Bell understood *him*—the difficult balancing act he had to maintain as the third son in a dynastic family, his reluctance to assume power, his need to act first as an Arab and second as a client of the British. Soon, Faisal was requesting weekly meetings with her to discuss everything from affairs of state to his family relations. She became his closest and most important adviser until her death five years later.[1]

King Faisal was not the only person who sought out Gertrude Bell's advice and counsel. Dozens of other Arab and British leaders of varying rank, including Winston Churchill, regularly met with her—in some cases continually over a period of twenty years—to discuss wide-ranging political and economic topics. Because of her expertise in Arab politics and culture, Bell was invited to join the British Foreign Service and later to become an adviser to the British government on Middle East affairs. Her paper "Self Determination in Mesopotamia" won her an invitation to the Paris peace conference of 1919. In it she offered advice on how to govern the region in the years following World War I.

Gertrude Bell's keen intellect, thirst for knowledge, self-assurance, and personal conviction were all qualities that contributed to her success. It was her deeply developed empathy, however, that set her apart. After winning highest honors—a "first"—in history and graduating from Oxford in 1889 (one of the first women to do so), Bell traveled throughout North Africa and the Middle East where she developed a deep empathy for the Arabs and Bedouins. A student of their desert cultures, she became fluent in Arabic and four other languages. Over time, she cultivated an uncanny ability to read the intentions and moods of the Arab leaders she dealt with. Bell understood the workings of other people's minds, and it was this capability that allowed her to develop her deep understanding of both Western and Arabic culture.

Bell, in short, had mastered the major foundations of empathy, and this was at the core of her extraordinary accomplishments. She had an abiding interest in people, humility, and a learning attitude; she was a superb listener, whether conversing with heads of state or local tribesmen; and she cultivated self-knowledge and self-control. To become the trusted adviser of King Faisal, and a confidante of many other Arab leaders, was a remarkable feat for any foreigner, especially a woman, in the Middle East of the early 1900s.

EMPATHY: THE KEY TO PERSONAL EFFECTIVENESS

Commonly defined as the ability to perceive other people's emotions and thoughts, empathy enables us to:

- Understand the character, perspectives, motivations, and values of the people we work with
- Form deep, meaningful, personal and professional relationships
- Respond to others in appropriate and effective ways

Ultimately, empathy enables you to learn about your clients, making you more innovative and effective as a professional. It also helps you create a rapport with your clients, allowing you to constantly exchange expectations about the work that you're doing. This is an important key to developing client loyalty, since client satisfaction is a function of expectations versus perceived performance. If you can understand and manage what clients expect, the odds go up dramatically that you will end up delighting them with your performance.

Here are some representative comments we heard from corporate leaders as they talked about their most important business advisers and the role of empathy:

- "The good adviser listens with the heart as well as the head."
- "The really empathetic professionals listen to what I mean, not what I say."
- "A session with a good adviser is a discussion, not a lecture."
- "The people I am comfortable going back to time after time . . . they are the ones who think about my needs and how to address them, not about the project they want to sell me."
- "The professionals I deal with must be genuinely interested in my issues and problems."
- "The adviser must know how to contextualize recommendations, making them both relevant to my company's unique problems and understandable to my executives and me."
- "The truly great advisers gain a deep understanding of my industry, of my organization, and, most important, of me as an executive and as a person—that's when a long-term relationship develops."

UNDERSTANDING EMOTIONS, THOUGHTS, AND CONTEXT

Empathy enables you to tune into your client's mood, frame of mind, and concerns. Understanding emotions is the first aspect of empathy: individuals who are good at this know when to press their point and when to change the subject. They can sense the mood of an audience and understand when they're losing the crowd and when it's appropriate to crack a joke. Many great orators—Martin Luther King, Jr. was a wonderful example—have a well-developed ability to perceive and be affected by emotions.

Empathy is also the ability to understand thoughts, to hear rather than just listen. When a client says, "I'll think about it," does he really mean it, or is this a brush-off? Part of this understanding is based on a grasp of how a client thinks. President Richard M. Nixon, for example, used to call up Secretary of State Henry Kissinger in the middle of the night and demand that a certain aide be fired immediately. "Get rid of the son of a bitch," he would shout into the phone. Sometimes, he would make three or four calls in succession, repeating the message again and again: "I want him out—have you fired him yet?" Kissinger always did nothing for at least a week; more often than not Nixon would never bring the subject up again. The message was not really to fire the individual, but rather, "I'm angry with this guy and distrust his loyalties. Keep an eye on him."

Understanding Context

Professionals who excel at developing broad-gauge relationships are skilled in yet a third type of empathy, which we call *contextual empathy,* or the ability to understand and appreciate the context in which a client operates. What are the forces and pressures acting on the client at the moment? How are her relationships with peers? With the boss? Is she happy at work? What's happening in the marketplace—or on a personal level—that may be affecting her moods, thought processes, and sensitivities? Being ignorant of, or insensitive to, this context is a common mistake of young professionals.

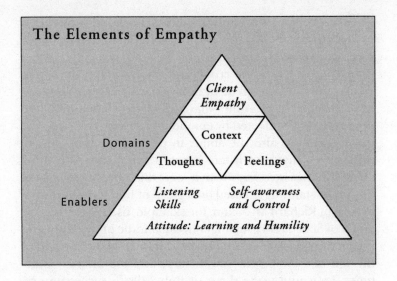

The Elements of Empathy

It is not untypical for consultants, attorneys, and financial advisers to become intensely focused on their message; after all, they have spent weeks or months researching what they are going to say. As a consequence they miss all of the nonverbal cues that could help them understand their client's emotional state and position their message so it could be understood and accepted. The risk is severe misunderstanding, as the poet Robert Frost notes: "Families break up when people take hints you don't intend and miss hints you do intend." The accompanying illustration summarizes these different aspects of empathy.

Good advisers are able to take their experience and concepts and contextualize them in a different way for each client. They must understand their client's value system and paradigms, which requires the exercise of empathy. For an executive who sees the world through the lens of shareholder value, a project to reduce personnel turnover will be bought on the basis that recruiting and training costs will go down, raising return on capital. A different executive might also value the economic benefits of the project, but ultimately be moved by the more intangible benefits of greater employee loyalty, job satisfaction, and a nurturing corporate environment.

Emotional, Rational, and Political Perspectives

Taking this a step further, you need to examine the emotional, rational, and political contexts of your client's thinking and decision-making processes. An investment banker, for example, was recommending an acquisition to his client, the chief financial officer of a securities firm. The banker's associates had fully covered the rational basis for the acquisition through their preparatory analysis, which included pro forma financials of the combined companies, the strategic rationale for the deal, payment mechanisms, and so on. The CFO, who was a candidate to succeed the CEO, was experiencing some significant discomfort that hinged on several unspoken emotional and political aspects of the potential transaction. How would the company's board and line executives view this initiative, for which the client was very much the spokesperson? Would it increase or decrease his standing among the directors, some of whom were exceptionally conservative? What if the integration process took too long or ran into problems? And what about the fact that the target company had its own exceptionally able finance head who was well known in the industry?

Managing this delicate situation required diplomacy, tact, and skill, and the risks made the client nervous. By understanding and explicitly addressing these political and emotional aspects of the deal—in private with the CFO—the banker gained his support and helped turn the transaction into a success.

Echoing the complexity and the importance of the emotional and political aspects of these kinds of transactions, one well-known corporate financier told us, "Mergers and acquisitions are not really about the figures—they're about managing the executives and the boards."

There are three fundamental preconditions for the exercise of empathy:

- The right attitude
- Self-awareness and emotional self-control
- The practice of specific empathetic listening skills

THE RIGHT ATTITUDE

Quite simply, you have to be interested in other people in order to be empathetic. Peter Drucker, one of our leading management thinkers, writes in *Adventures of a Bystander:* "I was always more interested in people than in abstractions. . . . People are to me not only more interesting and varied but more meaningful precisely because they develop, unfold, change, and become."[2]

A genuine interest in people can have a surprising impact on your relationships. Benjamin Disraeli, the Tory prime minister of Great Britain, had an enormous capacity for empathy and a corresponding effect on his acquaintances. A certain woman was once asked to compare Disraeli and his rival from the Liberal Party, William Gladstone, who also served multiple terms as prime minister. After dining one night with Gladstone, she remarked that she thought he was the cleverest man in England. "But after sitting next to Mr. Disraeli for the evening," she said, "I thought *I* was the cleverest woman in England."

Taking an interest in your adversaries can also be instructive. During World War II, the British general Montgomery used to post large photographs of the opposing German commanders on the walls of his personal quarters. He studied their characters at length, looking for clues and signs that would help him understand their strengths, weaknesses, and likely moves.

Some professionals, unfortunately, just aren't very interested in what other people think or say. They are either self-absorbed and egotistical—and therefore don't tune in—or they are too technically focused and more comfortable with things than with people. Large professional service firms—consulting, accounting, and law firms in particular—have grappled with this second type of person for many years: what do you do with someone who is technically brilliant but cannot relate to clients? Client relationships, especially long-term ones, are the lifeblood of any company. Service professionals who don't have client management skills have historically been relegated to second-class status. Firms struggle to create career paths for these individuals, calling them "subject matter experts," "expert contributors," or "technical resources" to distinguish them from mainstream professionals.

An Interest in Learning

The second element of the right attitude is genuine interest in learning. For many of us, part of the urge to empathize is ingrained from childhood, but much of it has to do with a desire to learn from others. The professionals who think they already know everything, however, have little interest in learning—why would they?

Some years ago, for example, an attorney with a large American law firm was supervising an assignment with a multinational company based in Mexico City. He had made a handful of trips to Mexico during the previous several years and mistakenly assumed he knew just about everything he needed to about the country and its culture. Furthermore, he perceived the legal issues his team of lawyers was dealing with to be fairly mundane and straightforward. He would fly down to Mexico City once a month for a day, ostensibly to supervise the work. Most of the morning he spent calling his office in New York to check messages—this at a time when long-distance calls from Mexico were exorbitantly expensive. After a long lunch and a perfunctory hello to the client, he would head out to the airport for his flight home. What could have been a major international beachhead for this firm turned, of course, into a one-off transaction.

Humility

Humility is the final part of having the right attitude. Unfortunately, humility tends to diminish as one's success grows. As financial consultant Fred Brown puts it, "When you're at the top of your game, you tend to stop listening. I have to make a concerted effort to ensure that I listen as closely to today's client as I did with my first one over twenty-five years ago." In contrast, one management guru told executives at a recent seminar that his new book contained "the only original management thinking to emerge in the last thirty years." He talked at the group for several hours and then departed, having learned nothing himself.

Many great client advisers have grown and become more open and empathetic through humbling experiences that they went through. When Gertrude Bell wanted to learn the Arab culture, for example, she did not begin by visiting heads of state. She went directly to the people and lived among them for months at a time in the parched desert.

Dr. Michael Gormley, a leading consultant to other doctors in London, spent a month at an alcoholic rehabilitation center (as a physician, not a recovering alcoholic), undergoing the same emotionally wrenching group therapy that all the patients went through, and the experience, difficult as it was, became a major catalyst in the development of his own empathetic skills. "On the first day, one of the patients came up to me and said, right to my face. 'You're just a Cambridge medical prick who's come here to observe us and thinks he's perfect.' It was a very difficult month for me, but that experience really developed my ability to empathize with patients."

Thomas More, as we noted in the last chapter, usually wore a hair shirt (an undershirt, painful to wear, made of bristly, itchy horsehair) under his satin and velvet robes in court. He wrote that "to be humble to superiors is a duty, to equals a courtesy, to inferiors nobleness." A hair shirt is not recommended to modern professionals, but it was an appropriate gesture at the time for someone wishing to remind himself continuously of both his religious convictions and his empathy for the poor. This link between humility and learning was captured beautifully by Mahatma Gandhi: "One must become as humble as the dust before he can discover truth."

An American executive, who was angry and about to break up a difficult partnership with a Japanese company, accidentally bumped into Peter Drucker in his Tokyo hotel. When he explained the situation, Drucker told him, "You get on that train the first thing tomorrow morning and go down there [to Osaka] and eat a little crow."[3] Apparently, the relationship improved significantly.

Empathy Wins Business

An executive at a large bank told us this story about how a consultant's empathetic style helped win a major contract:

> We faced a turning point in our asset management business and decided to hire a group of consultants to help us think through our options. Keep in mind that we're just about the best in this business, ranked in the top three in the country. So we invited several consulting firms in to present to us. The first group spent quite a bit of time describing a collaborative process where they would work with our executives to develop a set of strategic options for the business. Their background in the industry was very good, but they didn't overemphasize this point. They asked us a lot of questions during their session—what we thought of this trend, that merger, etc.
>
> The second group came from one of the really big-name consulting companies, where the consultants are known for their sheer brainpower. We were intrigued with using such a "brand name" company. They spent most of their presentation talking about the fund management business—the trends, the players, and so on. They went on for almost two hours about the state of the industry. Afterwards, the president of our asset manage-

ment company came up to me, red-faced, and said, in a furious tone of voice, "I did not learn *one* new thing from their presentation about our industry. Not one!" He refused to work with them. We went with the first group. They tried to help us define the problems, and they listened, whereas the second group set themselves up as investment management gurus and got shot down.

Clients do want to understand your experience and industry expertise, but rather than getting a lecture, they want to see how you use that experience to engage them creatively and understand their problems. The brainy consultants, failing in all three empathy domains, missed this point completely and lost a major piece of work with a prestigious client.

SELF-AWARENESS AND EMOTIONAL SELF-CONTROL

It is widely accepted that self-awareness and the ability to regulate your own emotions are fundamental prerequisites to the practice of empathy. This is common sense: if you can't tune into your own emotions, it's going to be a stretch trying to discern those of others. And if you are overcome by your own feelings, you'll never have the mental bandwidth to listen properly.

In his book *Emotional Intelligence at Work,* author Hendrie Weisinger succinctly states the case for the importance of self-awareness: "To be able to manage your anger you must be aware of what triggers it, and how this powerful emotion first comes upon you. . . . To short-circuit dejection so that you can motivate yourself, you must be aware of how you allow negative statements about yourself to sabotage your work. To help others help themselves, you must be aware of your emotional involvement in the relationship."[4]

Emotional self-control can follow once you achieve self-awareness. For professionals who want to develop broad-based relationships with their clients, keeping calm during the inevitable storms is critically important. Win Bischoff, CEO of the international merchant bank Schroders, puts it this way: "The real client leaders are the ones who put some distance between themselves and the velocity of the decision making. They don't shout and wave their arms. They are able to calmly give advice in times of stress, slowly peeling away the layers of the problem. At the same time, they are gradually bringing the client along." If you want to have deeper, longer-term relationships, the only condition under which executives will want you around them is if you yourself are consistently cool-headed.

EMPATHETIC LISTENING: A FORGOTTEN SKILL

"What keeps you up at night?" Carly Fiorina, now the CEO of Hewlett-Packard and previously a Lucent Technologies top executive and sales superstar, frequently asked her top clients questions like this. Intensely client-focused, Fiorina is constantly questioning and listening.

In talking about listening skills, we have to distinguish first between the individual professional and the firm or company she may work for. Clearly, "listening" at the institutional level is critically important for companies that sell complex services and products. Institutional listening to clients' needs and desires is achieved through mechanisms such as formal account reviews, client panels, focus groups, and client seminars. Our focus is different, however. We're concerned with your *personal* listening skills in the broadest possible sense. A company-level program to ascertain client concerns is laudable and necessary, but if the frontline professional who spends time with the client isn't able to tune in on a personal level, a collaborative relationship will be difficult to achieve.

Great client advisers are superb listeners. Their ability not only helps them gain information critical to their work, but gives their clients breathing space and allows them to think through the issues on their own. Empathy also underpins their personal and professional relationship with the client and helps it grow over time.

If the idea of listening as a key skill makes you roll your eyes a bit, just look at these statistics:

- The average businessperson typically spends about 40 percent of his day listening. A slight improvement in how effectively you listen will leverage a good chunk of your working day.
- A great deal of the communication in a conversation takes place through tone and nonverbal body language (perhaps up to half, although exactly how much is unclear—the studies on this subject are dated and limited in scope. Suffice it to say that a *lot* of meaning is communicated nonverbally). Tuning into nonverbal cues can greatly enhance your understanding of the hidden meanings in a conversation.

Several factors conspire, however, against even the best listeners:

- Culturally, authority and prestige accrue to the speaker in any given situation, not the listener. People who speak a lot in meetings—regardless of the content—are perceived by coworkers as having more leadership qualities.
- There is a time lag between understanding and listening. People speak 200 to 250 words per minute, whereas we can digest something like 300 to 500 words per minute. Listening makes us impatient! That's why so many of us finish other people's sentences.
- Experts develop great concentration in *telling*—after all, that's what an "expert" is paid to do. The same level of intensity needs to be applied to listening.

Poor listening skills can be a real career stopper. The protagonist in the following story torpedoed a wonderful opportunity because he couldn't listen.

The head of a consumer products company, wanting to shore up his marketing capabilities, invited an old colleague who was between jobs—an experienced marketing pro named Ted—to come see him. "Work for us as a consultant for a few months," the CEO told him. "Who knows, eventually you could even join us full-time. This is a great team." He repeated the offer of possible future employment several times, but left it vague and open-ended.

"Let me start by visiting your divisions," Ted replied.

A month later, after Ted had made the rounds of the company's various businesses, a raft of similar reports began trickling back to the CEO. "He's very, very bright . . . and has good ideas," one division president told him. "He knows our industry. But . . . he just doesn't listen. He does *all* the talking." Meanwhile, a yearlong consulting contract with Ted had already been drawn up and was waiting to be signed. The final straw was a planning meeting held a few days later. Ted awed the management group with his insights into the firm's marketing and channel strategy, proposing a clever five-point marketing program. Despite the fact that several executives disagreed with elements of Ted's proposals, Ted kept pressing the group to accept all of them, even blurting out at one point, "So at least let's cast in stone the five-point strategy that we all agreed on this morning."

At dinner that night he even told the CEO, "I've thought it over, and I'm ready to accept your offer and join full-time." When word of this conversation got around, a torrent of negative feedback from the rest of the executive team flooded the personnel director's office: "He doesn't listen"; "He's brilliant but he's too stuck on his own ideas"; "I can't get through to this guy."

Within a week Ted had no consulting contract and no job at the CEO's company. "We're having some profit pressures," the CEO told Ted in an apologetic telephone call. "I just can't justify bringing you on in the midst of all this . . . I hope you understand."

The real reason, of course, was that Ted had a terrifying lack of empathy. He lacked the interpersonal radar to see that his ego was getting in the way of his ability to work well with the team. Despite his brilliance, his inability to listen angered everyone he came into contact with.

For Laura Herring, president of The IMPACT Group, a highly successful and fast-growing employee relocation support firm, listening to clients is a key element of her business strategy and the secret of her success in developing new service offerings. Gary Gorran of Johnson & Johnson, one of her largest and longest-standing clients, says that "Laura and her people are constantly listening and asking questions."[5] This listening process enables Herring to develop a constant stream of additional services for her clients, and it creates an openness in her client relationships that encourages frequent, two-way communication. For example, when Herring once got word from some junior managers that an important program wasn't working as well as expected, she immediately huddled with her senior client and told him what was going on. "You have to help me figure out why this isn't working," she told him. He did. They fixed it, and he is one of her most loyal supporters five years later.

IMPROVING YOUR EMPATHY

Your capacity to empathize took years to develop, and it isn't going to change 180 degrees overnight. Many professionals who have become great client advisers, however, have demonstrated that change in this area is possible. Here are some suggestions:

Put yourself into unfamiliar situations where you have neither mastery nor control. This is exactly what Gertrude Bell did for many years as she explored the Arabian deserts. These challenges can be physical, such as learning a new sport or undertaking a wilderness experience like river rafting or rock climbing; or they can be intellectual—taking on assignments in a new industry, for example, where you have to listen and observe more than usual, and your sense of personal mastery is temporarily diminished.

Travel. Visiting foreign places can have an immediate effect on your empathy and your understanding of others. It's no accident that many writers, from the English romantic poet Lord Byron to the modern novelist Ernest Hemingway, have used travel to fuel their understanding of the human psyche and learn about the human condition. Henry David Thoreau's *Walden Pond* appears on the surface to be a study of nature, but it is in many ways the author's reflections on the civilization he left behind in Concord, Massachusetts.

When you leave the cocooned existence you call your home, you are suddenly exposed to a raft of new sights, smells, tastes, points of view, and sufferings. A surgeon we know routinely travels to South America to maintain his perspective and empathy as a doctor. One summer he'll hike the mountainous trail in Peru from Cuzco to Machu Picchu; the next he'll work on a rural agricultural project for several weeks. These experiences have the effect of sensitizing him to his patients' fears, concerns, and anxieties.

Accept occasional failures or setbacks and learn from them. Recent research into the careers of "extraordinary performers" has revealed the importance of failure as a personal motivator. Look no further than the lawyer Abraham Lincoln for an example of this: before he became the sixteenth American president at age fifty-two, Lincoln had endured more failures than most people could ever tolerate, including several family deaths and repeatedly unsuccessful bids for elected office. In the context of developing empathy—and, in particular, humility—missing the mark once in a while is salutary: it reminds us that we aren't infallible after all. Eating a bit of humble pie, a dish traditionally prepared from the entrails of a deer and served to the serfs after a medieval hunt, never hurt anyone.

Gain an understanding of your own basic strengths, weaknesses, and personality type. Some people intuitively understand their own emotional make-up, personal biases, and attitudes, but many of us don't, or we fool ourselves into thinking we do. Undergoing a standard personality assessment such as

Myers-Briggs can be extremely helpful to professionals. Based on Jungian concepts of personality preferences, Myers-Briggs helps you understand key aspects of your behavior and thinking processes, such as whether you prefer using facts or intuition, or the extent to which you are introverted or extroverted.

Learn to distinguish between observations and judgments. People who are highly empathetic usually have strong powers of observation—a quality that we'll come back to again and again in this book—but it's important to distinguish this kind of observation from judgment. For example, "He's too emotional about the subject to appreciate the reasoning in our report" is a judgment; "We haven't successfully communicated our logic" is an observation that will lead you to a very different prescription.

Stereotyping is another judgment that we often make: our understanding of what someone says is heavily influenced by that person's job title, gender, race, or perhaps some other factor. A recent study, for example, showed that African-American cardiac patients are poorly diagnosed by doctors compared to white patients. The same is true for women: research has shown that their complaints or descriptions of symptoms, compared to those of male patients, are less likely to be taken seriously by male physicians.

Always listen at the most involved level. Researchers who have studied listening skills typically identify three types of listening.[6]

- Level One: Engaging in empathetic listening, during which you listen deeply, actively observe, interpret nonverbal cues, and sense the underlying messages behind the words.
- Level Two: Hearing all the words, but not necessarily understanding their full meaning. Not observing or tuning into nonverbal cues (body language, tone).

- Level Three: Listening to only parts of the conversation, tuning out, or getting distracted for the rest.

Many of us are stuck at level two or even level three. Practicing affirmation—affirming and paraphrasing what your client has said to you—can help sharpen your focus on listening.

Recognize and eliminate your personal filters. Author Stephen Covey talks about four "autobiographical responses" that interfere with listening: "We evaluate—we either agree or disagree; we probe—we ask questions from our own frame of reference; we advise—we give counsel based on our own experience; or we interpret—we try to figure people out, to explain their motives, their behavior, based on our own motives and behavior." [7] Covey also has a nice expression for empathetic listening: he calls it "psychological air." When people sense you are not listening to them, they feel as if all the air in the room has been sucked out and they are choking.

Think hard about what your client is going to say. Many professionals rush from one client meeting to the next, their heads buzzing with their latest success or that new idea they want to present; they're totally concentrated on their own thoughts. President Lincoln, who was a master at reading other people, said, "When I go to meet with a man, I spend one third of my time thinking about what I am going to say, and two thirds of my time thinking about what he is going to say."

Ask guiding questions that help clients find their own answers. Open-ended questions are a good way to develop a broad introduction to someone's issues and concerns. ("How did that happen?" "What are your plans?" "How are things going in general?") Closed-ended questions are fine for gathering specific data, e.g., "What is your market share in North America?" But you need to ask additional, *guiding* questions that help clients clarify the issues for themselves and develop their own solutions. Examples of guiding questions might include:

- If you're successful in a year, what will that look like?
- After this project is completed, what changes should have occurred in your business?
- How do you determine the amount of risk you're willing to take?
- How would you approach this decision?
- What criteria are important to you?
- What have the barriers been in the past?

Guiding questions move the discussion beyond the basic facts and get clients to reflect on key issues and desired outcomes.

Seek honest feedback from clients about your performance and the conduct of the relationship. Very few professionals seek this kind of client-based performance review. Many large service firms do, of course, have a quality control function, where a partner who is uninvolved in the account meets with the client to solicit comments and feedback. This kind of institutionalized client-feedback process is important, but what we're talking about here, a one-on-one meeting between the professional and the client he serves, is quite different.

Here are the kinds of questions you ought to ask your client once or twice a year. Treat these as a guide; you'll need to word them in a way that suits your style and language, and there may be other topics you want to cover. Depending on your situation, for example, the use of "we" may be more appropriate than "I" for some of these questions:

- I'd like an honest assessment of our work together.
- Am I working on the most central and critical issues for you?
- Am I listening as well as I could? In what ways could I be a better listener to you and your organization?
- Are there any aspects of your business or parts of your organization I should understand better?

- Overall, how can I do a better job of helping you to meet your own objectives?
- How can I make doing business with me easier?

If your client says that you're doing *anything* less than a terrific job, you've got your work cut out for you.

COMMUNICATIONS STYLES: ADAPTING TO YOUR CLIENTS

Several thousand years ago, the Greek physician Hippocrates developed a classification method based on his empirical observation of hundreds of patients. He articulated four personality or physiological types: sanguine, choleric, melancholic, and phlegmatic. The sanguinary tended to be social and expressive; the choleric were driven, dominating personalities; the melancholic types were cautious, analytical thinkers; and the phlegmatic were steady, amiable individuals. In modern times, a great deal of research, including the Myers-Briggs profile we mentioned earlier, and dozens of books on this subject have only confirmed what Hippocrates intuited: there are indeed a few, fundamental personality types, and they align fairly closely to Hippocrates' original (and later, Jung's) system.

Professionals who excel with clients develop an understanding of personality types and adapt their communications styles appropriately. They know that some people are fact-based and task-oriented and want to get right to the point; others are reticent to express their views and have to be carefully drawn out; still others value the social nature of your meetings and want to dwell on personal and not just business topics.

Think about your current clients: you may have one, for example, who insists upon analytical, written documentation; perhaps another who likes face-to-face meetings and verbal reports. If you give informal, verbal briefings to the first client, he'll think you are sloppy and lack follow-up; if you

How Empathetic Are You?

✔ You know what issues and concerns keep your clients awake at night.

✔ You are rarely if ever surprised by a client's reaction to a particular person or situation.

✔ You do twice as much listening as talking.

✔ You understand how your clients like to communicate and have comfortably adapted to their style.

✔ You know what your own hot buttons are: you are aware of the behaviors and situations that set you off, are able to identify them, and can regulate your responses.

✔ Often, you understand that your clients *mean* something quite different from what they *say*. This doesn't surprise or bother you.

✔ You and your clients enjoy spending time with each other, and they routinely confide in you.

✔ You are comfortable seeking regular feedback from your clients about your performance as a professional.

provide the detailed memos to the latter, she will think you're not focused enough on the big picture and are spending too much time documenting things that are not important. These distinctions are not trivial; in fact, misunderstandings in this area are often behind the client engagements that go badly or that never result in repeat business.

For sure, human nature is such that you're not going to hit it off with every client you serve; but great professionals vastly expand their universe of relationships by being students of character and by consciously and methodically adapting their communications to each individual client.

• • •

ALTHOUGH EMPATHETIC abilities develop at a very young age, your capacity to empathize as an adult can be improved from whatever level it's at now. The three basic ingredients are having the right attitude (that is, an interest in people, a desire to learn, and a large dose of humility); being self-aware and in control of your emotions so that you can objectively listen and observe; and developing empathetic listening skills. These will enable you to tune into your client's emotions, thoughts, and context. A well-developed ability to empathize will not just enable you to see the hidden cues around you and therefore function at a much higher level with clients; it will open up the door to *learning*—of all kinds—in ways that will surprise you.

FOUR

DEEP GENERALISTS
Building Knowledge Depth and Breadth

An expert is a fellow who is afraid to learn anything new because then he wouldn't be an expert anymore.

HARRY S. TRUMAN

DAVID OGILVY, the advertising genius who founded Ogilvy & Mather, exemplified the expert who, to great profit for himself and his clients, became a *deep generalist.* Early in his career, he won the prestigious Rolls-Royce account. Instead of holing up in a conference room to brainstorm creative ideas for the ad campaign as many of his colleagues wanted to do, he launched an in-depth study of the company and its cars. He spent weeks interviewing Rolls-Royce engineers and managers and pored over every word that had ever been written about the company. In an obscure technical journal he read that "the ticking of the dashboard clock is the loudest sound the driver can hear at 60 miles per hour." Ogilvy had found his idea: what to an engineer seemed like a mere statement of fact became for a creative advertiser the basis for an enormously successful and award-winning campaign for Rolls-Royce. Ogilvy took this phrase, "the ticking of the dashboard clock . . ." and built a major print advertising program around it, using it as the headline for full-page ads in upper-crust British magazines. Later, other car manufacturers pirated Ogilvy's idea for their own publicity, and consequently *interior quietness* has for many years been featured as a key benefit in hundreds of other car ads.

Ogilvy was quite clear about his philosophy of learning: whereas many advertising professionals relied on "creative instinct" alone to develop new ideas, Ogilvy believed in carrying out in-depth research about every aspect of a company's products, customers, and competitors. In his classic book *Ogilvy on Advertising,* in a section entitled "Pursuit of Knowledge," he writes: "I once asked Sir Hugh Rigby, surgeon to King George V, 'What makes a great surgeon?' Sir Hugh responded, 'There isn't much to choose between surgeons in manual dexterity. What distinguishes the great surgeon is that he *knows* more than other surgeons.' It is the same with advertising agents. The good ones *know* more."[1]

This precept applies as well to professionals who become business advisers to their clients. Echoing David Ogilvy's observation, leadership authority Warren Bennis tells us, "The professionals who develop into really great advisers are *deep generalists.* They develop a unique blend of knowledge depth and knowledge breadth." Professionals who become deep generalists are able to add value in a greater variety of ways, more often and more consistently, than the average practitioner.

PROFESSIONALS WHO KNOW MORE

A deep generalist is someone who has a core expertise, say, organizational development or financial accounting, onto which he layers knowledge of related (and sometimes unrelated) fields. The result is a *business adviser* with technical depth rather than a *technical specialist.* Except for instances where there is a temporary shortage of a particular skill, such as some types of software programming, purely technical specialists are interchangeable commodities. The truly valued professional is the lawyer, accountant, consultant, or sales executive who not only brings functional expertise but who also understands the *totality* of her client's business. Eileen Friars, former president of Bank of America's credit card division, remembers one attorney who stood out and subsequently gained her long-term loyalty: "He got excited about the business side of things and thought creatively about the strategic issues. He looked at the deals in their totality, as opposed to focusing just on the lawyering, on the legal aspects."

Narrowband in a Broadband World

The evolution of both railroads and telecommunications provides apt analogies for this concept of the deep generalist. In the nineteenth century, there were many track gauges, or widths, used by American railroads, and most of them were narrow; the relatively wide-gauge track in use today had not yet become the standard. Wide-gauge tracks have many advantages over narrow-gauge ones, however: they are more stable and versatile; the driver can see farther around curves; and they permit higher train speeds. Analogously, today's broadband communication connections, like coaxial or fiber-optic cable, carry a variety of digitized formats—voice, video, and data—far faster than a narrowband link such as twisted-pair copper telephone wire.

Client advisers today need to adopt a broadband, wide-gauge approach to learning and knowledge; if you do anything less, you run the risk that your expertise will become a "stranded asset." You'll be like one of those isolated, narrow-gauge railways in the Colorado mountains that can no longer connect to the nationwide rail system.

Extraordinary professionals love to learn and become skilled at learning. Sir Brian Pitman, chairman of Lloyds TSB Group in London, sums it up by saying, "The great client advisers are constant learners who are not wedded to past concepts. They help accelerate learning within the organizations they serve." Indeed, in talking with professionals who have deep, lifelong client relationships, we have come to see that they all have an infectious zeal for acquiring knowledge. Bill

Leigh, who heads the Leigh Bureau, one of the preeminent speakers' bureaus in the country, tells this story—a typical one—to reinforce the point: "Some years ago, I negotiated a large TV deal, working with a very smart lawyer. This was a new field for me at the time, and I wanted to understand and experience it firsthand. The whole transaction ended up taking nearly *three hundred hours* of my time—and I was paid almost nothing. However, it was an intense learning experience for me: the deal was technically difficult, and I had to start almost from scratch. You have to make personal investments in order to learn."

Cultivating Deep Generalists

Among professional service firms, management consultants have explicitly struggled for many years with how to create deep generalists. The consulting firm McKinsey & Company was built on this concept: historically, McKinsey was a geographically based organization, with strong local offices staffed by generalist consultants who took a "top management" perspective. During the 1970s, however, new strategy firms, such as the Boston Consulting Group and Bain, emerged and began cutting into McKinsey's dominant position as *the* strategy firm. To counter these competitive threats and to better support its clients, McKinsey developed the concept of the "T-shaped" consultant, someone with deep knowledge of an industry or function, but who had sufficient experience in other fields to maintain a generalist approach to complex business problems. In the late 1970s, McKinsey overlaid its geographic office structure with a series of "functional capability groups" (e.g., global marketing) and "clientele industry sectors" (e.g., banking) in an effort to bolster formally its generalist approach with specific industry and functional expertise.

Early on at McKinsey, Marvin Bower, one of the founding partners most responsible for the modern culture and organization of the company, recognized the need to share ideas and experiences among consultants in order to create the generalist perspective he believed in so fervently. Bower hosted frequent lunches in the New York office, encouraging consultants to talk about their assignments and share war stories. Today, many service firms are making huge investments in information technology to institutionalize this type of experience sharing, moving it from the lunchroom to a firm-wide intranet. Although more efficient, and certainly necessary in large firms, these knowledge networks can't be anywhere near as much fun as Bower's old-fashioned get-togethers.

Many large service firms now matrix geography (generalists) against functions and industries (specialists). Usually, the specialist track dominates in a professional's development. This specialization, however, which jump-starts an individual's career, can eventually become a barrier to personal and professional development. Narrow specialization too often results in tunnel vision. The trick is to add peripheral vision to your tunnel vision, and thereby develop a holistic view of the client's issues and problems.

Becoming a deep generalist doesn't happen overnight. It's a slow evolutionary process, and the earlier you start, the better. It involves acquiring deep expertise and then adding—sometimes simultaneously, at other times sequentially—complementary knowledge.

Developing your core expertise comes first. If you are a service professional, this is defined initially by your field—advertising, law, consulting, finance, and so on—and later by your specialty within that field. If you are in executive sales, the sales function itself, as well as your industry and your product suite, defines your basic expertise. As we have said, deep expertise alone does not create the kind of lasting client relationships that this book is about, but it will engender respect and credibility and become the starting point for relationships.

In establishing your initial specialty, however, you have to aim high: in today's fiercely competitive market, no client is going to be impressed by anything less than outstanding subject matter expertise. You need to demonstrate *distinction* in a domain, not just competency. The tenacity shown by Amos Tuck School professor J. Brian Quinn can be instructive: he read or reviewed five thousand books and professional journals to prepare for a single MBA course in innovation. Later, Quinn became a presidential adviser on the subject.

WHEN THE STUDENT IS READY

A prerequisite to becoming a deep generalist is to cultivate a learning attitude. This attitude, and its consequences, can be summed up by an ancient but still fresh Zen proverb: *When the student is ready, the teacher will appear.* The elements of this powerful statement deserve a closer look:

- *The student:* Great learners think of themselves as perpetual students. In the ancient world the outstanding example was Aristotle; in today's field of management it's Peter Drucker. Even when teaching, these learners are working to expand their own knowledge. Drucker has said, "Students without a great deal of experience don't learn anything from me because I don't learn anything from them."[2] As the great Zen master Shunryu Suzuki wrote, "In the beginner's mind there are many possibilities, but in the expert's there are few."[3]
- *Readiness:* Having a student mindset isn't enough, however. You have to be ready to learn, often by unlearning old precepts or concepts that are no longer valid. Most people aren't ready to accept new ways of looking at old problems. The first response often is: "We've tried that and it doesn't work." The next reaction is: "Perhaps it has some merit." Later, they tell you, "It's true and we already thought about it a long time ago." Students who are ready lack the "not invented here" attitude; instead they rapidly identify and incorporate new information and ideas.

- *The teacher:* Most of us think about teachers in a fairly formal sense—university professors, mentors, authors, perhaps even our students or protégés. Avid learners know that teachers come in every shape and form and often are disguised. Our clients are teachers, as are our spouses and families. The books and magazines we read are teachers, and so are all of our most difficult experiences. Both our best and worst competitors are teachers. Strangers you meet in chance encounters—perhaps the next passenger you sit down with on an airplane—may turn out to be teachers.

  "When young people come to me now complaining about their horrible bosses," Geraldine Laybourne, the chairman of Oxygen Media says, "I say, 'Aren't you lucky,' because the more examples of bad management you see, the more you'll learn."[4]

- *Appearance:* Ready students are constantly on the lookout for people and experiences they can learn from, and they know these teachers can appear at any time. One day, while Paul McCartney was on his way to John Lennon's house for a songwriting session, he asked the driver of his car if he was working hard. "Hard?" the man responded. "I'm working eight days a week!" After listening carefully to the driver's tale of endless chauffeuring, McCartney sat down with Lennon that afternoon and penned the famous Beatle song "Eight Days a Week."

Aristotle: The World's Greatest Learner

There was probably no greater lover of knowledge and learning than Aristotle, the teacher, philosopher, and scientist who lived from 384 to 322 B.C. At a time when books were scarce and laboriously handwritten on rolls of papyrus, Aristotle personally owned one of the largest libraries in Greece. A neighbor referred to the great philosopher's home outside

of Athens as "the house of the reader." Consultant to influential people, head of his own academy (the Peripatetic
School), organizer of the body of facts known to the ancient
world, Aristotle embodied the attitude of a perpetual student. There was hardly a field or endeavor—biology, zoology,
physics, art, logic, philosophy, mathematics, government,
and many others—that Aristotle did not study and master.
His system for classifying the animal kingdom, for example,
endured for 2,000 years. Ultimately, Aristotle's greatest contribution to learning was that he organized knowledge so
that it could be methodically studied and passed on to others. Since his time, we take for granted that there are "bodies
of knowledge"—physics, medicine, economics, etc.—that
can be systematically studied as well as reviewed, tested, and
questioned.

Alexander the Great, who had conquered most of the
known world by the time he was thirty, benefited from three
years of tutoring during his teens by the master from Athens.
Although Aristotle did not advise Alexander in the sense that
we are discussing in this book—that is, as a "client"—this ancient philosopher does represent the love for learning that
takes the adviser both deeper into an area of expertise and
wider across the full range of knowledge. Aristotle instilled his
passion for learning in the young Alexander, who, according
to legend, sent back to his teacher unusual species of plants
and animals that he found on his conquests abroad. Back
home, Aristotle put the gifts to good use, inviting scholars
from across the ancient world to study these new discoveries.

THE LEARNING HABITS OF GREAT PROFESSIONALS

The knowledge acquisition strategies of client advisers
are fundamentally different from those pursued by experts,
both in terms of what they learn and how they learn it. Advisers roam far beyond their core expertise as they constantly
absorb new information in a variety of arenas, and they employ multiple methods of learning. They also engage in deep,

client-centered learning that enhances their ability to be insightful and add value. The accompanying diagram illustrates these differences.

Let's first examine the three learning arenas: core expertise, ecosystem, and personal interest.

Core Expertise

Most professionals spend the vast majority of their learning time just trying to keep up with new developments in their fields. Whether it is gaining on-the-job experience, going to a workshop, or reading a book or an article related to their areas of expertise, these professionals seek to drill deeper into that core of knowledge that defines their expertise.

Having truly outstanding depth and mastery in your chosen field is a prerequisite for getting new clients to listen to you and then to stick with you over time. Just staying current in your core expertise can be overwhelming—and not just because of the extremely long hours that we all work. The

Learning Focus

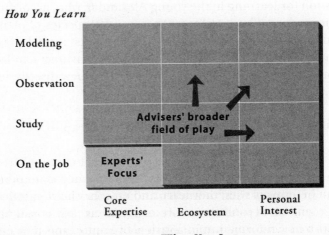

How You Learn

Modeling

Observation

Study

On the Job

Advisers' broader field of play

Experts' Focus

Core Expertise   Ecosystem   Personal Interest

What You Learn

half-life of knowledge is now shorter than ever. In fields such as software and in some medical subspecialties, for example, your knowledge base can become obsolete in just a couple of years if not months. Therefore an enormous effort is required to keep up. Unfortunately, just being up-to-date in your field alone is not sufficient to inspire client loyalty.

Ecosystem

Every professional applies his expertise to some larger *ecosystem*. Often, this ecosystem is the world of business and management, although many professionals also work in ecosystems such as healthcare or government. In this wider zone of learning, many experts drop out. How many attorneys are familiar with the latest thinking in corporate strategy? How many information technology consultants have a grasp of behavioral psychology or marketing? The ecosystem you work in has many parts to it. It includes:

- Your client's competitors, suppliers, and customers
- The strategic forces driving change in the industry
- Other macro-trends affecting your client, such as international developments and government policy
- Your client's own company—its organizational structure, products, distribution channels, and technologies
- All of the other functional disciplines, such as strategy, marketing, operations, information technology, and finance, which surround your particular expertise
- Adjacent or parallel industries

In addition there is a *personal* ecosystem that you must be aware of. It comprises information about your client's aspirations, goals, and values as well as professional status and familial situation. Few professionals delve into even a small portion of this knowledge. Yet this kind of mastery is precisely what enables you to develop tailored, innovative solutions and truly stand out in your client's eyes.

Both management consultant James Kelly and investment banker Nancy Peretsman, whom we introduced in chapter 1, are so effective precisely because they plunge into the ecosystems that surround their clients. Peretsman, for example, spends a great deal of time reading about and studying the industries and the environment—new media, the Internet, communications, and so forth—that her clients operate in. It's understanding the context around her clients that gives her so many good ideas.

Moving to Europe in the midst of his career as president of the MAC Group, James Kelly added a whole new expertise—international business—to his quiver. As globalization heated up in the mid-1980s, his understanding of the international environment that his clients operated in greatly enhanced his effectiveness and ability to add value.

Personal Interest

Learning for pleasure, for its own sake, whether it is learning a foreign language, traveling, reading history or philosophy, or pursuing a hobby, is in short supply today. Many professionals find that just keeping up on their home lives and doing a minimum of reading about their field are more than they can handle. Yet the learning zeal of great professionals doesn't stop at business books or areas strictly related to their profession. Noted client adviser Orit Gadiesh, head of consulting firm Bain & Company, tells us: "I read about one hundred books a year. Many of them have nothing to do with business. I actually think this is one reason business leaders enjoy talking with me: my perspectives go way beyond talking shop."

You never know how your personal interest learning may one day connect with professional opportunities and your effectiveness with clients. At a major management consulting firm, one consultant had pursued a personal interest by studying French in college and subsequently spending a year living in Paris. Years later, while he was based in London, his firm acquired a French consulting company. Management decided to send one of their own experienced partners, who had good relationships with the rest of the company, to serve as country head for France and to help integrate the acquisition. A careful internal search identified the French-speaking consultant as virtually the only professional out of hundreds who possessed the linguistic and cultural skills to handle the assignment. Once in France, this consultant had to employ a broad range of knowledge acquisition methods that went well beyond just on-the-job learning; he engaged in a deep study of the French language as well as careful observation and modeling of successful French consultants. The combination of his management experience and his cultural knowledge and sensitivity ultimately was very effective in handling French clients.

Becoming an Explorer

In the last two categories—ecosystem and personal interest—great client advisers engage in *exploratory learning.* Once they establish their expertise, they spend a lot of time in undirected, curiosity-driven exploration. "I read eight different newspapers a day, and each one gives me a somewhat different perspective," says Warren Bennis. "Rather than over-exploiting my past work," relates C. K. Prahalad, "I have completely changed my research focus over the last two years." These are typical comments from great learners, who are, in fact, inexhaustible *explorers.* They have a childlike desire to learn about everything in their environment, the way a toddler wants to empty every drawer in the house.

The analogy of the explorer as exemplary learner is useful to keep in mind. As we mature from children into adults and learn about constraints, develop an aversion to "wrong" answers, and become smug in our expertise, our curiosity wanes. We no longer ask seemingly absurd (but important) questions such as "Can bobcats eat glass?" (posed recently to one of the authors by a six-year-old child). Much of Albert Einstein's adult work had its origins in playful questions he used to daydream about as a teenager. For example, at the age of sixteen the young Einstein asked himself what it would be like for an observer to travel alongside a light wave: would he ever surpass the light wave? He also wondered what would happen to the objects in the pocket of someone who was inside a box falling down a long shaft: if he took them out of his pocket, would they drop to the bottom of the box or remain suspended in air?[5]

We go from wanting to know everything to thinking we know it all. Unlike the young offspring of many animals, however, whose responses to their environments are genetically preprogrammed, young humans can immediately adapt their behavior and responses to external stimuli. We are designed to interact with and learn about our surroundings. Some people retain their youthful curiosity and inquisitiveness and remain explorers as adults. Paolo Novaresio, an Italian historian, writer, and traveler, says this about the explorer mindset: "Play . . . is the mechanism that allows us to continue to explore as adults. . . . The explorers have always been dislocated individuals (before they even depart), anomalous and outsiders. In some way they remain 'children,' with their minds free of the inhibitions of the society in which they live."[6]

HOW WE LEARN

If you want to develop into a deep generalist, a final aspect of learning to consider is *how* to learn, which is a function of both attitude and the specific learning strategies you adopt.

The most effective learners cultivate an attitude of *mindfulness,* an old Buddhist concept that has been explored in a modern educational context by Harvard psychologist Ellen J. Langer. She defines *mindful learning* as having three elements: the continual creation of new categories (e.g., different frameworks); openness to new information; and an implicit awareness of more than one perspective.[7] Mindfulness essentially means cultivating a flexible, open intellect. The opposite of mindful learning is allowing yourself to be trapped in old paradigms, being unreceptive to new information and ideas, and rigidly looking at the world through a single perspective.

You can also accelerate your learning by using all of the knowledge acquisition methods listed down the left side of the diagram entitled "Learning Focus":

- *Direct experience:* This is how most professionals do the bulk of their learning—on the job, day to day, by doing. The best learners, however, go well beyond experiential learning.
- *Study:* This consists mainly of reading, but extends to formal education, seminars, workshops, and so forth.
- *Observation:* Although clearly used on the job, observation represents a knowledge acquisition method by itself. How carefully do we really watch the people and things around us?
- *Modeling:* This approach is used very effectively by many exceptional professionals, who typically identify and emulate successful role models early in their careers. The mentoring process, for example, is based on modeling.

HOW MUCH TIME DO YOU SPEND LEARNING, AND WHERE DO YOU SPEND IT?

The first key difference in the learning habits of ordinary versus extraordinary professionals is that the latter spend *more total time* dedicated to active learning and knowledge acquisition. Even though a lower percentage of their time is spent reinforcing their core expertise, for example, they end up spending more absolute time strengthening this core than the average professional spends.

The second difference between the learning habits of experts and of advisers is in terms of where they spend their time. Experts spend the majority of their time becoming more expert in their chosen subject. Advisers also continue to cultivate their expertise, but they work to give it increasingly greater context. They also engage in more "random" learning, which is done for pleasure and interest, but which has the effect of bolstering their intuition and ability to synthesize. Client advisers thus spend perhaps as much as one-half of their learning time in the exploratory learning zones, ecosystem and personal interest, whereas typical experts might spend only a small fraction of their time there, a fact that Harry Truman lamented when he commented on the expert who feared learning anything new because "he wouldn't be an expert anymore."

The same is true if we look at how professionals learn, or the methods they use to acquire knowledge. Experts do the vast majority of their learning experientially—on the job—whereas advisers supplement their experience-based learning with reading and study; they develop acute observation skills that enhance their ability to learn under a variety of circumstances; and they use successful individuals around them as role models.

A Deep Generalist without Peer: Peter Drucker

Peter Drucker, the man who almost single-handedly established the modern profession of management, is an inspiring example of a great client adviser who revels in all three of these learning arenas. As a young man in Vienna during the 1920s and early 1930s, Drucker opened himself to a variety of individuals and experiences that laid the foundation for his later eclectic, breakthrough writings on management. He experienced long evenings with his parent's circle of intellectual friends (which included Freud); he witnessed the collapse of the Austro-Hungarian empire and the rise of the Nazis; and he participated in a famous Viennese salon where leading figures of the day would hold forth in debate and discussion at a private home. He earned his Ph.D. in public law and international relations, but had equally steeped himself in economics and history by the time he graduated. When he began his study of General Motors, which resulted in his seminal book *The Concept of the Corporation* (1946), Drucker had worked as a journalist, an editor, a banker, a securities analyst, and a university professor, to name just a few of the professional disciplines he had undertaken.

Drucker has an uncanny ability to observe and learn from the people around him. His book *Adventures of a Bystander* is full of finely drawn portraits of individuals ranging from his fifth-grade teacher to the intellectual Fritz Kraemer, "the man who invented Kissinger." And from each, Drucker draws life lessons that would probably have escaped most of us.

So in Drucker's case, what has all this knowledge depth and breadth produced? Under his tutelage, management has emerged as a broad discipline rather than a specialty. Biographer Jack Beatty sums this up by stating that Drucker has taught management "as an integrating discipline of human values and conduct, of social order and intellectual inquiry, one that feeds off economics, psychology, mathematics, political theory, history, and philosophy. In short, management is a *liberal art*."[8] Drucker's contribution to the modern practice of management includes many fundamental concepts we now take for granted, including management by objectives (MBO); decentralization; and the concept of the knowledge worker. His deep knowledge of history puts modern phenomena in a new context for many of us. The American Heart Association, for example, reorganized its field operation after Drucker described to its management how the British had governed India with just 1,000 young men.[9] A recent Drucker article on information technology, "The Next Information Revolution,"[10] draws insightful parallels between modern information technology professionals and marketing executives on the one hand, and the printers and publishers of the seventeenth century on the other.

Drucker hasn't come up with all these insights just because he's smart. Rather, it is his unique blend of raw intelligence and knowledge depth and breadth. All of this comes through in his work with clients. The former chairman of Citicorp, Walter Wriston, recalled his work with Drucker during the 1960s and 1970s: "His perspective was so broad and wide—he always seemed to see something that no one else did. I taught a class with him just last year at Claremont, and it was so much fun . . . he just astonishes you with historical facts that put current issues in perspective. He is a constant learning machine!" Other clients echo these comments: "He makes you see the whys to the issue and not just the answer." [11]

Broad Knowledge Sparks Innovation

This theme of blending the specialist's expertise with broader perspectives reoccurs in the next chapter where we examine how great client advisers add value through big-picture thinking—synthesis—rather than analysis. It is a pervasive issue in many fields: the highest value seems to be created by individuals who take a multidisciplinary approach, despite the fact that we are all endlessly pushed to specialize.

This tension was the impetus behind the founding of the Santa Fe Institute in 1984 by Nobel laureate Murray Gell-Mann, former National Science Foundation director Edward Knapp, and several other leading scientists: namely, that modern scientists are so specialized that no one outside their fields can even read the research papers they write. At the Santa Fe Institute, teams of scientists and professionals from diverse fields—physics, mathematics, biology, history, and operations research, for example—work together on a project basis. The output of the Santa Fe Institute has been red hot and includes ideas such as complexity theory, computer simulations that learn and evolve, and new perspectives on the origins of life. Consultants and academics from around the world now make regular pilgrimages to New Mexico to walk barefoot on this hotbed of new concepts.

Rajat Gupta, the worldwide managing director of consultants McKinsey & Company, sums up the practical advantages of a broad, multidisciplinary perspective when he says, "Some of our best people are those who studied literature or the classics, and who later received business training. These people tend to understand the array of forces at work in organizations, and they approach decisions in a very well-rounded way. My advice to young people is to avoid the urge to focus too early."[12]

THREE LEVELS OF CLIENT LEARNING

Professionals who become advisers to their clients develop into deep generalists, in short, through both the systematic and casual pursuit of knowledge depth and breadth. There is a particular aspect of this knowledge acquisition, however, that needs special emphasis: learning about your clients. As we stated in chapter 1, doing a competent job and having "satisfied" clients alone will not bring clients back to you year after year. Doing outstanding work, however, and constantly adding value through the insights you bring and the personal and professional relationship you develop will earn you deep loyalty.

Developing in-depth knowledge about your client is the best and quickest way to get in a position where you can contribute insights and create the foundation for a long-term, collaborative relationship. Client learning occurs on three levels, and at each succeeding level you become more and more valuable to the individual you serve. From the broadest to the most narrow, the three levels are:

- *Your client's industry:* Today, most clients insist on a certain degree of industry knowledge and expertise. You have to be fluent in the issues that your client's particular industry faces and the position of her company within the industry. Although an important first step, this knowledge alone will not differentiate you as a professional.

- *Your client's company and organization:* As you build knowledge about your client's strategy and operations, your ability to suggest new ideas and solutions increases dramatically. An understanding of the people in the organization is also critically important. Whether you advise a department head or a CEO, the more you know about that person's direct reports, the more helpful you can be as an adviser.

- *Your client:* At the top of this pyramid you get to know your client both personally and professionally. You develop an understanding of her strengths, weaknesses, and preferences. You learn when to push hard and when to step back. You appreciate her world view, or paradigms, and know how to sell your ideas and get them across most effectively. At this level of client learning, you are in a unique position to add extraordinary value.

These three levels are depicted in the following illustration.

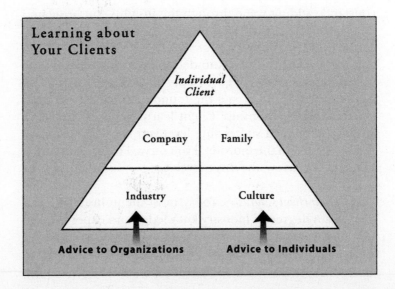

Learning about
Your Clients

Individual Client

Company   Family

Industry   Culture

Advice to Organizations   Advice to Individuals

If you are an accountant, financial consultant, or other professional who advises individuals rather than organizations, there is an analogous hierarchy, shown on the right-hand side of the illustration "Learning about Your Clients," that you have to master, and it also consists of three levels:

- *Culture:* An individual client will have a very different value system, world view, and risk propensity depending on his culture. Culture in this sense has many different manifestations—it could denote a distinct racial, ethnic, or religious group, or even refer to a geographic location. Personal debt accumulation, for example, may be encouraged and even admired in one culture but anathema in another.
- *Family:* Whereas the corporate lawyer or consultant studies the organization of the company he advises, the individual adviser has to understand the family of his client. The number, type, and quality of family relationships will all temper the nature of the advice given.
- *Client:* Again, at the top of this pyramid is the individual about whom you must develop a broad understanding.

When you have mastered all three of these levels, your ability to anticipate client needs, bring fresh solutions and ideas, serve as a sounding board, and provide comfort and reassurance to your client is at its peak. This is why empathy is so important to this equation: you don't achieve this level of client knowledge without a healthy ability to empathize.

Developing Unique Knowledge

Remember that your goal has to be more than just developing general knowledge about your client. You need to learn things about his organization and his company that even he doesn't know; you need to be in a position to actually teach him about aspects of his business—customer needs, organizational dynamics, technology issues, and so on—that he was previously unaware of. New knowledge represents real value for your client; recycled, old information is fairly useless.

In the early nineteenth century, the Rothschild bankers in Europe had a secret weapon—carrier pigeons—that provided them with information about major events, such as Wellington's victory over Napoleon at Waterloo, well before any of their clients found out. The French statesman Talleyrand once sighed that "the English ministry is always informed of everything by the Rothschilds ten to twelve hours before Lord Stuart's dispatches arrive."[13] This "information edge" gave the Rothschilds an enormous competitive advantage.

Allen Freedman, chairman of insurance giant Fortis, summed much of this up when he explained to *The Wall Street Journal* why he moved his business to investment bank Donaldson, Lufkin, and Jenrette in order to follow his longtime banker, who had left Union Bank of Switzerland: "When you go into battle, you want to have people with whom you've worked before, and whose behavior under adverse conditions can be predicted. It took me years to train this guy in my strategy. He's seen enough of our transactions to know what we're good at and what we're not good at."[14] By successfully tackling all three of these learning levels—industry, company, and individual client—this particular banker earned a *client for life.*

BECOMING A DEEP GENERALIST

So how do you set about becoming a deep generalist rather than a subject matter expert, to *knowing more,* as David Ogilvy suggested? There is no set formula for developing the breadth of knowledge that is characteristic of great professionals. We have, however, observed certain habits and practices among the advisers we have studied.

Learning through Teaching

The best learners like to teach, and teaching helps them learn. For Aristotle, learning and teaching were inextricably linked. He believed that you couldn't truly master a subject unless you could teach it and communicate your knowledge to others. Peter Drucker has the same philosophy: he loves to teach because he learns so much (if the students are experienced!). Many other great historic advisers, in fact, have been teachers: Henry Kissinger was a professor at Harvard for many years before becoming Nixon's secretary of state, and General George Marshall, Roosevelt's wartime adviser, put in long stints teaching at the army's war college and other field training centers.

When you teach something, you have to organize and systematize what you know. This process solidifies your thinking, pinpoints the gaps, and forces you to go deeper into the subject matter.

There are plenty of opportunities for professionals to teach. They include internal company training (if you work for a firm), seminars for clients, taking a speaking slot at an industry conference, guest lecturing at an undergraduate or graduate program in your field, writing, or actually teaching a course at an educational institution.

Exploring

One of the biggest barriers to promotion into senior management for corporate managers is having a narrow, overly technical perspective, and the same is true of professionals. If you are an accountant, you have to develop knowledge of the functions—marketing, sales, engineering, and so on—that interrelate with finance. A consultant has to understand how an area of focus—be it information technology, logistics, or personnel—fits into the client's broader business strategy.

Another important area for exploration lies entirely outside the business ecosystem. It includes culture, politics, and religion. In order to understand your own cultural and national context—and biases—you have to become knowledgeable about others. There are many ways to do this, including living abroad if your personal situation permits it, traveling, studying, having a diverse group of friends and colleagues, and so on. You can get an excellent start in this area by looking at Will Durant's *The Story of Civilization* series or *A History of Knowledge* by Charles Van Doren. No single book is going to make you a deep generalist, but these volumes are fascinating to read and represent a concise summary of most of the important ideas, cultures, and discoveries of the last 3,000 years. In a couple of evenings of reading, you'll learn about the importance of the Greeks and the impact that printed books had on seventeenth-century Europe. Is any of that at all relevant? Just ask Peter Drucker. Keep in mind, however, that educating yourself about history and culture needs to become a longer-term habit; collecting a few unrelated facts or random trivia won't help much. As Alexander Pope said in his *Essay on Criticism,* "A little learning is a dangerous thing/Drink deep, or taste not of the Pierian spring . . ."

The Role of Play

Studies have shown that many highly creative learners have a childlike perspective when it comes to ideas. They "toy" with new ideas, without fear of criticism or disapproval, rearranging them and looking at them from many different perspectives. Like children, they frequently ask "why?" Einstein saw playfulness as "the essential feature in productive thought." Newton wrote, "I do not know what I may appear to be to the world; but to myself I seem to have been only like a boy playing on the seashore, and diverting myself in now and then finding . . . a smoother pebble or a prettier shell than ordinary whilst the great ocean of truth lay all undiscovered before me." Interestingly, contemporary research on play has produced evidence that adults who engage in play have superior cognitive abilities.[15] We don't know if one leads to the other, but there appears to be a correlation.

Powers of Observation

Extraordinary professionals have well-developed powers of observation. No matter where they are—at work, with their families, or at play—they are always listening and watching. Isaac Newton's neighbor used to think he was insane. She would observe him through his bathroom window in the bathtub, where he would lie for hours staring at soap bubbles until the water was ice cold (we wonder exactly what this neighbor was really up to!). Newton wasn't wasting his time, of course; he was carefully watching the behavior of the bubbles, the surface tension that kept them rigid, the diffraction of light from his window as it struck them. His mind was racing. Similarly, Louis Pasteur, the French bacteriologist and vaccine pioneer, made a major discovery about anthrax by observing a small patch of discolored soil on a farmer's land. Pasteur's observation uncovered the fact that the farmer had buried a sick pig under the spot. Until that point, no one could figure out why anthrax seemed to stay in the ground forever. When Pasteur investigated, he discovered that worms were burrowing deep into the soil and bringing the anthrax back to the surface.[16]

One professional tells the story of a summer job where he worked as a lab assistant to a marine biologist. When he arrived to start work, the biologist gave him a wet, cold fish, told him to study it, and disappeared. After an entire day of staring at the fish, the youthful apprentice nearly died of boredom. After a second day of observation, he began seeing patterns in the scales, and other features of the skin and eyes, that he hadn't noticed before. When he was finally released from the assignment at the end of yet a third day (we hope the fish was on ice at this point), he had begun to make careful sketches of the fish, finding additional details that had escaped him during the first two days.

Asking "why?" makes the connection between observation and learning. It's not enough just to listen carefully and watch closely; you have to keep wondering why and trying to develop explanations for what you see. If you do this systematically, you will slowly convert random observations into knowledge.

Knowledge Acquisition As a Daily Routine

Many of us, as adults, compartmentalize learning. We do it in chunks—going to a seminar, taking a week off for a workshop, or enrolling in a graduate program. Learning has to be like exercise or diet: it should be embedded in your lifestyle. It could be time set aside each day to peruse several newspapers, or twenty minutes before bedtime dedicated to a book you're reading.

Reading new things *immediately* is also a good strategy that many effective learners employ. If you pile up articles, books, and papers, with the intention of reading them at some future date, you'll rarely get around to them. Furthermore, in the interim something more up-to-date or urgent will take their place. Peter Schwartz, a renowned futurist and author of *The Art of the Long View,* says this about staying current: "You may wonder how I keep track of all the material I gather. I have no elaborate filing system; no database, for instance, and no millions of articles in folders with tags recording their location. I used to maintain such a system and found I never used it. I hardly ever went back to the files. Instead, I concentrate on educating myself; on passing information through my mind so it affects my outlook; on tuning my attention as if it were an instrument . . . don't worry about your files; worry about your perceptions." [17]

Enlarging Your Professional Focus and Experience

Just because you're successful at change management consulting or consumer brand advertising doesn't mean you

Are You a Deep Generalist?

✔ Clients ask for your advice and respect your judgment about issues that extend beyond your core professional expertise.

✔ You enjoy exploring subjects that have nothing to do with your work.

✔ You find something interesting about everyone you meet and every situation you encounter.

✔ You often notice things other people don't—details in a landscape, a particular fact from a presentation, a nuance of behavior.

✔ Your job is an important source of learning for you, but it's only one of many. A lot of your knowledge acquisition comes from broad-based reading, study, discussion and debate with friends and family, pursuit of outside interests, and careful observation of successful individuals.

✔ You've made changes in your professional focus—learning a new industry or a new specialty, moving to a new location, or even undertaking a major career shift.

✔ You excel at your core specialty and constantly keep up to date in it.

have to maintain that focus for the next twenty-five years. Most of us are tempted to do so; it builds our reputation as experts, and we stay in our comfort zone. Many of the effective professionals we have studied continue to develop their original expertise—their distinctive competency—but they also layer new knowledge on top of it. We have seen this take the direction of new industries, new types of clients, or new specialties altogether.

Clients, like all of us, are attracted to new ideas and concepts. Baltasar Gracián, a wise seventeenth-century Jesuit priest and adviser to Spanish noblemen, wrote that "you will be esteemed as long as you are new. Novelty pleases everyone because of its variety. A brand new mediocrity is more highly regarded than an extremely talented person to whom we have grown accustomed. When eminences mingle with us, they age more quickly."[18] You can counter this phenomenon by constantly adding to your professional repertoire and broadening your experience.

To MATURE from subject-matter expert to trusted business adviser, you have to adopt a student mindset. You need a knowledge acquisition strategy that takes you well beyond your core expertise and utilizes multiple methods of learning. Client learning has to be a central focus of your efforts: depth and breadth of knowledge, together with an intimate understanding of your client and his world, form a powerful combination that will fuel your ability to be insightful and consistently add value.

Just as empathy opens the door to learning, you need to become a deep generalist in order to activate your big-picture thinking skills—your powers of synthesis—that will truly differentiate you as an extraordinary professional.

FIVE

THE BIG PICTURE
Cultivating Powers of Synthesis

Most managers become so involved with their own companies that they get lost in the trees—it's hard for them to pull back and take a global perspective, to see the big picture. Great advisers help you do this.

REGINALD JONES, *former chairman and CEO, General Electric*

IN THE MIDST of his career as a diplomat and influential adviser to the powerful Florentine Council, Niccolò Machiavelli was forced out of office in 1512 when the existing republic fell and the Medici merchant family seized power. Falling victim to the changing political winds of the Renaissance city-state of Florence, Machiavelli was accused of being a traitor, imprisoned, and tortured before finally being acquitted and released. With little money, and his pride broken, he retreated to his modest country house in the tiny village of Sant'Andrea outside of Florence. There, during what would turn into a seven-year exile, he produced one of the most penetrating and enduring political analyses ever written: *The Prince.*

During his rural exile, Machiavelli spent mornings at the local tavern, socializing and playing cards with friends. In late afternoon, his serious work began. Machiavelli took a bath, donned his finest clothes, and settled into a comfortable armchair in his small, rustic study. Dozens of rare books by great historians and writers—Livy, Cicero, Ovid, Dante, and Petrarch—lined the walls of the room. Here, Machiavelli spent hours in intense concentration, reading and rereading the mostly Latin and Greek texts that chronicled the tumultuous histories of Persia, Rome, Carthage, Spain, and other empires.

Although he took great pleasure in learning for its own sake, Machiavelli had in mind several concrete objectives: first, by writing a book about princely power, he hoped to demonstrate his political sagacity to the newly installed Medici ruler and possibly secure a post in the prince's administration; second, and more important, he wanted to develop and disseminate a set of ideas that would help bring stability and unity to Italy.

Whereas today we study corporate chief executives and the organizations they lead, Machiavelli analyzed princes and governments. Cloistered in his farmhouse, he distilled the lessons of 2,000 years of history into a brief handbook for rulers. A practical guide to obtaining and keeping power, *The Prince* was given as homage to the Florentine leader Lorenzo de' Medici. While it isn't clear that *The Prince* made an impression on Lorenzo, this short work has since found a strong following with many rulers and political scientists. Adored by some leaders and abhorred by others, *The Prince* is one of those rare books that has stood the test of time (King Henry III of France reportedly had a copy of *The Prince* in his pocket when he was assassinated in 1589!). Although we don't endorse the more ruthless aspects of Machiavelli's proposed leadership approach, which in any event has to be viewed in the context of his war-torn, unstable sixteenth-century world, many of the lessons articulated in *The Prince* are still surprisingly fresh 500 years later.

Because of its insights into leadership and the use of power, *The Prince* is an important work for modern professionals who advise clients. If you aspire to be a big-picture thinker, the book is particularly instructive because it is an example of a prodigious *synthesis,* a brilliant distillation of the *underlying patterns* that characterize successful rulers and their policies. To develop his synthesis of the key elements of princely power, Machiavelli employed many of the skills, tools, and practices that we'll discuss in this chapter.

THE INGREDIENTS OF BIG-PICTURE THINKING

First of all, Machiavelli had put the *foundations* in place to develop his synthesis. His thinking was driven by a clear, overarching purpose: to achieve a unified, stable Italian state. In Machiavelli's time, Italy as a country did not exist; instead, there were five city-states that vied with each other for power and influence. Furthermore, foreign armies from France and Spain routinely attacked the Italian city-states. Machiavelli viewed stability and unification as important ends that could be achieved only through the leadership of a strong, skilled prince. He had also established the other foundations for synthesis: an understanding of the whole picture and a sense of the most strategic issues. Between his years of experience working as a diplomat for the Florentine republic and his vast readings, he had developed an unusually thorough grasp of the workings of sixteenth-century European politics and military strategy, and an appreciation for the key factors of political stability throughout the ages.

With these elements in place, Machiavelli then utilized a number of *tools and techniques* for his synthesis. Through his extensive study of political and military history, he drew out the patterns and commonalities among successful rulers; he used analogies and metaphors to clarify lessons for his own age; he employed multiple perspectives, in turn taking the point of view of large, powerful states as well as of small, defenseless countries; and he cleverly framed his conclusions using artful juxtapositions, categories, and groupings. The first chapter of *The Prince*, for example, is about how to annex another principality—analogous, perhaps, to the modern advice given by business professionals on how to integrate a corporate acquisition. Machiavelli distills five key insights on how to accomplish this objective, drawing on a series of historical examples from Roman times. He then sums it up quite neatly, using France's King Louis VII's failure to conquer Italy as the case in point. Machiavelli ends the section by advising conquering princes to always exile the family of the old prince and to never change taxes in the conquered territory (translated for today's reader: when you make an acquisition, you have to put in your own management, and you shouldn't mess with employees' compensation).

Finally, Machiavelli employed many of the *habits of mind and practices* that enhance the use of these tools and aid synthesis. He took advantage of his time in exile to relax, think, and reflect. He engaged in intense concentration, day after day, as he researched and wrote *The Prince* in the small study of his farmhouse. And he practiced integrated, holistic thinking, studying science, history, literature, and military strategy with equal depth and emphasis.

Synthesis versus Analysis

"Synthesis" comes from a Greek word meaning "to put together into a whole." The essence of synthesis is being able to identify overarching patterns and themes, to see, in effect, the big picture. The ability to synthesize, which is really at the root of strategic thinking, is one of the reasons an adviser is more valuable than an expert. Professionals who can see both the individual trees in the forest and the state of the entire forest are good synthesizers.

To understand synthesis, contrast it with analysis, the stock-in-trade of many professionals. Synthesis and analysis are *complementary opposites* because we need both of them. Without a good understanding of the individual elements of an issue or problem, you'll never produce a good synthesis, and if you don't go beyond just analysis of the problem, you'll be of limited help to your client. They are also opposites because analysis and synthesis involve fundamentally different processes. Analysis is concerned with breaking things down into elements and examining each piece according to a set of prescribed, logical steps; synthesis, in contrast, entails building up an idea, concept, or framework out of the details, often in an illogical, nonstandard, or roundabout way.

All too often, analysis slavishly employs the same old frameworks; when this happens, it becomes a commodity, which clients buy by the pound. Good synthesis—a thinking process that identifies patterns, simplifies and frames the most critical issues, creates a new idea or develops new conclusions from old data—is a scarcer and more valuable activity. It helps clients prioritize their issues and understand what it is they actually need to do, rather than just giving them a snapshot of what is.

Henry Mintzberg, professor of management at McGill University and an authority on strategy, clarifies the differences between analysis and synthesis by distinguishing strategic planning from strategic thinking: "Planning has always been about analysis—about breaking down a goal or set of intentions into steps . . . and articulating the anticipated consequences or results of each step. Strategic thinking, in contrast, is about synthesis. It involves intuition and creativity. The outcome of strategic thinking is an integrated perspective of the whole enterprise."[1]

Clients who actively use professional advisers also see the distinction between analysis and synthesis quite clearly. One executive made the point as follows: "If you just want information, you get an expert or a consultant. But that's not a real adviser. The adviser provides new perspectives and new ways of looking at the same old issues. He helps you see the big picture."

Here are some other typical phrases we've heard clients use to describe longtime advisers from whom they buy products or services:

- "He gives me a global view."
- "She provides additional perspective and helps me to reconceptualize the problem."
- "He brings big-picture thinking to the discussion."

- "They help me consistently focus on the important, strategic issues . . . the level of the conversation is elevated."
- "He handles the details, the tactics, but is also able to see the overall strategy."

Most great discoveries and ideas have been the result of synthesis: someone develops a hunch and only later (if ever) gathers the data to prove it. Isaac Newton, who was a scientist, educator, and adviser to the British government, performed what is generally considered one of the greatest acts of synthesis in scientific history when he developed his laws of motion. Tucked away in a remote rural cottage while the plague swept through Cambridge, Newton explained, in one fell swoop, the basic physical laws of the universe—knowledge that had eluded mankind for thousands of years. He took all the discoveries and theories of Gilbert, Galileo, Descartes, Kepler, and others, integrated them into his thinking, and then saw the unifying principles and patterns. "I stood on the shoulders of giants," he later wrote.

In the business world as well, many management concepts—decentralization, management by objectives, the importance of company culture, the learning organization, and so on—emerged as principles or generalizations that were based on synthesis, not quantifiable analysis.

As we saw in the case of Machiavelli's *The Prince*, there are three major ingredients necessary to develop good synthesis. First, the *foundations* have to be in place. These consist of an overarching purpose or goal that conditions your thinking and motivation; a clear view of the whole picture, not just a piece of it; and a sharp understanding of the most critical, relevant issues within that whole picture. Second, you need to utilize specific *tools and techniques* for synthesis, such as simplifying frames, multiple perspectives, and pattern identification. Finally, there are some *habits of mind and practices*—for example, taking time for reflection and staying involved in hands-on client work—that will help you effectively use these tools and arrive at the big picture. The accompanying illus-

Cultivating Powers of Synthesis

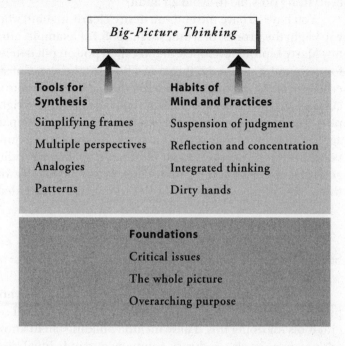

tration sets out the major ingredients of big-picture thinking. Let's look carefully at each one of them in turn.

LAYING THE FOUNDATIONS FOR SYNTHESIS

The first stone in the foundation of a good synthesis has to be a sense of *purpose*. Just as Machiavelli had in mind an overarching goal in writing *The Prince*—a stable, unified Italy—so should modern professionals as they set out to formulate conclusions and recommendations to their clients. Are you trying to keep your client's company from being taken over, or is the goal really to obtain the best price? Are you trying to develop a winning strategy or staunch the red ink and save your client from bankruptcy in the short term?

Does your client want to minimize taxes at all costs or do everything possible to avoid an audit?

You have to have the end you desire clearly in mind when you begin the process of synthesis. In 1985, for example, attorney Marty Lipton developed the so-called poison pill defense for companies under the threat of a hostile takeover. Considered one of the major innovations in the field of corporate securities law, the poison pill, essentially a shareholder rights plan that makes it prohibitively expensive to buy a company against the will of management, was a response to the junkbond financed takeover boom of the 1980s. The overriding goal that drove Lipton's thinking was providing clients with the ability to choose whether or not to remain independent.

Seeing the Whole Picture

Next, you have to develop an understanding of the whole picture. In chapter 4 on deep generalists, we suggested several tools for doing this. These include building client knowledge at three levels—industry, company, and individual client (or culture, family, and client)—and developing a deep, contextual understanding of your client's entire ecosystem.

The attempt to develop a holistic conception of the corporation and its ills has been one of the driving forces behind mergers in the services industries. Electronic Data Systems (EDS), for example, bought the management consulting firm A. T. Kearney with a view toward being able to offer clients broad transformational projects that cut across operational and strategic issues; for similar reasons, Computer Sciences Corporation acquired the consulting firm Index. Now accounting firms are adding law practices, and law firms are eyeing accountants. One of the theories driving all this consolidation is that managers cannot treat individual, functional problems in isolation, since they always form part of an integrated whole. A second reason given—the need to be equipped to serve global client needs—is often a euphemism for forced industry consolidation that results from slowing growth.

The importance of seeing the total picture is exemplified by this story from another field altogether—medicine. Some years ago a young woman was sent to see Dr. Michael Gormley, the renowned English physician whom we introduced in chapter 3 on empathy. She worked as the personal assistant to a high-powered executive in the London office of a large multinational corporation. Suffering from chronic tonsillitis and fatigue that seemed resistant to all treatments, and constantly missing work, she visited several doctors in search of a "cure." Her executive boss was desperate to get her cured so she could get back to work once and for all. The first doctor who saw her suspected that her problem was something more serious and sinister than mere tonsillitis, but he couldn't quite figure it out.

Rather than immediately sending the young woman off for a battery of expensive diagnostic tests (the equivalent to analyzing the problem to death in a corporate setting), Gormley took the time to develop a detailed medical, personal, and professional profile of the patient. It turned out that her boss was a tyrant, insisting that she show up at 7:00 A.M. on some mornings, for example, which required her to get up at 4:30 in order to catch the train into central London. She was, furthermore, simultaneously pursuing a graduate degree at night school and providing financial support to an ailing parent. She hated her job and felt trapped. The tonsillitis was real enough, but the young woman's impossible boss and the complications of her personal life had weakened her immune system and made her illness advance from acute to chronic. The big-picture solution wasn't more tests or antibiotics but rather a blended approach of palliative medical treatment, rest, and a readjustment of her work situation. Her improvement was immediate.

Identifying Critical Issues

For managers, *critical issue selection*—the ability to identify and focus on the most appropriate and relevant priorities and problems—is a fundamental skill. The inability to identify the critical issues is a principal reason for failure and dismissal in management jobs. If cost cutting is the most pressing short-term issue and an executive focuses on marketing, her tenure will be short-lived. The pages of *The Wall Street Journal* and *Fortune* are routinely filled with tales of otherwise highly talented CEOs who put their energies into misplaced and ill-timed priorities and consequently are ousted by impatient and unhappy boards.

For professionals who want to evolve from specialists into broad-based business advisers, this ability to prioritize is even more important: clients expect you as an outside adviser to help keep them focused on the most important problems and priorities. How do you do this? First, by constantly screening these issues against the ultimate purpose at hand. You have to ask, "Which issues will really affect the outcome I seek?" Second, you need to distinguish between symptoms and causes. A CEO might bring in a psychologist to counsel senior executives who are in conflict, for example, but the root cause might be a compensation system that is driving them apart rather than personality differences. Their interpersonal dynamics, in short, do not represent a priority issue; the compensation system, however, does.

The ability to frame and communicate the critical issues in each situation gives an edge to any professional. Eric Silverman, who heads the Global Project Finance group at the New York law firm of Milbank, Tweed, describes how big-picture thinking can vastly increase the impact you have on clients and improve the tenor of your relationships with them. He tells us:

A major energy company struggled for a year to put together a multibillion-dollar financing package. A number of financial institutions were involved, but the package never quite got off the ground. The company finally got a large bank to come in and support the deal, guaranteeing its success. This bank—a latecomer to the whole process—insisted that we come in as attorneys to review the entire project. The energy company itself, the other financial partners, and their legal advisers were adamantly against our involvement, and they aggressively tried to keep us out. The original banks in the deal were afraid we would slow down the project by months and essentially redo a lot of the legal due diligence that had already been painstakingly undertaken.

So when my firm arrived, the environment was hostile—at best we'd be paid for our time and ushered out as soon as possible. Most law firms would have brought in a cast of thousands and insisted on reviewing every single aspect of the deal. Instead, we used a very small staff. Then, we isolated the top five or six legal issues—out of hundreds—that we felt were truly strategic and brought these to the consortium management. They were delighted: we weren't milking the situation and calling everything into question. The points we chose to review and analyze were ones they had struggled with for a year, so everyone was motivated to resolve them. The main client ended up calling us back repeatedly to assist with other, unrelated deals. Instead of a one-off transaction, this has become a very long-term relationship.

All too often, professionals get caught up in the details of their work. You might spend weeks analyzing the results of an advertising campaign or conducting a legal review of a major contract. When you see your client, you want to get across all the richness of the work you've completed, including the details of how you arrived at your conclusions. Often, this documentation is necessary. But when it comes to communicating your ideas and conclusions, you have to consider that most people are able to absorb and remember *three main points* during any major presentation or discussion. The trick for client advisers is to make sure that those key points are clearly communicated, and that they're the right ones in the first place. The following story, told by a consultant about a project for a major client, illustrates this point clearly:

> We spent over six months analyzing the operational performance of a large industrial company. We wrote up our analysis and conclusions in a 200-page document that laboriously documented all of our findings, which were substantial—many parts of the company were underperforming, and severe operational deficiencies needed to be addressed.
>
> Coincidental with the end of the engagement, a new chief executive was appointed to run the company. We hoped to continue our work, and I sent a copy of our report to the new CEO. A number of weeks passed, but I heard nothing back. Finally, I called the CEO to discuss the work. His terse response was, "Can't you give me an executive summary of what you've done? What's the big picture you're trying to get across here?" Somehow, the report's complexity obscured the handful of critically important points that we were trying to make. There was in fact a two-page executive summary in the front of the document, but in retrospect it was actually too brief to be convincing to the CEO.
>
> After working on it for a week, we finally produced a fifteen-page synthesis of the key conclusions and recommendations. The CEO called me up about ten days later, his tone now enthusiastic: "Thanks for the new report," he said to me. "Now I finally understand what you guys were trying to say." We've worked for the company for many years since.

Before any client meeting or presentation, ask yourself: if someone encounters my client in a week and asks him what we said today, how would I like him to respond? What are the main points I want him to remember? You'd better have these clearly in your own mind.

TOOLS AND TECHNIQUES FOR SYNTHESIS

Once the foundations are in place, there are five specific techniques that you can use to undertake synthesis and develop the big picture for your client.

Develop simplifying frames. Framing is the essence of synthesis. It organizes and explains complex phenomena by reducing them to a few, simple dimensions. A good frame (or framework) highlights the most relevant aspects of the issue or problem, shows how they interrelate, and then connects to your overarching purpose or goal. Often, frames provide a picture or visual representation that makes it easy to rapidly understand the key relationships. Aristotle recognized this, writing that "it is impossible to even think without a mental picture." Frames can be quite simple; indeed, some of the most ingenious ones are very elementary in their construction. Like good business strategies, they seem basic and obvious when viewed in hindsight.

Remember that there is a huge gulf between simple and simplistic. Good frameworks that are simple use just a few dimensions or concepts that together explain most of what's going on; simplistic frameworks, in contrast, ascribe too much explanatory power to a few variables. Many popular diet regimes are like this; they are based on an easily understandable prescription, such as eating fruit or avoiding protein, whereas weight levels and general health are predicated on more complex factors. The same can be said for most management fads—they are simplistic, overly narrow attempts to find the silver bullet that will result in corporate success.

One concept to keep in mind when developing frames is the principle of Ockham's razor. William of Ockham, a medieval scholastic philosopher and monk, argued that "entities are not to be multiplied beyond necessity," writing on a later occasion that "what can be done with fewer is done in vain with more." A corollary of his simplicity principle is that given several competing explanations for a problem, you should prefer first the one that requires the fewest assumptions. Only after that explanation is proven wrong should you proceed to the next most complex set of assumptions. Good synthesis follows Ockham's principles by focusing on the simplest but most comprehensive explanation that relies on the fewest assumptions.

Let's look at two well-known frameworks that have become influential:

1. *The growth-share matrix.* In the 1960s, Bruce Henderson at the Boston Consulting Group developed the growth-share matrix, a framework that categorizes the businesses in a company's portfolio and prescribes strategies for them based on their market share and the overall growth rate of the industry they operate in. The matrix identifies four types of businesses:

- *Stars:* High market share, high industry growth—these are the winners in your portfolio and should be aggressively supported.
- *Question marks:* Low market share, high industry growth—these businesses have a questionable future. Major investment will be required to improve their position.
- *Cash cows:* High market share, low industry growth—these are businesses that throw off cash that can be milked to fund "question mark" or "star" divisions.
- *Dogs:* Low market share, low market growth—these are unattractive businesses that need to be substantially restructured or divested.

Henderson reduced the hundreds of variables that can affect performance and competitive position down to these two principal ones—market share and industry growth—thus vastly simplifying the task of evaluating businesses within a portfolio. Although contemporary research has rendered the original growth-share matrix somewhat antiquated, it had a major impact on strategic planning for many years. The term "cash cow," for example, is an integral part of our management vocabulary thirty years later.

2. *Stephen Covey's time management model.* In his first book, *The 7 Habits of Highly Effective People,* Stephen Covey set out a very simple time management framework that has since led to a number of additional books (such as *First Things First*) as well as a huge training business in time management. His model classifies all of your activities along two dimensions: degree of importance and degree of urgency. Covey's matrix has four quadrants, and everything you do can be positioned in one of these quadrants. The idea is get rid of activities that are not urgent and not important (e.g., watching TV or reading junk mail) and focus more and more of your time on tasks that are in the "not urgent but important" quadrant, such as pursuing personal development, building long-term relationships, and so on.

Covey's time management matrix is quite basic, and while other authors have addressed the same concepts in one form or another, the simplicity and clarity with which he framed it gave it its power and popularity. Rather than focusing on *efficiency*—how to do more in a single day—Covey reframed the problem by creating a model that emphasizes the *effectiveness* of your time and its link to your major personal and professional goals.

We learn several things about framing from these examples. First, there is no "formula" for how you frame. Sometimes, as in the case of the Boston Consulting Group matrix, quantitative analysis underpins the frame, and then judgment is applied to tease out the patterns and critical issues (Boston Consulting Group had done quite a bit of research on the "experience curve" and the impact of market share on profitability). Frequently, however, the frame is qualitatively based. Covey's time management system is not a "data-driven" concept; it was created from observation of the most critical factors or issues and an understanding of how they interrelate. Also, frames have to simplify. There is nothing more confusing and irritating than a framework that has dozens of moving parts. The essence of framing is a reduction to basic components and drivers.

Use analogies and metaphors. Analogies are a powerful way to create new ideas and to transfer concepts from one domain to another. Charles Merrill, the founder of the modern financial behemoth Merrill Lynch, tapped into the power of analogy when he brought stocks and bonds to the masses. Early in his career as a banker, he helped finance several of the burgeoning retail store chains, such as J. G. McCrory, which were focused on the mass market. Merrill quickly adopted this new concept of mass merchandising and used it to reconceptualize and restructure the stockbroking business, which had previously served only the very wealthy, in order to make investments accessible to the average man and woman. Merrill was so enamored of this analogy that even his corporate offices in New York were decorated with large murals depicting chain stores, such as Safeway. For over seventy years, Merrill's original mission statement, "To Take Wall Street to Main Street," has given the company its direction.

Marvin Bower, one of the founding partners of McKinsey, spent the first several years of his professional life working for the blue-chip Cleveland law firm of Jones, Day. When he subsequently joined James O. McKinsey in his growing accounting and consulting business in 1933, management consulting in the modern sense of the word really didn't exist. In fact, companies were a little suspicious of McKinsey and other so-called "company doctors" who were beginning to set up shop. Bower decided early on that their new consulting business—like his old law firm—had to develop and adhere to a set of ethical and moral standards and principles. He called it the Professional Code. Throughout his career, Bower emphasized this code of conduct—borrowed analogously from the legal profession—and it was a significant factor in helping to establish McKinsey & Company as the world's leading strategy consulting firm.

Modeling as well as analogy played a key role in Bower's learning strategy. He later said, "I got a chance to work with Mr. Ginn, the senior partner. Because I had heard so much about him and the firm he had shaped, I made it an immediate objective to learn why it had been so successful. From observation and analysis during my Jones, Day years began the formulation of the program I later brought with me to McKinsey."[2]

Analogies become apparent when you are constantly engaging in "crossover" thinking, asking yourself, "What else is this like? and its variant, "What else is like this?" When Leonardo da Vinci designed a famous staircase, for example, he modeled it after a spiral seashell he had plucked off an Italian beach.

Storytelling is a powerful communications form that is heavily based on the use of analogy and metaphor. Some of the most powerful communicators—politicians and religious figures in particular—rely heavily on the use of stories and fables to get their points across. Well-crafted stories have sharply delineated characters, a brief plot, and a lesson to be learned. They are effortlessly digestible and easy to remember. The setting of a good story often has nothing to do with your audience's context, but the moral does. Good stories go beyond the use of analogy, by the way, often representing a superb overall synthesis in very few words. Professionals who become good at storytelling are able to impart vivid imagery that sticks in people's minds.

Develop multiple perspectives. In 1917, the Indian spiritual leader Gandhi went to the province of Champaran to help resolve a particularly bitter and long-standing dispute between the impoverished indigo farmers and the local planters. Gandhi was dedicated to "truth in the collection and interpretation of data," and rather than automatically taking the side of the downtrodden farmers, he systematically interviewed not only the villagers but the planters and local British officials as well, to understand all of their perspectives. This enabled him to isolate different aspects of the problem: the desperate financial condition of the farmers was to a great extent the responsibility of the planters, but many other problems, such as illiteracy and poor sanitation, were the responsibility of the villagers and had to be solved by them. The dispute was satisfactorily resolved.[3]

"We think too small," said the Chinese leader Mao Tse-tung. "Like the frog at the bottom of the well. He thinks the sky is only as big as the top of the well. If he surfaced, he would have an entirely different view." Part of the essence of synthesis is looking at the world with the broadest possible view. If you adhere slavishly to a single perspective, it will inevitably limit and even distort your thinking. This is, in fact, one of the primary reasons why otherwise successful companies fail: they refuse to relinquish their traditional, narrow frames of reference and the assumptions that go along with them.

In the early 1970s, for example, U.S. automakers held dearly to a narrow perspective that allowed the Japanese to gain a huge share of the U.S. market. Their basic point of view was a financial one: many of the top executives at General Motors had come through the finance organization, and the belief was "We are in the business of earning a return for our shareholders" (as opposed to "We are in the business of making great cars that everyone wants to buy"). Furthermore, they were convinced incorrectly that Americans wouldn't like small cars and that their customers valued styling over quality. The result was a steady loss of market share.

Professionals acquire a number of perspectives that help them develop the big picture. First, every constituency involved in the problem you are trying to solve has a particular point of view, and you need to understand it. Whether the issue is one of business strategy, legal practices, or financial policy, chances are you will reach a better understanding of your options and their implications if you review the situation from the perspective of each of these groups. Constituency groups in a corporate setting can include employees, top management, customers, the capital markets, suppliers, and the press.

The ability to understand the perspectives of multiple constituencies has very practical implications for client advisers. A mid-sized company, for example, was sued by a customer for breach of contract. Both management and its legal advisers concluded that the case was completely without merit and that there was virtually no way they could lose if it went to trial. However, managers of this company were contemplating a merger with another firm that, if successful, would give them a preeminent market position. On the basis of the legal issues involved, there was no question but that they should go to court. After discussions with several shareholders, however, as well as their investment bankers, they realized that from the capital markets point of view a pending lawsuit would overshadow and possibly stymie any future merger efforts. Management gritted its teeth and made a financial settlement that cleared the way for the merger strategy.

There is a second type of perspective that great client advisers acquire, which we call a multidisciplinary perspective. This is depicted in the illustration "Understanding Multiple Perspectives," in the boxes labeled "Functions" and "Disciplines."

Depending on our training and specialty, we all tend to adopt a particular functional or discipline-based point of view. If you are an advertising professional, you will look at corporate issues through the lens of marketing and brands; if you are a reengineering consultant, you see everything in terms of processes; an economist focuses on supply and demand; and so on. The challenge is to understand and appreciate the perspectives of other corporate functions, such as marketing or manufacturing, and other disciplines like economics or organizational behavior. Author and strategist Michael Porter's five-forces model of competition, for example, blends the traditional perspective of an economist with that of a business strategist. This doesn't mean you have to become expert in all of these specialties, but rather develop an

Understanding Multiple Perspectives

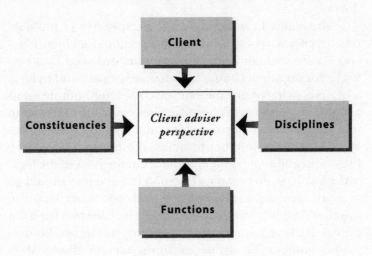

understanding of basic frameworks and principles. It goes back to being a deep generalist.

Reverse your thinking. Reverse thinking is a form of synthesis that involves completely rearranging the pieces to create a new whole. Sometimes, in other words, it is possible to reconceptualize a problem or situation by reversing or radically reorganizing the chain of events or order of information. In the 1960s and 1970s, the typical sequencing for technology product introductions (e.g., mainframe computers and photocopiers) started with the government market, moved into the business segment, and then "trickled down" to consumers. Since the first product models were extremely expensive, large, and typically full-featured for the most demanding users, it was logical (or so it seemed at the time) to start with the customers who could pay the most and who would use all of the bells and whistles.

In the 1970s, product strategists at Canon proposed an unorthodox approach for the copier market. They *reversed* this flow and targeted the consumer market first with inexpensive machines, and then moved up to businesses and government. By taking these strategic moves, they created huge economies of scale, achieved low unit costs, and seized significant market share from Xerox. Canon turned "trickle-down" into "trickle-up."

Reverse thinking concepts are now embedded in modern office equipment such as computer printers. Normally, a company will charge a higher price for a product that costs more to manufacture and distribute. Quite the opposite is occurring with some printer models: the low-speed, less expensive (five pages per minute) version of one printer, for example, is the same as the high-speed model except that it contains a special chip that slows it down. Because of the extra chip, it costs more to build than the higher-priced version—a complete reversal of typical pricing logic.[4]

As is the case with other tools for synthesis, there is no cookie-cutter approach to developing reverse thinking. You can start the process, however, by asking a series of questions that challenge the status quo: Why does this have to be done this way? What if instead of creating a new position, we redistribute the responsibilities? What if we turned this process on its head?

Look for patterns and commonalities. Big-picture thinking is sometimes referred to as *pattern thinking.* If you can "identify the constellations of significance in the otherwise chaotic flow of information,"[5] you are well on your way to synthesis.

One of the best ways to develop your pattern thinking skills is to organize and codify. In chapter 1, we outlined the seven core attributes of great client advisers. These seven attributes emerged from the organization and codification of the findings from about 100 high-level, in-depth interviews and the contents of over five hundred books and articles. Examples of this type of organization abound: Howard Gardner's seminal book on the theory of multiple intelligences, *Frames of Mind* (1983), sets out seven distinct types of intelligence; educator and strategy expert Michael Porter articulated three generic business strategies in his first book,

Competitive Strategy (1980); Abraham Maslow developed a hierarchy of needs with five levels; and so on.

The high-yield (or "junk") bond market, considered one of the greatest innovations in twentieth-century finance, was developed by Drexel banker Michael Milken, who could see patterns in the performance of obscure bonds. Observing that the default rates of high-yield bonds were lower than expected given their high interest rates, Milken concluded that they were an above average investment on a risk-return basis. He then convinced hundreds of large investors around the world of his findings, and with ready buyers for these securities, the 1980s takeover boom was born. Although there are today widely varying opinions about Milken's professional conduct and personal scruples, the enormous impact that his innovations have had on corporate finance cannot be denied.

Henry Kissinger: An Extraordinary Big-Picture Thinker

Part of recognizing patterns is the ability to see *commonalities*. Many of us look for differences, yet it can be more productive to look at similarities—to try to identify the common ground between different issues, phenomena, or constituencies. The case of Henry Kissinger, adviser extraordinaire, shows how a grand strategy can be crafted by discerning commonalities rather than differences.

Henry Kissinger was a master not just of pattern thinking, but of virtually all the tools of synthesis that we've been discussing. Secretary of state under Presidents Richard Nixon and Gerald Ford, Kissinger has been for the last fifteen years an influential consultant to multinational corporations. "At the core of his brilliance," writes biographer Walter Isaacson, "was an ability to see the relationships between different events and to conceptualize patterns. . . . He sensed . . . how an action in one corner of the world would reverberate in another, how the application of power in one place would ripple elsewhere."[6]

Although unquestionably gifted with a powerful intellect, Kissinger crafted for himself an education that provided much of the grist for his later inventiveness in the field of foreign policy. Growing up in Germany during the rise of the Nazis, he was routinely bullied and beaten by other youths because he was Jewish. After his family fled Germany in 1938, Kissinger had the advantage of the multiple perspectives afforded by a bicultural upbringing.

Like Peter Drucker, Kissinger has been a constant learning machine. As a freshman at Harvard in 1947, he was renowned for his voracious study habits. His undergraduate thesis is still legendary at Harvard: with the modest title "The Meaning of History," it weighed in at 383 pages and provoked the "Kissinger Rule" that thereafter limited theses to 150 pages.

Kissinger's most memorable act of synthesis was his conceptualization of the triangular balance of power between China, the Soviet Union, and the United States, a framework that—obvious in hindsight, but almost unthinkable at the time—endured for a full twenty years after he left office. In 1968, Russia was the major threat to the United States, whereas China was a pariah, a political outcast. Kissinger felt that a rapprochement with China would pressure the Soviet Union into moving closer to the United States and subsequently force all three nations into a more stable relationship with more closely aligned national interests. Both Russia and China, he believed, would seek a common bond with the United States. This strategy was neither intuitive nor obvious at the time; in fact, there was great resistance in the State Department and in other quarters to meeting with the Chinese at all. Kissinger, of course, was not alone in pushing for the China strategy; Nixon was also enthusiastic about it, and other leaders, such as Charles de Gaulle, had hinted at the growing importance of China. Kissinger was, however, the strategy's main architect and advocate.

Like Machiavelli—and perhaps the comparison is no accident—Kissinger had a brilliance for big-picture thinking that drew on a variety of factors, including a deep and broad

education, exposure to a variety of perspectives (from the
Nazis to American democracy), the clever use of historical
analogies, and an insatiable appetite for learning.

HABITS OF MIND AND PRACTICES
THAT ENHANCE SYNTHESIS

So far, we've covered specific tools and techniques that
you can use to cultivate your powers of synthesis. There are
some additional "habits" that can help these tools work and
facilitate your ability to see the big picture. These habits have
been identified through our own studies of great professionals, and they are confirmed by what experts on the nature of
creativity and innovative thinking have gleaned from over
thirty years of extensive research.

Suspension of Initial Judgment

Analytical thinking is based on making careful judgments at each stage of the thought process and then validat-
ing every step or conclusion. Synthesis requires a suspension
of judgment (at least until you've made up your mind and are
ready to take a final position on the matter) in order to allow
"unrealistic" alternatives or ideas to be allowed into the discussion. Many great discoveries were either accidental or the
result of "mistakes." Marconi pursued his (ultimately) successful experiments in the belief that radio waves followed
the curvature of the earth (they don't). Penicillin and x-rays
were also "mistakes," which developed into life-saving medical breakthroughs. For this reason, General Motors executive Charles Kettering once said, "If I want to stop a research
program, I can always do it by getting a few experts to sit in on
the subject, because they know right away that it was a fool
thing to try in the first place." [7]

The Use of Humor

Humor—a talent for which not everyone has—shares several characteristics with creative, synthetic thinking. Clever jokes and stories often present unexpected solutions and juxtapose ideas or concepts that normally would not go together. The best jokes—like good thinking—often end with an unexpected punchline. Savor, for example, the twist in this old story:

> During the Soviet occupation of Czechoslovakia, a rainbow appears over Prague, ending in the middle of St. Wenceslaus Square. A Czech soldier and a Russian soldier rush to the square to find the treasure, which sits squarely under the end of the rainbow. Arriving at the same time, they vie for the gold.
>
> "OK," says the Czech, "let's share it like brothers."
>
> "No way," responds the Russian, shaking his head. "Let's share it fifty-fifty."

Time for Reflection

"I lived in solitude in the country," said Albert Einstein, talking about the sources of his great ideas, "and noticed how the monotony of quiet life stimulates the creative mind."[8] Some researchers in the field of creativity, in fact, believe that insight occurs during the reflection and relaxation that follows a period of intense activity and work. J. P. Morgan used his yacht *Corsair* for this purpose. Moored far out in New York harbor, away from the frenetic pace of the financial markets, the yacht provided Morgan a seclusion where he would take in the sea breeze, relax, and think. When trying to resolve a difficult negotiation or industrial dispute, Morgan might bring executives out to his boat for several days as his guests. There, he would listen while they talked for hours. Usually, a compromise would slowly be reached as Morgan brokered a solution.

Today, our minds are rarely silent. The average businessperson receives hundreds of e-mails and voice messages a day, and vacations for many of us are action-packed weeks more likely full of family activities than opportunities for repose and contemplation. Commenting on this phenomenon, Andrew Heyward, the president of CBS News, said, "Whenever I have a free moment now, I turn to e-mail. It's probably taken away the last few minutes in my life that were available for reflection."[9] For many modern-day client advisers, solitude unfortunately comes only during long airplane rides, and then the time is often spent working on a laptop computer or making calls from the plane's phone system.

While some professionals manage to set aside annual time for reflection—best-selling author Ken Blanchard, for example, takes a "mini-sabbatical" each summer at a country house, working solely on his next set of ideas and his writing projects—most of us in practice have to aspire to some regular, daily, or weekly space for reflection. It can be helpful to have a quiet place you can retreat to from time to time, even if only to the public library. Thomas More, chief adviser to King Henry VIII, built a small, secluded study on his property in Chelsea, away from his main house. He wrote that a man must "choose himself some secret, solitary place in his own house as far from noise and company as he conveniently can, and there let him sometime secretly sit alone, imagining himself as one going out of the world."[10]

The Power of Concentration and Observation

As noted earlier, songwriter Paul McCartney has a marvelous talent for picking up small details around him and turning them into hit songs. Similarly, the highly successful advertising campaign "If you're out of Bud, you're out of beer" was apparently based on a comment overheard in a bar by a copywriter. (A customer, so the story goes, asks the bartender for a Schlitz, and upon learning that they had sold out, he replies, "When you're out of Schlitz, you're out of beer." The copywriter appropriated the idea for the Budweiser account he was working on.)

Learning to concentrate is also a key to synthesis. In attempting to explain Newton's intellectual breakthroughs, John Maynard Keynes wrote: "I believe that the clue to his mind is to be found in his unusual powers of continuous concentrated introspection. . . . His peculiar gift was the power of holding in his mind a purely mental problem until he had seen straight through it."[11] Kissinger was similarly known for his ability to concentrate intensely.

How do you develop this kind of concentration? A lot of it has to do with clearing your mind of other distractions. Recall the image of Isaac Newton sitting for hours in his bathtub until the water was cold, pondering how the light was diffracted through his soap bubbles. Part of the secret as well lies in developing an obsessive dissatisfaction with your answers. Great thinkers keep concentrating because they aren't happy yet with the results they're coming up with. Seeing the imperfections in their early ideas, they push and then push some more. Don't be satisfied with your first thoughts—they may end up providing the insight you seek, but they might not, as well. As Mihaly Csikszentmihalyi, the author of the best-selling *Flow,* says, "Some of the most creative people I've interviewed say the reason they are creative is that they can throw away the bad ideas much quicker than other people can."[12]

Holistic, Integrated Thinking

Based on the pioneering research done by Nobel Prize winner Roger Sperry and others, current theory suggests that the right and left hemispheres of the brain undertake distinct functions. Modern scanning techniques are offering some confirmation of this division of labor: the left side of the brain processes logical, analytical thinking, and the right side handles our more intuitive, conceptual thinking. Problems arise when we develop and exclusively use one type of thinking over the other, something often encouraged by our educational system, which, at least in the United States, tends to emphasize left-brain, analytical approaches to problem solving. The result, at one extreme, is the engineer who is good at number crunching but can't write a sentence; and at the other, the talented artist or writer who can't balance his checkbook and makes a shambles of his finances.

Many of our greatest thinkers and creators, in contrast, have cultivated both sides of their brains. For Leonardo da Vinci, who was both a prolific inventor and a master artist, "art and science were indivisible." [13] Recall, in fact, how advertising great David Ogilvy studied and mastered both the art of creative ad copy and the science of statistical research methods. While no one knows for sure whether specific exercises can enhance one side of your brain versus the other, you should certainly give yourself freedom to pursue a broad range of personal learning that traverses both science and the humanities. Consider this: it is no accident that so many revolutionary inventions and discoveries—the printing press with cast metal type,[14] lead pencils, the mechanical clock, and so on—were made during the Renaissance, a period when many scholars, scientists, and artists were equally exploring science, mathematics, art, history, and literature.

Dirty Hands

A nineteenth-century French diplomat, showing disdain for Anglo-Saxon pragmatism, is said to have remarked, "It will work in practice, yes. But will it work in theory?"[15] Intense concentration of thought and the development of theoretical frameworks are key ingredients in effective big-picture thinking, but it is also true that *doing* is just as important. This is a dilemma for professionals who work in large companies: as you become more senior in an organization, you are exposed to more and more projects and client situations at a very top level; yet at the same time you may actually do less and less hands-on work with specific client issues and problems.

Ideas and innovations often flow from the actual doing, however. Investment banker Nancy Peretsman, whom we introduced in chapter 1, believes she should never stray very far from hands-on client work: "Investment banking has gotten very functionalized at big firms—you might see only a narrow slice of the deal. I like to stay involved in all aspects of a transaction, from start to finish. For example, a year ago I advised on the merger of CDnow and N2K, two Internet-based CD companies. For that size transaction, most senior bankers would delegate the work to a junior team. I felt there was something important to learn, however, so I dug in myself—it took months of my time. Yet based on what I learned during that period, I came up with the idea of linking the new company with yet a third, Columbia House. Without having gotten my hands dirty, I would never have had the insight, confidence, or credibility to approach Time-Warner about Columbia House."

Machiavelli himself was not just a political theoretician; he relished getting hands-on experience. One of his strongly held beliefs was that a government should create a national militia (or army) rather than rely on mercenaries whose loyalties are always suspect. Not one to just sit at a desk, he convinced the Florentine government to create an experimental regiment that Machiavelli personally led into battle. It had limited success—Machiavelli was better at writing than soldiering—but experiences like this shaped and reinforced his thinking.

IF WE LOOK back over the examples of great synthesis discussed in this chapter—the growth-share matrix, the poison pill, the five-forces competitive model, the junk-bond market, and others—there are many commonalities in terms of how these breakthrough ideas were incubated. First, most of their developers used some or all of the tools we've described, such as framing, pattern thinking, and multiple per-

Are You a Big-Picture Thinker?

✔ Before you start any assignment, you are very clear about the overall goals and purpose and have discussed these with your client.

✔ You are drawn to summarize and crystallize the key issues inherent in any given client situation—you are vaguely uncomfortable until you lay these out in your own mind.

✔ You like to collect facts and analyze them, but what really motivates you is asking *why* and trying to understand what they mean.

✔ You develop a strong personal point of view about an issue, but you value and seek out other perspectives as you formulate that view.

✔ Sometimes clients visibly respond when you sum up a situation for them or make recommendations. You get comments such as "Now I see"; "Aha!"; "That puts it in perspective"; "I see the relationship"; or "That's a good way of putting it." They will often repeat what you've said and even use your language as they explain it to others.

✔ Clients often like to sit down with you to "get your perspective" on an issue or situation of importance to them.

spectives. Second, these individuals were totally immersed in the day-to-day practice of their professions—they were doers as well as thinkers. Third, these frameworks were not just the result of blue-sky brainstorming, but derived from an understanding of both the details and the big picture. And finally, the principals involved all had a deep knowledge of the entire ecosystem in which they worked. One of Milken's biographers, for example, ascribes his extraordinary success as a financier to the fact that he had mastered every functional aspect of banking: securities issuance, trading, sales, corporate finance, and mergers and acquisitions (functions which, by the way, make quite distinct demands on the left and right sides of the brain). Similarly, Bruce Henderson of Boston Consulting Group and Marty Lipton of Wachtell, Lipton had a very broad and deep understanding of the companies and industries they dealt with.

Strong big-picture thinking skills will greatly enhance your ability to arrive at sound judgments. Rather than being a purely analytical exercise, which is how most books on decision making portray it, coming to judgment involves equal amounts of analysis and intuition, of left- and right-brain thinking.

SIX

AN EYE FOR WINNERS
Developing Great Judgment

One cool judgment is worth a thousand hasty councils. The thing to do is to supply light and not heat.

WOODROW WILSON

A DECCA RECORD COMPANY EXECUTIVE, responsible for advising management on which new music groups to sign up, had just finished listening to the latest demonstration recording from an aspiring British rock 'n' roll band. With only a moment's reflection, he turned to the group's young manager and shook his head. "Sorry," he said as he got up to leave the room. "We're not interested. Guitar groups are on the way out." The year was 1962. The aspiring rockers happened to be, at the time, a little-known group called the Beatles. They went on to sell over a billion records, tapes, and CDs, but not with Decca.

Only months earlier, newly inaugurated President John F. Kennedy had authorized, under pressure from key advisers, a mission that turned into one of the most disastrous foreign policy blunders in U.S. history. Known as the Bay of Pigs invasion of Cuba, a small group of U.S.-backed Cuban-American volunteer soldiers landed in Cuba with the objective of overthrowing the Castro regime. When they ran into heavy military resistance, the United States withdrew its support, and the operation collapsed. The incident was a major international embarrassment, and it set the stage for the Cuban missile crisis in the following year.

Bad judgments? Clearly. Avoidable? Possibly. But both accounts lend support to the old adage: If your advice is correct, no one remembers; if it's wrong, no one forgets.

In hindsight, bad judgments always seem particularly egregious, and good judgments appear especially brilliant; but in fact the quality of judgment is extraordinarily difficult to evaluate. Contrast the Bay of Pigs and Beatles rejection debacles with this example of what turned out to be a very shrewd judgment:

In June of 1993, Microsoft made a verbal offer to buy America Online (AOL), the Internet service provider. The price per share they were willing to pay valued the company at $268 million. AOL had only 250,000 subscribers and faced stiff competition from other online services like CompuServe and Prodigy, which were larger.

At a tense and dramatic board meeting, AOL directors pondered the fate of the company. Directors supporting an immediate sale made comments like, "We never know when the bubble will burst," and "We could get vaporized." One director who was against the sale pleaded, "Do we want to be a footnote on Bill Gates's resume, or do we want to be the king of the online industry?" AOL CEO and founder Steve Case was against selling but saw both sides, later saying, "I recognized that if we sold, everyone would make a bunch of money and we could all just go off. It wasn't without its possibilities."[1] By a narrow margin of one vote, the board decided to remain independent. Today AOL—which has since acquired and merged with Time Warner—has over 30 million subscribers. Steve Case, who is still AOL's CEO, is a billionaire. In the end, Case's and other board members' beliefs in the value of independence and the importance of making a difference in the new online world won the day.

THE MANY FACETS OF JUDGMENT

A clear-cut judgment? In fact, but for a hair's breadth, Steve Case of AOL and the Decca record executive could have experienced radically different futures. In the case of AOL, the decision not to sell out was decided by *one vote* cast by a director who arrived at the very last minute from Europe. The Decca executive actually had a second chance at the Beatles: when the group's manager, Brian Epstein, pressured him to reconsider his original decision, he took a train to Liverpool to watch the foursome live at the now-famous Cavern Club. It was pouring rain that night, however, and there was a long line at the door of the club. Unwilling to endure the cold, wet wait, he returned to his hotel and never saw them perform. "I should have known by the line in front of the club that there was something special about this group," he later told a Beatles historian.

The best judgments, in fact, can become suddenly unhinged by unforeseen or unpredictable developments. Just look at the multibillion-dollar Iridium satellite telephony project, which was conceived in a 1980s world where cell phones were limited and expensive. By the time it was operational in 1998, the widespread diffusion of low-cost, terrestrially based cellular telephones rendered the service practically obsolete, and Iridium filed for chapter 11 bankruptcy the following year.

The quality of a judgment is difficult to evaluate because we tend to assess decisions based on the consequences they produce rather than the soundness of the judgment process used to reach them. A sound judgment is logically airtight—perhaps the Iridium satellite phone project was an example of one—but it can be punctured by unknowable future events, and the decision makers viewed, in hindsight, as having exercised flawed judgment. Conversely, poor judgments can be compensated for by ideal circumstances—bad managers can look good in a fast-growing market, for example, even though they've made poor decisions. You have to examine each situation carefully, in other words, before jumping to conclusions. Was a seemingly bad decision the result of inherently poor judgment or the unfavorable circumstances that followed? Did a decision turn out well because of keen judgment or because events (e.g., the Federal Reserve Bank lowered interest rates) were just overwhelmingly in our favor?

Robert Frost's famous poem "The Road Not Taken" beautifully illustrates the dilemma of choices. Frost describes a walk in the woods where he encounters two diverging roads, one of which at first seems more worn than the other. Because of the ending—"I took the one less traveled by/And that has made all the difference," the poem is interpreted by many as a salute to individuality and the importance of being a nonconformist (remember all those college dorm-room posters announcing, "I took the road less traveled," with a photograph of two diverging paths in a fog-laden forest?). In the second stanza, however, Frost tells us that actually the roads have the same amount of wear—the second path *isn't* less traveled. In other words, the choices look very similar. The poem, then, is not about being a nonconformist or contrarian, but rather about the enormous difficulty of decisions and the dilemmas inherent in having to choose alternate paths (someone ought to inform the poster industry about this). In retrospect, Frost tells us, we like to think we were contrarians, but in fact at the time of judgment it's impossible to tell where each choice will lead us; and we can never go back.

The key to good judgment lies in balance—in carefully blending facts, experience, and personal values to arrive at a decision. Let's look at the case of J. P. Morgan, an extraordinary decision maker who achieved precisely this balance.

John Pierpont Morgan: The First Relationship Banker

In December 1900, J. P. Morgan learned that industrialist Andrew Carnegie wanted to expand his steel operations into finished products, which was the very market dominated by Morgan's own steel companies, Federal Steel and National Tube. Concerned that the same overcapacity and chaos that had reigned in the railroad business would spread to steel, Morgan hatched a plan to create a steel colossus—a large trust company with the clout to reduce costs and prices, expand the market, and globalize. Just a few weeks later, Morgan sounded out Carnegie on his willingness to sell his steel company to Morgan's trust, which was named U.S. Steel. After a reflective game of golf, Carnegie scratched a number—$480 million—on a slip of paper and had his key lieutenant, Charles Schwab, deliver it to Morgan. Morgan took one look at the figure and, without a moment's hesitation, announced to Schwab, "I accept your price." Later, he said to Carnegie, "Mr. Carnegie, I want to congratulate you on being the richest man in the world" ($480 million in 1900 was the equivalent of $9.5 billion today).

Morgan did not carefully study Carnegie's steel operations and assets before accepting his asking price. Rather, he based his rapid judgment on a premise that was revolutionary at the time: expected future cash flows. He reframed the question from "What are Carnegie's steel assets worth now?" to "What will they be worth in the future?" Most businessmen at the time looked at the value of current assets, but Morgan knew that the future potential of U.S. Steel was so great that $480 million was an entirely acceptable price.

Morgan was the most powerful banker of the nineteenth century. He and his partners held 72 directorships in 112 enterprises and controlled one-fifth of the railroads in the United States. We tend to think of Morgan as a commanding CEO, but he played an equal role as an adviser. From 1870 to 1910, few major industrial or business decisions were made without his influence or involvement. Kings and queens sought him out for his financial insights, and during his career he advised half a dozen U.S. presidents on economic and financial affairs. After an audience with Morgan, Pope Pius X reportedly said, "What a pity I did not think of asking Mr. Morgan to give us some advice about our finances!"[2] Later, Morgan and his bank did in fact advise the Vatican on its investments.

Pierpont Morgan did not want to be just a financier. One Morgan biographer notes that early in his career, "Pierpont began to style himself as far more than a mere provider of money to companies: he wanted to be their lawyer, high priest, and confidant. This wedding of certain companies to certain banks—'relationship banking'—would be a cardinal feature of private banking for the next century."[3]

Morgan exemplified many of the most important qualities of extraordinary client advisers, such as conviction and big-picture thinking. Above all, however, Morgan possessed extraordinary judgment, an ability to formulate, under stress, rapid decisions, usually about high-stakes issues. Although Morgan had a precise and mathematical mind, he was not prone to lengthy and exhaustive analyses. A lawyer who knew him commented, "Morgan has one chief mental asset—a tremendous five minutes' concentration of mental thought." Typically it would take him no more than a few minutes to grasp the key issues inherent in a very complex financial deal and then come to conclusions.

Moreover, he could quickly size up a business and its management team, determining whether and by how much to extend credit. In the period of his ascendancy U.S. financial markets were largely unregulated. There were no rating agencies such as Standard & Poors to evaluate systematically the health and viability of companies. There was no Federal Reserve Bank to regulate the economy. It all came down to the banker's imprimatur: if Morgan endorsed a firm, it could issue stock and borrow money. Without the stamp of approval from a major bank, companies were stuck. Morgan's bank prospered because of his uncanny ability to judge the strength and potential of a given enterprise.

Was Morgan simply born with this good judgment? No. He cultivated it through measured risk taking; an intense, lifelong study of the financial markets; and by maintaining a focus on the important issues in each situation. The incisive, rapid judgments he reached were, ultimately, based on a delicate blend of facts and deep experience, tempered by Morgan's personal value system that heavily emphasized stability and order.

THE IMPORTANCE OF KEEN JUDGMENT

Consultants, attorneys, bankers, accountants, and other professionals are involved in high-risk, high-stakes decisions every day: Should the case go to trial or be settled out of court? Should a microchip manufacturer invest another $1 billion to increase production capacity? Do the company's financial statements represent the actual condition of the business? A keen judgment is one of the most valuable assets a professional can have. Few clients, for obvious reasons, go back to a professional whose judgment is poor. Many of the executives we have interviewed, in fact, remember all too clearly the poor judgments offered by some of their advisers, even though the incidents occurred years ago.

Good judgment, in contrast, is invaluable to clients. Win Bischoff, chairman of the British merchant bank Schroders, recalls a seminal decision he made and how the accurate judgment of his adviser contributed to Schroders' international success:

It was in the early 1980s, and we felt we needed to recapitalize our U.S. bank, which engaged in commercial lending. We were convinced we could issue debt to do this. I went to see the head of Warburgs [a major British merchant bank], David Scholey, to seek advice. In the space of an hour he delivered an unequivocal set of judgments. Issuing debt would be all but impossible, he offered, quickly turning the conversation to the topic of Schroders' overall strategy, and the need for us to assess it in detail at this critical juncture.

We were already considering undertaking a strategic review, and Scholey's advice was important encouragement. We subsequently made a series of important decisions, including eventually selling the U.S. bank instead of recapitalizing it, as well as making other strategic choices that enabled us to prosper as an institution.

That short, singular conversation, and the rapid-fire but incisive views provided by Scholey, became a significant influence on our thinking.

Instinctively, Scholey did several things when asked to advise Schroders. First, he made a rapid, intuitive judgment about the feasibility of issuing debt. The situation fit a pattern in his experience, and he knew what the answer was without hesitating. In the process, he thought two or three steps ahead, and was able to visualize the chain of events following a hypothetical debt issue by Schroders, and the negative consequences that could ensue. In effect, he helped Bischoff avoid a potentially bad judgment. Second, he reframed the question Bischoff was asking. The right question wasn't "Should we recapitalize our American bank?" but "Should we be in the U.S. banking business at all?" Since that time, Schroders' market value has increased fifteen-fold, from about $300 million to $5 billion today.

FIVE JUDGMENT TRAPS TO AVOID

Before we look at the specific practices that allow great professional advisers to arrive at high-quality judgments, we have to understand how to avoid bad judgments. First, bad judgments can be deadly for an organization; second, they will ruin your reputation as a professional—your clients will never forget the poor decisions you recommend; and third, it's very common to make mistakes of judgment, since so many factors can cloud our decision making. The fact is, avoiding bad decisions is one-half of the battle: even if you don't make particularly good ones, you can muddle along and survive, whereas a poor judgment can put you out of business, for good. The exceptional professional, therefore, constantly examines his client's thinking and behavior to help prevent these wrong turns.

Here are five of the most important judgment traps that professionals should be aware of as they advise their clients:

I. Weak Premises: Starting Out on the Wrong Foot

Many clients approach a problem or decision with wrong or partial facts at the outset, resulting in a chain reaction of faulty thinking. The two most common errors that bias clients are *anchoring*—the decision maker allows himself to get "anchored" on a specific starting number—and *availability*, the tendency to use the most available, recent, or vivid information.

If two real estate appraisers, for example, are asked to assess a house that is already for sale, their valuations will vary based on what selling price they're given. The appraiser who thinks the house is for sale at $200,000 will assign a lower valuation than the second appraiser who is told it's on the market for $250,000, even though it's the same house. Where you start often determines where you end up.

Clients can get anchored in many ways. Incumbent corporations in deregulated industries like telecommunications and utilities, for example, often get anchored in their old growth paradigms. Compared to their historic growth rates of 3 percent or 4 percent a year, achieving 5 percent or 10 percent now seems wondrously high. But the new standard, in order for a company to be considered a "growth" business, is more like 15 percent annual growth. Because many of these companies are anchored on the old standards, they end up being acquired.

Whatever happens to be the most available, recent, and vivid data can also bias us. This perception bias can operate when managers go out and talk to just a few customers and then draw sweeping conclusions about their company's products and positioning. Bad personnel decisions are often rooted in this judgment trap—we sometimes pick people we already know for a job rather than the most qualified candidate.

2. Confirmation: Seeing What You Want to See

Many people start out wanting to confirm—consciously or unconsciously—what they already believe and tend to ignore subsequent evidence that contradicts their beliefs.

The confirmation trap is often triggered during mergers or acquisitions. Some years ago, two large professional service firms decided to pursue a merger, which, if completed, would have resulted in large financial payouts to management. A subsequent study commissioned to assess the cultural compatibility of the two companies pointed out very major differences in the two cultures, and an unbiased observer would have concluded that the organizations were virtually incompatible and shouldn't merge. Some partners who read the report, however, came to the opposite conclusion—that there was a strong cultural fit. They ignored the differences that the study cited, or reframed them as "strengths" that would actually aid the merger. As a result, the two firms went through significant post-merger trauma as their different cultures clashed, resulting in bitter conflicts and an exodus of partners.

3. Overconfidence:
Underestimating What It Takes to Succeed

Overconfidence is probably the most common and fatal judgment trap. In his book, *When Giants Stumble,* historian Robert Sobel chronicles famous business blunders by major corporations. He sums up by saying, "If there is any single moral to the tales [about corporate failures] it is that for all but one of these entities failure was preceded by great success."[4] Business success, Sobel cautions, can breed overconfidence and complacency.

Clearly, the Decca record executive cited at the beginning of this chapter was suffering from a major case of overconfidence (and maybe incompetence as well) when he so brusquely turned down the Beatles. A famous historical example of overconfidence is Germany's invasion of Russia during World War II. Adolf Hitler, buoyed by easy victories over Poland, France, and other European countries, became filled with hubris as the war progressed. He then ignored the warnings of his generals and insisted on invading Russia nearly a month too late. His armies were virtually destroyed by the combination of the severe Russian winter and the unexpectedly large number of Russian troops that Stalin was able to mobilize.

Several other classic judgment traps that are related to overconfidence include an over-reliance on *rules of thumb* and a *misunderstanding of base-rates*. Rules of thumb include "When writing an ad, use sentences of no more than twelve words," or "Summer is the best time of year to sell your house." We tend to simplify our experiences and reduce them to easy-to-remember rules and guidelines. Problems arise when these cherished rules just don't apply. For example, Long Term Capital, a hedge fund manager, had leveraged $160 billion worth of securities with just $4.8 billion in capital (the underlying value of the derivatives was estimated at $1 trillion). The company bet large sums of money that the yields on twenty-nine-year government bonds would converge with the yields on thirty-year bonds—something that had always happened in the past (this expected convergence was a "rule of thumb"). In July and August of 1998 the yields actually diverged and Long Term Capital lost virtually all of its capital, nearly causing a global panic in the process.

Misunderstanding or ignoring the underlying statistics regarding an event is also common. For example, most studies on the success of corporate acquisitions demonstrate that 50 to 60 percent of acquisitions are considered failures within five years. The figure is even higher for cross-border mergers, which only succeed 30 percent of the time. Yet many executives pay no attention to these sobering statistics.

4. Prior Commitments: Making New, Inappropriate Commitments Based on Previous Ones

Prior investments or decisions can unduly influence the formulation of new commitments: once we take a stand or position, we often resist changing our mind. This phenomenon may explain why President Kennedy gave the go-ahead for the Bay of Pigs incursion—it was already planned, organized, and ready to go when he was elected. Companies frequently ignore an analogous rule of finance—don't consider sunk investments when making new ones—and they mistakenly pour good money after bad.

In his classic book *Influence: The Psychology of Persuasion,* Robert Cialdini cites many examples of how even very small prior commitments can induce level-headed individuals to agree to things that make no sense. In one study, for example, homeowners consented to have large billboards encouraging traffic safety installed on their front lawns, simply because they had previously agreed to put a small sticker bearing a similar message in the corner of a window![5]

5. Groupthink: Believing That It's "Us Against Them"

The author Irving Janis, in a book entitled *Groupthink,* identifies eight symptoms that can distort judgments and behaviors.[6] These include:

- An illusion of invulnerability, which leads to excessive risk taking
- An unflinching belief in the morality and rightness of the group
- Stereotyped views of adversaries as either evil or incompetent, and therefore not worth dealing with

Corporate organizations often suffer from groupthink, and it can lead their managers to make poor judgments.

When Mexico deregulated its long-distance telephone market, for example, several large U.S. telecommunications companies entered the Mexican market believing they could easily dislodge the national phone company. They held its management in disdain and considered it a stodgy, unworthy competitor. To their surprise, they sustained heavy losses as the national company beat them at every turn with innovative marketing and pricing strategies.

During World War I, this attitude resulted in the slaughter of tens of thousands of soldiers in Turkey. In *The Broken Years: Australian Soldiers in the Great War,* Bill Gammage describes the first Australian soldiers who went into action at Gallipoli: "They thought themselves the equal to twenty Turks, they bowed to no man, and with the eagerness of children they restlessly awaited their glory."[7] Within nine months they had suffered appalling casualties and were forced to creep away in defeat.

How to Avoid Bad Judgments

You need to be constantly vigilant for signs that your client is about to fall into one of these judgment traps. Do you see a client using rules of thumb that are shopworn and outdated? Has your client already made up his mind and just wants your stamp of approval? Do you have clients who rush to judgment based on too much "intuition" and too few facts, or who grossly underestimate what it will take to succeed?

Here are some specific actions you can take as an outside professional to help your client avoid lapses in judgment:

- Always vigorously challenge your clients' assumptions. What makes their starting number right? What would justify a number that was 50 percent less or 50 percent more? Do their customers really only buy on price? Do their products really have the highest quality? Introduce as much contradictory information as you can and ask lots of "disconfirming" questions whose answers might undermine the initial premise.

- Keep yourself up-to-date on key statistics and research in your field—remember, there's a lot of folklore out there. Beware of accepted wisdom: the "dogs of the Dow" stock-buying strategy, for example—popular for many years with investors—has worked poorly during the last five years. (This popular investment strategy involves buying the ten stocks in the Dow Jones Industrial Average with the highest dividend yields during the previous year; holding them for one year; and then going through the same selection process again for the following year, picking a new group of ten).

- Be careful how you ask and frame questions. "Do you feel the market is saturated now?" is a leading question; a better phrasing would be "What is the market potential?" Many professionals ask questions that are biased and reflect what *they* think or what they feel their clients *already* believe.

- Try to identify independent thinkers who can help challenge your clients' thinking. These can be outside speakers, for example, or perhaps mid-level managers who see the need for change more clearly than top management does.

- Finally, don't ever let yourself be used simply to confirm something a client already believes—your collusion may help undo the client. An assignment like this may help out with short-term bookings, but it won't build your reputation as a professional with integrity and an independent point of view. (The exception would be the case of a legal advocate who commits to demonstrating the truth of her client's story in court).

WHAT IS SOUND JUDGMENT?

What is sound judgment and how does a professional develop it? We are concerned with a definition of judgment that is the ability to arrive at opinions about issues; the power of comparing and deciding; good sense.[8]

The elements that contribute to sound judgment can be expressed in a formula with three basic parts:

$$\text{Judgment} = (\text{Facts}) \times (\text{Experience}) \times (\text{Personal Values})$$

The facts about the issue at hand—too few and you'll be hipshooting, too many and you'll risk overanalyzing the situation—represent the first major input. Experience, which fuels intuition, is the mechanism by which the adviser adds to and processes these facts. Good decision makers then filter the resulting options through a strong set of personal beliefs and values.

Historically, good judgment was associated with age and experience. The elders in a society were considered the wisest, and therefore they were consulted on the most important decisions. Today, there are several, contradictory schools of thought on what constitutes good judgment and decision making. Most researchers in the field embrace the cognitive model and believe that solid judgments can only be reached through a highly logical, step-by-step, rational process, focusing almost exclusively on the factual inputs described in our judgment formula. Many popular books have been written that propose this approach, and they're filled with elaborate, quantitative tables and charts, which decision makers are supposed to use in order to come to sound conclusions. Unfortunately, research into decision making in the real world clearly demonstrates that good decision makers rarely undertake this much rational analysis.

Another, smaller group of scholars believes that judgment is essentially intuitive, and that most real-world decisions are made with little analysis. Based on our own research into professionals and the clients who employ them, we believe that the best decision makers blend these two approaches—cognitive and intuitive—and they add a third dimension, which is the personal value system.

FIVE STEPS TO GOOD JUDGMENT

Great professionals excel at a number of specific practices that underpin sound judgment. They:

- Frame problems appropriately at the outset
- Engage in creative but selective fact gathering
- Use intuition: they leverage their personal experience to find similar patterns and relevant analogs
- Filter their judgments through a clear set of personal beliefs and values
- Are honest enough to learn from experience

I. Frame the Problem

The first critical step is to identify the right problem and frame it correctly. Diagnosing the wrong problem is one of the most common mistakes that professionals make, regardless of their field. Many corporate executives will ask consultants to help "reorganize," when the real problem—for example, ineffective communication or poor leadership—often has nothing to do with organizational structure.

Professor Joseph Bower of Harvard Business School, who actively consults to industry leaders, told us the following story about problem framing, or rather, *reframing*:

> The head of a large company called me in to advise on a major revitalization program that he wanted to launch. He had identified a host of problems with his organization structure, distribution network, technology platforms, and so on. He was also going to engage a large consulting firm to help with the effort. I sat in on the kick-off meeting with the CEO and his fifteen top executives. For two hours the CEO waxed eloquent about the need to change, and the new program he was about to launch. There was little discussion, and the meeting

ended. Afterward, I sat with the CEO and he asked me for my reaction. I looked at him and said, "Did you see the faces in that room? There isn't one of your top executives who buys into your program. I think that's your real problem." Initially, he was stunned, but then he nodded his head. He began to smile. "You're right," he said quietly. "They're not on board at all, are they?"

Ironically, that was the end of the consulting assignment for both me and the large firm he had lined up. In his mind, the engagement had been a success and was over. The real problem had been identified and he set to work fixing it, personally. The consultants were a bit stunned, but to me it was a good outcome. The CEO subsequently replaced half his senior team with outsiders, and they went on to be quite successful.

2. Engage in Creative but Selective Fact Gathering

Horserace handicappers use historical data on horses to set the odds for each race. In a classic study, a group of professional handicappers was asked to make predictions for various races. In the study they were given increasingly more facts about each horse and then, after absorbing the new batch of facts, asked to predict its performance. For the first round, they were given only five facts on each horse; for the second round, ten; the third round, twenty; and finally, forty pieces of information on which to make a judgment. What happened? After each round, the handicappers' confidence in their judgments increased. But their accuracy stayed the same![9] After a minimum threshold of key facts is reached, having more information does not increase the quality of decision making. In certain business situations where time is of the essence, gathering more information can actually *decrease* the quality of decisions because key actions are delayed as managers conduct more and more analysis.

While somewhat counterintuitive, the idea that more information and expertise isn't always helpful has been borne out in a variety of settings. In our largest corporations, for example, the careful review and analysis of decisions by large numbers of internal staff experts and external professional advisers often decreases rather than increases the quality and robustness of decision making. This may happen because excessive analysis screens out promising creative ideas that do not stand up to the scrutiny of traditional financial benchmarks.

3. Use Intuition to Leverage Facts and Personal Experience

Intuition is a powerful tool for making judgments. Just look at this example: a fire chief leads his men into a house where a kitchen fire is burning. It is a relatively small fire and shouldn't be a problem for the half-dozen trained fire fighters arrayed to put it out. Suddenly, the chief has a terrible feeling about the fire. Without thinking, he orders his men to evacuate immediately. They rush outside, and as they leave the house, the entire first floor collapses in an explosive inferno. They have just escaped with their lives. When a postmortem is done on the situation, the chief believes that his "sixth sense" perceived the danger and saved him and his men.[10]

Researcher and author Gary Klein, who studies decision making under pressure, recorded this case, and he knows that it wasn't the chief's extrasensory perception that saved the day (Klein's book *Sources of Power* examines how people make decisions in real life as opposed to the laboratory). Using innovative interview techniques, Klein reveals the real reason: the chief's experience-based intuition. The fireman sensed that, even though the fire was small, it was generating an unusually large amount of heat. Furthermore, there was very little noise—it was too quiet for such a hot fire. In fact, what had happened was that the basement was on fire, and what seemed like a kitchen fire was actually a huge basement conflagration leaking upstairs. Subconsciously, the chief compared this fire to similar fires in his experience. It didn't fit established patterns, and this set off warning bells. He knew something was wrong—he didn't know exactly what yet. So he ordered a retreat to reexamine the situation from a safe vantage point.

The example of the kitchen fire illustrates the first key component of intuition: *the subconscious analysis of patterns.*[11] We often experience it as "gut feel," but a better description would be "experience feel." After we have seen many, many similar cases, we develop an ability to sense whether a new example fits—or diverges from—the patterns we have come to recognize. Chess grandmasters function very much the same way. They spend most of their time studying games and positions, and they develop the ability to rapidly size up any situation they encounter on the chessboard. As you can see, developing your powers of observation, a theme we highlighted in the previous two chapters on learning and synthesis, will help sharpen your judgment skills. In order to leverage your experience, you have to cultivate the ability to observe intensely what is going on around you.

The second step in using intuition involves imagining how the decision will play out. Various researchers use expressions like "mental simulation" or "imagining the outcome" to describe this. Very skilled professionals can rapidly simulate scenarios in their minds. Bain & Company CEO Orit Gadiesh implicitly refers to this when she tells us: "The good client advisers always keep three or four moves ahead. They are constantly imagining steps two, three, four, and five of the process while their clients are still focused on step one."

The intuitive part of judgment also involves the ability to identify *analogs*—to be able to say, "This here is like that over there." In the last chapter we saw that analogies are also an important tool for synthesis. Here, we are trying to use analogies to make better judgments, to enhance our understanding of the immediate decision we have to make. American military advisers during World War II, for example, might have foreseen the attack on Pearl Harbor if they had studied the history of the Russo-Japanese war. In that situation, the war was also preceded by a Pearl Harbor–like attack on the Russian fleet at Port Arthur in 1905.

4. Incorporate Your Personal Values and Standards

Good judgment, or at least judgment that is consistent with your own character, is also based on having a strong, explicit set of personal beliefs and values that guide your decisions (chapter 7 on conviction treats this subject in depth).

The following story, told to us by the chief executive of a $2 billion company, illustrates the power of an adviser's personal value system. You may not agree with the values, but you can't argue with the result:

> Some years ago, we faced a class action suit from a group of dealers, which potentially was going to cost us $50 million. We believed we had done nothing wrong, but our lawyers advised us that if it went to court, we stood only a 50-50 or worse chance of winning. A major distributor, who used to be the chairman of my company, originated the suit. He had died just shortly after the suit was filed, and on his deathbed he had his sons swear they would not relent in their pursuit of the lawsuit.
>
> One of my long-standing advisers is a minister who excels at taking principles from the scriptures and applying them to business problems. I explained the situation to him, and he gave me this advice: he told me to go see the sons of the major distributor (who had just died) and tell them that we were donating $200,000 to a charity of their choice "to honor their father." "He was the founder," I was to tell him, and "this is to honor him." I did this, and they accepted. Then my adviser told me to go around and personally visit each distributor who was a party to the lawsuit. He told me to ask them what their issues really were and what they needed. I spent six weeks traveling to see them. At the end of this, I offered to settle for something like $2 million over three years.

Eventually they settled for $1 million up front. This advice saved the company tens of millions of dollars and helped reestablish the loyalty of our key distributors.

The pharmaceutical company Merck's development of Mectizan, a drug for river blindness, is another example of how a clear set of personal values can and should influence business decision making. In *The Leadership Moment*, Professor Michael Useem of the Wharton School of Business chronicles the story of Roy Vagelos, who was the head of Merck's laboratories in the 1980s. Vagelos made a personal decision to support development of a revolutionary drug that could cure or forestall the spread of river blindness, which is caused by a devastating parasite infection affecting 60 million people in developing nations. The problem was that none of the customers for Mectizan could afford to pay for it.

Vagelos advised Merck's management committee, and later, when he became CEO, its board of directors, to support the production and distribution of Mectizan—for free, forever. This was a huge and risky decision that by 1997 cost Merck $200 million in lost income. Yet Vagelos never hesitated. A physician himself, he deeply espoused a personal mission to "preserve and improve human life." His own beliefs and values were carefully factored into his decision making.

5. Don't Be Misled by Your Experience

On November 23, 1951, Ivy League rivals Dartmouth and Princeton played a hotly contested football game. The game was marked by fierce rivalry and very rough play on the field. Princeton's star player broke his nose and a Dartmouth player broke his leg. Afterward, a bitter dispute erupted about the way the game was played, with each side accusing the other of unsportsmanlike conduct. A psychologist from Dartmouth, Albert Hastorf, and a researcher from Princeton, Hadley Cantril, teamed up to study the incident. They surveyed students who had seen the game, and they showed a

film of the game to students at both colleges who had not attended the match. Predictably, each side reported that the
other team had committed the most infractions. Even with
the benefit of objective evidence—a film that recorded everything—the students couldn't agree. The researchers concluded, "It seems clear that the 'game' was actually many
different games. It is inaccurate and misleading to say that
different people have different 'attitudes' concerning the
same 'thing.' For the 'thing' simply is *not* the same for different people."[12]

As this example illustrates, although it would seem very
natural for us to learn from experience, memories are "re-
constructed" after the fact and sometimes not very accurately.
Researchers in the legal field, for example, have found that
"eyewitness" accounts can be very unreliable. In short, we
tend to see what we want to see.

Physicians can be particularly susceptible to this phenomenon. A study done many years ago asked a group of experienced doctors to assess who among 500 children needed
tonsillectomies. They concluded that about 50 percent
needed to have their tonsils removed. They then separated
out the 50 percent whose tonsils were deemed healthy and
asked another group of doctors to examine them. Again, just
under 50 percent were deemed in need of surgery to remove
their tonsils. The "healthy" children were again culled from
this group and assessed by yet a third group of doctors. Incredibly, nearly 50 percent were still diagnosed with un-
healthy tonsils requiring removal!

There are three major pitfalls that prevent us from learning from experience:

- *We claim credit for all successes.* Not all good things are
  due to our genius; luck and happenstance affect a lot
  of outcomes. We have to recognize this and develop a
  measured understanding of our capabilities.
- *We minimize and dismiss failures.* Often, we will reframe
  events with hindsight so they are more favorable to us,
  or we simply forget them. This keeps us from learning.

- *We distort actual events, in our favor.* Like the students at Dartmouth and Princeton, we allow personal biases to color our recollections.

You can enhance your ability to learn from experience by doing a few simple things. First of all, keep track of your advice. Six or twelve months after the fact, ask yourself if you would give the same advice, or if, perhaps, you would say or do something different. Second, think about how past events might have turned out differently. Research has shown that you can reduce hindsight biases by looking at how the results of decisions could have been different. It's not enough to say, "Why did things turn out the way they did?" You also have to ask, "How else might it have turned out, and why?"

TECHNIQUES TO DEVELOP BETTER JUDGMENT

Based on our observations of professionals who have great judgment, here are some suggestions for improving your own decision-making ability:

Overinvest in problem identification. Lack of up-front investment in thorough understanding of the issues that the client faces is one of the biggest mistakes professionals make. At least 50 percent of the time, the "problem" presented by your client will change and evolve from the one you discussed at your initial meeting. It is a dangerous mistake to accept your client's first "problem statement" at face value.

Examine alternative problem definitions. Be creative in examining all the root causes of the issue at hand. Harvard's Joseph Bower, in our earlier example, correctly identified that his client's first problem was executive alignment and buy-in, not antiquated processes or information systems.

Make sure the problem is really a priority. Given the strategy, goals, and current situation of the organization or individual you're dealing with, does it make sense to work on this problem? A few years ago, a major bank had lost nearly $500 million in just twelve months. Management began soliciting multimillion-dollar bids to develop a "cultural change" program. Was this really the place to start, given the huge losses and other associated problems of cost efficiency and strategic positioning that the bank faced?

Ask "disconfirming" questions. As we mentioned earlier, you can avoid the confirmation judgment trap by asking questions and collecting data that you suspect might disprove the initial hypothesis.[13] For example, the United States decided to drop the atom bomb on Japan in 1945 because of a firm belief that the Japanese would never surrender. U.S. officials believed that an invasion of mainland Japan, which would cost an estimated 1 million Allied casualties, was the only other viable option. But what if the following question had been seriously pursued: "Short of dropping the atom bomb or invading the mainland, what event could lead the Japanese to surrender?" This line of inquiry, if advanced in a thorough manner, might have revealed other options to the Allies, including the obvious one of just waiting for a few more weeks, since constant American firebombing had already destroyed a large number of Japanese cities.

Develop both standard and outlandish alternatives. We often put boundaries around our thinking, and this severely limits the range of alternatives or possibilities we are able to consider. What if we do nothing? What if we do the opposite of what everyone is suggesting? An outlandish alternative proposed at a Drexel Burnham brainstorming session in 1983 was the concept of an "air fund" for corporate acquisitions— a fund with no money in it. At first, the idea seemed absurd. But it eventually evolved and developed into the "highly confident" letter that Drexel would send out prior to a takeover. Basically, the letter stated that Drexel was highly confident the financing could be raised in the high-yield bond market.

There was no money available yet, just the promise of billions of dollars soon to materialize.

Engage in prospective hindsight. Try stating a question about the future in two different ways:

- How likely is it that our closest competitor will take ten points of market share away from us in the next two years and surpass us in revenue? Give reasons why this might occur.

Here is a slightly different version of this question:

- Pretend it is two years from now. Our closest competitor has increased its market share by ten points and surpassed us in revenue. Explain how and why this has happened.

When a hypothetical event is stated as a reality—as in the second question above—people are far more creative in coming up with reasons for why it could happen, and the quality of their thinking improves dramatically.

Understand your client's tolerance for risk and uncertainty. Every client has different levels of tolerance for risk, and this tolerance will vary from situation to situation. Several years ago, for example, a leading European travel company commissioned a group of consultants to review its U.S. operations. Although the firm's U.S. office was at a serious disadvantage against bigger players, and losing money, the consultants believed that with a great deal of work and further investment it could grow and achieve greater market clout and economies of scale, finally becoming profitable.

Their conclusions bothered the CEO, however, and he asked a friend, a former top executive in the travel business who had retired, to come see him. Sitting over lunch the next week, his friend said, "It all comes down to what management really wants here. So what do you really want out of your U.S.

operations? And what risks will you tolerate?" The CEO paused, since no one had bothered to ask him these questions in quite this way. He replied, "I basically need to show the flag in the United States. The business doesn't have to be big—in fact it can be very small—we just need a visible presence. And I can't risk it *ever* losing any money. I just cannot afford it anymore—the government won't put up with the losses." The CEO declined the follow-on consulting contract and instead spent a month downsizing the U.S. office to the point where it could break even under any circumstances. The CEO was happy, and so were his shareholders, who were more interested in national representation—"showing the flag"—than market share. The consultants, in short, had misjudged their client's appetite for risk and misunderstood his business objectives in the United States.

Enhance your ability to reach for patterns in your experience. You can deepen your effective experience by learning from other, more seasoned peers. Get them to share stories and anecdotes. You might consider questions like: "What was the most difficult client you ever had? What was the most awkward professional moment of your career, and how did you handle it? Have you ever taken on a case that seemed hopeless? Why?" Stories are a powerful means of enhancing your experience.

BECOMING A GOOD THINKER

Good judgment flourishes, first of all, in the absence of bad judgments. Great professionals help their clients avoid the many subtle judgment traps that can lead to poor decisions. Then they actively exploit each part of the judgment equation in a balanced fashion. They combine known facts with their experience and assess the alternatives through the lens of their beliefs and values.

By becoming a deep generalist, cultivating your powers

Do You Have Good Judgment?

✔ When your clients face tough choices, they often use you as a sounding board. They share their dilemmas with you.

✔ You're right more than 50 percent of the time.

✔ You have the confidence to make judgments relatively quickly. You identify and marshal the key facts and perspectives that you need, but it doesn't bother you if you don't have *all* the facts.

✔ If you're asked by a client to judge an issue where you lack experience and important information, you're not afraid to come out and say you just don't know.

✔ You're honest about your track record at giving advice and making recommendations. You've made mistakes and learned from them.

✔ You're very aware of your clients' tolerance for risk and loss, having discussed this openly with them.

of synthesis, and developing good judgment, you will be well on the road to becoming a *good thinker,* a person aptly defined by Vincent Ruggiero in his book *The Art of Thinking:*

Good thinkers produce both more ideas and better ideas than poor thinkers. They become more adept in using a variety of invention techniques, enabling them to discover ideas. More specifically, good thinkers tend to see the problem from many perspectives before choosing any one, to consider many different investigative approaches, and to produce many ideas before turning to judgment. In addition, they are more willing to take intellectual risks, to be adventurous and consider

outrageous or zany ideas, and to use their imaginations
and aim for originality.[14]

IF YOU ARE able not only to demonstrate sound judgment
yourself but also help your clients arrive at their own good
judgments, your value as an adviser will increase significantly.
By developing a reputation among your clients as a good
thinker, you will be asked back by them again and again.

SEVEN

THE POWERS OF CONVICTION
Drawing Strength from Your Values

*I have found that the greatest help in meeting any problem with
decency and self-respect and whatever courage is demanded, is to
know where you yourself stand. That is, to have in words what you
believe and are acting from.*

WILLIAM FAULKNER

THE ROOM WAS SILENT as the world's most powerful chief
executive began to speak. Surrounding President
Franklin Roosevelt at the conference table were key cabinet
members and the top officers in the U.S. military. It was
November 14, 1938, and in an atmosphere of isolationism
Roosevelt was struggling to mobilize the United States for the
inevitable war with Germany. His latest plan, an impractical
compromise, was to get Congress to appropriate funds to
purchase 10,000 airplanes, but to appease the isolationists,
he recommended that no budget be set aside for crews or
ground forces.

As Roosevelt outlined his proposal, heads nodded in
sympathetic agreement. One by one, he asked his advisers
what they thought. "Good plan, Mr. President," they each in-
toned as Roosevelt went around the table. General George
Marshall, newly appointed deputy chief of staff of the army
and one of the most junior officials in the meeting, came last.

172

Experienced in European trench warfare and knowledge-able about the German military, Marshall came to his new job with a deep sense of conviction and integrity. He knew what it would take to wage war on a global scale.

"Don't you think so, George?" the President asked Marshall. "Good idea, isn't it?"

The faces in the room blanched at Marshall's reply: "Mr. President. I'm sorry," he bluntly told Roosevelt, "but I don't agree with that at all."[1]

Roosevelt gave him a startled look and abruptly ended the meeting. As the other shocked generals and cabinet sec-retaries left the room, they each shook Marshall's hand to bid him good-bye. Secretary of the Treasury Henry Morganthau whispered to him, "Well, it's been nice knowing you." Every-one knew that Marshall would soon be removed from his post and sent to some far-off military installation. Quite the oppo-site happened, however. From that day onward, Roosevelt adopted Marshall, one of the few of the president's men who had the courage of his convictions, as his closest military ad-viser. Just a year later, Roosevelt pinned another three stars on his shoulders, appointing him secretary of the army.

Born in 1880 in Uniontown, Pennsylvania, George Mar-shall was reared in a Victorian world that profoundly valued integrity and duty. As a teenager, he was not a very capable student. In fact, until he was into his second year at the Vir-ginia Military Institute, he showed no special promise. In the military, however, he shone. Whatever weakness Marshall had in the academic realm was more than made up for by his per-sonal qualities—his honesty, dedication, conviction, disci-pline, judgment about people, and ability to reflect.

As secretary of the army, Marshall's conviction was so strong, so sincere, and so rooted in his beliefs that no one could remain unmoved when he expressed a view. All of his actions were driven by an intense sense of duty to his country, his belief in democratic principles, and his desire to do the right thing at all times for the American people. His convic-tion about the proper troop levels and theater war strategies was a major factor contributing to the defeat of Germany and

Japan. In the face of widespread isolationism, both among the American people and in the U.S. Congress, Marshall understood the delicate balance and diplomacy needed to secure a credible military buildup in the European theater. Marshall advised both the president and members of Congress, many of whom said at the time that it was Marshall's intense conviction and lack of ulterior motives that persuaded a reluctant Congress to approve the necessary spending.

Marshall's dedication to his principles never ceased. Several years before his death, he agreed to be interviewed by a historian. He set two conditions, however: the historian had to be chosen by a disinterested third party and *none* of the profits from the resulting biography could go to either Marshall or his family.

CONVICTION:
THE ELIXIR OF MOTIVATION AND DRIVE

One of the strongest common denominators among the hundreds of extraordinary professionals we have observed and studied is the intensity of their convictions. Like a powerful elixir, conviction impels us to accomplish great things. It amplifies our other qualities and enables us to push to our limits. If we have a good idea, it becomes twice as powerful if it is backed with conviction. If we have a difficult goal to achieve, it is conviction that enables us to persist through setbacks and obstacles.

Clients recognize and are deeply affected by the power of conviction. "If you want to have an impact, you have to have conviction. The authoritative delivery of a judgment is absolutely key," one leader told us. Other clients made similar comments:

- "I have observed many great professionals over time. The really good ones almost have an aura when they come into the room. There is an instant connection of belief and corresponding conviction. I'm not talking about the 'gurus' here but rather the really solid client advisers."

- "The adviser's words have to be backed by deep values and principles. This gives him genuine conviction."

Demonstrating Belief and Winning Others Over

Steve Kerr, a former business school dean who now heads Corporate Leadership and Development for General Electric, is a personal adviser to CEO Jack Welch. Commenting on the importance of conviction, he tells us: "When you're advising a smart, well-informed executive, you have to be extremely persuasive—you must have enormous conviction. You may, for example, persuade someone like Jack Welch of your point of view only one time out of five, and that's assuming you're very convincing to begin with. If you're faint-hearted about your views, you won't be effective at all."

The word "conviction" is derived from the Latin word *convictum*, which means "that which is proven or demonstrated." A personal conviction thus has the sense of a belief based on something you have proven or demonstrated to yourself. To *convince*, which is the next step after formulating your own convictions, has associations with the Latin verb *vincere*, "to win." Not only do great professionals have strong convictions, but they are skilled at winning over or persuading their clients. You can be a brilliant big-picture thinker and arrive at incisive judgments for your clients, but unless you are able to develop a deep belief in your point of view and win your client over to it, you will be ineffective.

Conviction also has to be accompanied by integrity. The first element of integrity, which we'll examine in detail in the next chapter, is discernment of right and wrong. Great professionals, therefore, have convictions that are ethical and moral. There have been plenty of individuals who have had deep, powerful convictions that are totally at odds with the principles and values of a democratic society; look no further for examples, than the racist Ku Klux Klan or "militia" leaders.

George Marshall demonstrated his integrity and selflessness in 1942, when it came time for Roosevelt to select a commander of Operation Overlord, the invasion of mainland
Europe. Marshall was the highest-ranking officer in the U.S.
military, and the command, implicitly, was his to have. As
much as he wanted the post, Marshall was also convinced
(and Roosevelt felt the same way) that he was far more valuable to the war effort if he stayed in Washington. Marshall
never lobbied Roosevelt for the job, however. He simply re-
mained silent on the matter, freeing up his chief to choose
General Dwight D. Eisenhower to lead the invasion. Marshall's conviction about the right thing to do for his country
made him stand aside and forgo the most prestigious operational command in military history.

Conviction is fundamentally rooted in three aspects of
personality: your own particular set of personal experiences;
your beliefs and values; and your sense of mission. This personal conviction underpins what we call daily conviction—
the conviction and persuasiveness you demonstrate in your
work as you express points of view and make recommendations to clients. Finally, your daily conviction is intensified
and supported by your ability to read audiences, the sharp-
ness of your communications skills, and the palpable energy
you marshal behind your words.

We are, of course, concerned with true conviction, not
rhetorical techniques for persuasiveness. Extraordinary professionals often have both, and the combination can be a powerful force to reckon with. Rhetoric and shallow salesmanship,
however, are marketing devices; and if you indulge in these
without substance and integrity, your clients will eventually see
through them, and their trust in you will dissolve.

CORE BELIEFS AND VALUES:
THE BEDROCK OF YOUR PERSONAL CONVICTION

General Marshall had a firsthand understanding of the
European battlefields and what it would take to win against a

large, well-entrenched army such as the Germans had deployed in 1939–40. His resulting beliefs about military strategy fathered his deep convictions about how the Allies would have to fight World War II. Churchill's inclination was to engage the Germans in a piecemeal fashion, attacking their flanks, whereas Marshall was convinced that the Allies could never unseat the Germans unless they attacked them with overwhelming force in their heartland. It was no easy task to face down the powerful and persuasive British prime minister, but on numerous occasions Marshall vehemently argued his viewpoint with Churchill and eventually prevailed. Such personal conviction evolves from one's own unique experiences and the specific values and beliefs that spring from them.

Conviction is, ultimately, belief in yourself and your abilities. When you know what you stand for and feel strongly about it, you become a confident, convincing, and persuasive individual. You radiate a genuine assuredness that is attractive to colleagues and clients alike. It gives you the strength to exercise the independence and objectivity that are hallmarks of great client advisers.

John Adams, the second U.S. president and one of America's founding fathers, relied on his beliefs to guide him through many difficult times. He wrote to a friend, "I have been twenty years, in the midst of Politicks, and through the whole of it, invariably constant to the same Principles and the same system, through all Opprobriums, Obloquies, Dangers, Terrors, Losses and Allurements." [2]

The philosopher Alasdair MacIntyre eloquently describes the roots of our beliefs and values:

> I am someone's son or daughter, someone else's cousin or uncle, I am a citizen of this or that city, a member of this or that guild or profession, I belong to this tribe, that clan, this nation. I inherit from the past of my family, my city, my tribe, my nation, a variety of debts, inheritances, rightful expectations and obligations. These constitute the given of my life, my moral starting point. This is in part what gives my life its own moral particularity. [3]

Linda Srere is an extraordinary client adviser who exemplifies how professionals reach into their personal and professional experiences to draw strength and clarify their beliefs. Srere is chief client officer for advertising agency Young & Rubicam, and CEO of their large New York office. She is intensely client-focused ("as a policy," she says, "I call or visit at least one client every working day"). Moreover, she constantly searches for ways to add value to her clients, sometimes leaving one of them a weekend voice message with a new idea she's developed. Listen as she describes some of the events—good and bad—that have fueled her sense of conviction and her success as a professional:

> Early in my career, I was working at Ogilvy & Mather on the General Foods account. After eight years of work and a major investment, they were about to launch a new product called soy bacon. It was my responsibility to review all of the test market results, reanalyze them, and prepare a presentation for the client. I found that the product just wouldn't succeed nationally. Due to unusually high hog prices during the test marketing, the soy bacon was artificially cheap for consumers. But the pricing differential wouldn't be favorable anymore for long-term, nationwide distribution.
>
> After consulting with my management, and with as much conviction as I could muster, I told the client the product wouldn't fly. He agreed, and they killed the launch. That incident enhanced my reputation for honesty and professionalism, and since then I have become known for having the courage of my convictions.
>
> At age thirty-three, I was diagnosed with a very threatening illness. This was a life-altering experience: suddenly, I realized I might not be around anymore. I fought back and ultimately was cured. This put a lot of things in perspective for me.
>
> These and other experiences have solidified the values in my life: integrity, honor, trust, courage, loyalty, and perseverance. They made me realize I have to be

able to live comfortably with any decision I make in life—I have to make decisions because they seem right, regardless of the consequences. These are the standards I measure myself against, and they're the things that underpin my convictions.

Professor Joseph Badarraco, who teaches ethics at Harvard Business School, calls the process of identifying your belief system "Becoming who you are." He says, "Tracing the 'roots' of one's values means understanding their origins, evolution, and importance. It involves an effort to understand which values and commitments really have, up to the present, defined a person's moral identity."[4]

The Origins of Belief

The sources of your beliefs can be varied. They can spring from a religious upbringing, from a particular type of family experience, or from tragedy. In *The Courage of Conviction,* Phillip Berman asked thirty-three prominent men and women to talk about their beliefs and how they put them into practice. Invariably, these individuals recalled formative personal experiences that had occurred years earlier to explain the roots of their present-day conviction. Elliot Richardson's story is typical. A lawyer and former attorney general under President Nixon, Richardson refused to fire special Watergate prosecutor Archibald Cox when ordered to do so and, because of this refusal, was himself fired by Nixon. Reflecting on a key moment in his past, he once described feeling a sense of interconnectedness that later underpinned his enormous integrity in the face of intense pressure from the president of the United States:

Walking beside the Charles River and thinking hard as I walked, I suddenly understood that no person's identity can be fully defined except in terms of others: family, friends, teachers, fellow workers, other members of the same community and the same heritage. Each unique and inviolable self exists in the midst of a web of inter-connecting relationships with other people. To be a complete person is to be a part of others, and to share a part of them. This is what we mean by love. This is why giving is natural.[5]

Personal experiences inexorably lead to the creation of each person's set of core values and beliefs. Not everyone has conviction, however. The difference is that individuals with great conviction are able to tap into these experiences, frame them in a positive light, and then walk away with an explicit understanding of the values and beliefs that naturally flow from them.

A SENSE OF MISSION

It's been said that "we all arrive on Earth with sealed or-ders." From our unique life experiences and the belief system that emerges from them, each of us discerns a sense of mission that guides and drives us. This mission is the final element that defines our personal conviction. If we don't have a clear idea about where we're headed and what our purpose is, it's hard to have a great deal of conviction and confidence. We'll return to the importance of what we call a *mission orientation* in the final chapter of this book. Suffice it to say that once you are able to discern your core beliefs and values, these, combined with the personal and professional choices you have made, begin to shape your sense of personal mission.

FROM PERSONAL CONVICTION
TO DAILY CONVICTION

What about day-to-day conviction, which is what your clients see? Personal conviction—knowing what you believe in—gives you a sense of self-assurance and confidence that underlies your daily conviction about the issues and problems your client faces. In other words, if you are certain in your core being, you will be able to radiate confidence about your opinions and findings.

Daily conviction is also strengthened by honing your judgment skills, which we reviewed in chapter 6. When your judgments are informed equally by fact and experience and tempered by your value system, your confidence in your own opinions and views will rise.

There are, in addition, several enablers of your daily conviction—skills that enable you to be convincing and persuasive when you express a view. These include:

- *Empathy for your audience.* Great professionals who are convincing have a knack for reading their audiences. They constantly scan the audience, reading both verbal and nonverbal cues. Are people falling asleep? They change the pace. Does one particular point elicit great interest, raising the energy level? They pause temporarily to take advantage of the interest and engage their listeners at a deeper level. No matter how you plan your communication, you have to be prepared to change tactics on the spur of the moment. You may have planned a one-hour slide presentation, for example, but after twenty minutes you should be prepared to shorten it and revert to using flip charts if necessary. The CEO of DaimlerChrysler once did exactly this just before a speech to a group of employees of the merged automakers. A discussion session with some of the managers prior to the event raised a series of issues that were of great concern to the U.S. employees. The CEO subsequently dumped his carefully prepared speech and centered his talk on the list of issues developed just minutes earlier. He received a standing ovation.
- *Communications skills.* You won't convince anyone of anything if you can't communicate effectively. You

have to be able to organize your thoughts and summarize the key points you are making both before and after you elaborate on your arguments. Commenting on the importance of clarity, the nineteenth-century Austrian statesman Metternich said, "Anything that is good in itself must be capable of being expressed clearly and precisely. The moment I come across words that are not very clear, I am left with the conclusion that they are either mistaken or deceitful."

- *Energy.* Clients have to sense your energy when you speak or write—your enthusiasm and belief need to be tangible and genuine. Author and executive coach Debra Benton talks about infusing communications with strong physical, mental, and emotional energy.[6]

  Calibrating your energy level can be compared to gauging the effectiveness of your accent when you try to speak a foreign language. If you speak French with what you think is an appropriate intonation and pronunciation, your speech will usually come across as very flat; if you exaggerate your French accent to the point that it sounds embarrassingly overdone, however, you've probably got it just about right. The same is true of personal energy: to be effective as communicators, we have to project it at a much higher level than we use customarily.

Think back to the memorable speakers you've heard. Good speakers typically have an intuitive understanding of their audiences. Their messages are clear, crisp, and concise. And the best ones resonate with personal energy.

WHY SOME PROFESSIONALS LACK CONVICTION

Sometimes, professionals have trouble being convincing. They hesitate and waver. As we've said, the root of the problem may lie in an inability to get in touch with a set of strong, personal beliefs. Sometimes, though, the lack of conviction is due to self-erected barriers. Here are four typical ones:

- *"I'm not an expert."* Often, professionals feel they can opine only in areas where they possess deep expertise. Obviously, you don't want to be a hip-shooter who offers opinions on everything. The best client advisers, however, combine knowledge depth and breadth with a broad-based understanding of their client's industry, company, and organization. This combination enables them to provide useful advice and perspectives that go beyond just the technical details of the assignment. They know that simply asking good questions and applying common sense are often more powerful than expertise.

  The Silicon Valley–based law firm of Wilson, Sonsini, Goodrich & Rosati, for example, has tripled its revenues in five years, and each year it takes dozens of high-technology companies public—more than any other law firm in the country. A recent *Fortune* magazine profile on WSGR stated, "Clients . . . seem to put an unusual degree of trust in the company. They routinely turn to WSGR for business strategy advice." Their attorneys have accumulated a breadth of experience in the world of high-tech start-ups, and they are able to convincingly add value to clients in subjects outside their core legal expertise.

- *"I might be wrong."* Of course you might. But when you *believe* something is true or right—based on your assessment of the facts and your intuition—you have to express conviction. Even the smartest, most capable professionals make mistakes. Few consultants speak with more conviction and wisdom than Peter Drucker, for example, and yet he has been occasionally wrong (he reportedly suggested to the head of General Electric that under no circumstances should any of the company's senior executives be given incentive pay or bonuses; they should all be put on a straight salary). The point here is that Drucker has been right many other times, and if he had not been persuasive at those moments, few would believe his good advice.

- *"I don't have enough information."* You will never have all the facts. Recall from chapter 6 on judgment that sometimes having more facts actually decreases the quality of decision making. You often have to be willing to draw conclusions based on sketchy data. You can always frame your opinion with some qualification—"This is my preliminary view"—but it still has to be conveyed with conviction, not insecurity.
- *"My client's conviction is far greater."* Often, your client is going to hold some very strong convictions. Remember the words of General Electric's chief learning officer Steve Kerr, who routinely has to be convincing with CEO Jack Welch: an experienced, talented client will of course have strong views, and you may only occasionally manage to persuade him. William Esrey, the CEO of Sprint, used to be a partner at the investment bank Warburg Dillon Read, which he still uses for advice. When one of the bankers at the firm was asked if Esrey, an ex-investment banker himself, challenges his advice, he replied, "98 percent of the time!"

Just like corporate leaders, professionals have to win over others to their point of view in order to be effective, but because they're outsiders, their task can be even harder. Managers often believe that their company accepts the advice of outside professionals more readily than their own, but the opposite is often true: an organization with an entrenched culture, for example, tends to reject any recommendation that comes from the outside.

DEVELOPING YOUR OWN CONVICTION

There are a number of specific things you can do to increase and intensify your own conviction:

Get in touch with your core values and beliefs. This is a highly personal exercise, and there is no "right" way to do it. Start by

posing yourself the following questions and carefully thinking through your answers:

- What were some of my most intense and memorable
  experiences as a child, and what did I learn from them?
- What are the most valuable professional experiences I
  have had, and what I did I learn from them?
- Who have been my role models in life, both professionally and personally? Who helped me become the
  person I am? What did I learn from those individuals?
  What did they stand for as people? What were their
  values?
- What are the most important things for me in life?
  Why are they important?
- On a professional level—implicitly or explicitly—what
  guides my behavior? What standards or principles
  drive me? Where did these come from?

Finally, try to summarize what you've learned. Can you
create a list of five or six core values that implicitly guide your
behavior and decision making? Can you identify three or
four of your beliefs that you follow in your professional life?

Young & Rubicam's Linda Srere articulates some values
(integrity, honor, trust, courage) and some beliefs (you have
to spot and promote talent early) that she lives by. Occasionally, there is something in your past that you don't want in
your own life, and this becomes a driving force in the alignment of your own values. Financial consultant Fred Brown,
scion of a famous banking family, made a conscious decision
not to be just like his father: "He was a terrific, successful
man," Brown explains, "but he was unbalanced. His work and
material success were everything. I looked at him and
thought, I want something more, I want balance in my life."
Leaving behind the frenetic life of a successful stockbroker
and becoming a personal financial consultant was part of his
balancing process. Now Brown instills this balance in his
clients, who have been coming back to him for years.

Some professionals formalize their values into a written,

personal mission statement. In his famous *Autobiography,* Ben Franklin wrote out his thirteen "virtues," complete with a weekly chart to encourage their practice. Others just keep them in the back of their minds as a guide. How you articulate them is a personal choice.

Use your integrity to screen your convictions. Your convictions should always have integrity to them—a consistency and wholeness with respect to your beliefs and values. Sometimes, we convince ourselves—and then others—of things that, deep down, we don't fully believe in. If you're really good at the arts of persuasion, your inner doubt may never show through. But often, the person you're dealing with will perceive, even if on an unconscious level, the weakness in your conviction. Something in your tone of voice, your body language, your eyes, or your language tips him off. His belief in what you're saying is diminished. Afterward, if your conviction turns out to have been transitory, the trust between you and your client can be irrevocably damaged.

During the 1972 presidential campaign, Democratic presidential candidate George McGovern chose Senator Thomas Eagleton as his vice-presidential running mate. During background checks, it was revealed that Eagleton had been treated for depression and had undergone electroshock therapy. Despite an outcry, McGovern went on national TV to declare that "I am 1000 percent behind Senator Eagleton as my running mate." Within twenty-four hours, however, McGovern dumped him from the ticket. This incident seriously damaged McGovern's credibility and the public's belief in his convictions.

Employ logic as well as facts. Facts are important, but conviction grounded only in facts is very fragile, since supporters on each side of an issue can invariably marshal their own set of facts to support their particular views. The debate over whether or not Americans were economically better off at the dawn of the twenty-first century, for example, became endless and inconclusive. Prominent economists and experts produced mountains of statistics and evidence, supposedly to prove the question either in the affirmative or the negative, but the question was never settled. Einstein's general theory of relativity, on the other hand, was constructed using impeccable logic; the specific observation that confirmed it, the bending of the sun's rays during a solar eclipse, was not made until several years later.

If your conviction is based on solid principles and well-reasoned logic—and you have some key facts at your disposal as well—you will be far more effective in persuading clients than if you just bombard them with statistics.

Have a clear message. In 1996, the situation in Bosnia had deteriorated, and President Slobodan Milosevic's police and army units were threatening the lives of thousands of Bosnian civilians. General George Joulwan, the Supreme Allied Commander for Europe and NATO military chief, asked to meet with President Clinton and his cabinet. He believed strongly that NATO intervention was necessary to prevent a massacre in Europe's heartland, but he had to convince a group of reluctant politicians. General Joulwan, like many of the historical figures we have profiled, was both a great leader and a great adviser. He tells us:

> As NATO Commander, I had to convince thirty-six nations to work together, to develop a common political will. There was also an enormous need for clarity about political guidance. In October of 1996 I went to see President Clinton and his cabinet at the White House. Remember that this was a president just a year away from an election: if the United States went into Bosnia, and things went badly, it could have cost him his reelection. I explained why it was essential for NATO to intervene. I felt very, very strongly that it was the right thing to do, even though there were risks. I then set out four conditions for the success of the mission: First, clarity of command at all times. Second, unity of command. Third, we had to have clear, robust rules of engagement—eventu-

ally they filled seventeen pages. Finally, I required them to make timely political decisions. They agreed. The conditions were fulfilled, and the operation was a success. We didn't lose one soldier.

Like another famous general before him—George Marshall—Joulwan showed enormous personal conviction, which persuaded a skeptical audience and prevented the deaths of many innocent civilians. The unequivocal clarity of his message was an integral part of his ability to convey his convictions and be convincing.

Focus on your passion. People who are *passionate* are convincing. That's why it's so important for professionals to identify and gravitate toward an area of interest that really excites them. One young man, for example, left a large bank to join a prominent management consulting firm. He spent the first two years working on a series of strategic planning assignments. Although he was bright and energetic, his performance was uneven; he found the detailed analysis required for these projects boring and could never get energized about the routine client reports and presentations. When asked to help roll out the findings of one study in a series of educational workshops, however, he began to excel. His passion wasn't strategic analysis or figuring out which acquisition made sense—it was teaching and expanding the intellectual horizons of the managers he worked with. Having recognized his passion, he subsequently moved into the firm's management education practice, where he did outstanding work. In front of a single client, trying to explain a workplan or the findings of a study, his passion—and corresponding conviction—were limited. In front of a class full of managers eager to learn, however, he felt energized, passionate, and full of conviction.

Ann Medlock is the director of the Giraffe Project, an organization that publicizes individuals who have "stuck their necks out" for something they believe in. They run the gamut from the lawyer who has quit his six-figure partnership position to open a storefront legal clinic for the poor, to the mother who has lost a son to urban violence and now devotes herself to speaking and reaching out to community groups on gun control. Medlock's project has documented nearly 1,000 cases of outstanding citizens who have become, in her parlance, "giraffes." When asked what she sees in common among the hundreds of individuals she had studied, all people with great conviction, Medlock says, "For most of these people, the outcome they are working for has great meaning to them. It fuels their generative powers. They are passionate about their cause. Many of them are also enjoying themselves immensely. When I asked the lawyer in Atlanta who had opened the storefront legal clinic how long he'd keep it up, he replied, 'I'll never quit doing this. I'm having too much fun.' "

Choose to believe. The process of clarifying your values and beliefs is usually one of detection rather than creation. In other words, you find out who you already are—you don't create a persona for yourself from scratch. Purposeful choice, however, is often a part of your determination. Your past contains many elements you can draw on, and you can exercise free choice in determining what you embrace and what you reject. Evangelist and presidential adviser Billy Graham, for example, has said, "I made a conscious decision to become a Christian." Likewise, Fred Brown told us, "My father was a great man but I was determined not to sacrifice my personal and family life the way he did. I chose a life of greater balance." The beliefs and values that drive your conviction have to come from within you, but often it requires an act of will and a conscious choice to decide that you will never compromise your integrity or that you will apply a standard of excellence to everything you do professionally.

Test and challenge your convictions. Convictions don't have to remain unchanged throughout your entire life. You may alter some of them, and you most certainly will add new ones as you gain more experience and reflect on what's important

---

Do You Have Conviction?

✔ If a client asks what's important to you as an individual and as a professional, your answers are immediate and clear. You know what your core beliefs and values are.

✔ There are certain key experiences in your past that you refer to from time to time. They give you strength and inspiration, even the negative ones.

✔ You feel a sense of mission as you pursue your career, which is a passion rather than an obligation. Your financial compensation is important to you, but it doesn't drive your choice of work.

✔ You communicate strongly and forcefully. You feel and project passion and energy when you talk.

✔ When you speak with clients, your message is unequivocal. If someone asks them a week later about what you said, they can easily remember your key points.

✔ If a client has fixed, dogmatic views, you aren't dissuaded from trying to change his mind.

---

to you. The famous figures whom we remember for their enormous conviction—people like Gandhi and Abraham Lincoln—had belief systems that developed and evolved. Lincoln, for example, wasn't always adamantly against slavery; his opposition to it grew gradually, until it became a firm conviction. Rather than feeling smug about your convictions, you should welcome people to challenge them. Discussion and debate will cause them to evolve, improve, and ultimately strengthen.

THE GREAT client advisers mentioned in this chapter all have strong convictions rooted in their integrity and individual belief systems. Their beliefs and values, in turn, lead them to discern a sense of mission that further galvanizes their persuasive abilities. And they bolster their conviction with well-developed communications skills, creating a powerful combination. If you get in touch with your own beliefs and express yourself with conviction that is surrounded by passion, energy, and clarity, you'll be surprised at how effective you can be with your clients. You will become energized, and your other strengths will be amplified and sharpened.

EIGHT

WHAT MONEY CANNOT BUY
Creating Trust through Integrity

> QUESTION: *Is not commercial credit based primarily upon money or property?*
> J. PIERPONT MORGAN: *No, sir, the first thing is character.*
> QUESTION: *Before money or property?*
> J. PIERPONT MORGAN: *Before money or anything else. Money cannot buy it. . . . Because a man I do not trust could not get money from me on all the bonds in Christendom.*
>
> J. P. MORGAN'S
> *1912 Congressional Testimony*[1]

AMERICA IS SLOWLY BECOMING a low-trust society. In 1960, 58 percent of Americans surveyed felt that "most people could be trusted," but when asked the same question in 1993, only 37 percent replied in the affirmative.[2] Evidence of low trust is everywhere: politicians routinely lie, litigation proliferates, and the confidence we have in a variety of professional figures—doctors, lawyers, consultants, stockbrokers, journalists, and others—appears to be at a low ebb. Even our trust in respected institutions such as local police, the FBI, clergy, and the military has waned in recent years.

A lack of trust in business and personal dealings carries many costs. Corporate managers and public officials, for example, are reluctant to share information that could empower their organizations, resulting in sharply reduced employee loyalty. Transaction costs, such as legal fees and overly detailed contracting, are major expenses for both corporations and individuals. And because of a fear that they will be sued, many employers refuse to give recommendations for former employees—the two parties, in essence, don't trust each other.[3]

Service professionals, who have historically enjoyed a reputation for unimpeachable integrity, have contributed their fair share to the diminution of trust that clients place in them. Stories are reported in the press—and also occasionally circulated among clients—about investment banks whose client loyalties are a function of deal size rather than prior commitments; about consultants who oversell and put inexperienced staff on projects; of lawyers who create conflicts of interest by allowing themselves to become financially intertwined with their clients; and so on. Litigation against large professional service firms, once rare, has become commonplace.

The basic patterns are all fairly familiar by now: confidential information is misused; a client's interests are put last rather than first; standards are compromised in order to retain client business; and conflicts of interest are not disclosed. As the service industries become more competitive, there is an increasing tendency to compromise principles in order to meet growth and profitability objectives. Integrity, inexorably followed by a decline in trust, is the casualty.

Great professionals, however, never concede their integrity in order to win. They may be bold and determined in pursuit of their objectives, but integrity and their clients' needs—not selling the next assignment, not earning a large bonus, not pleasing their boss—come first. And if there ever is a conflict between the two—between what a client wants and what the professional's integrity dictates—integrity always wins out.

YOUR MOST POWERFUL ALLY

Trust is especially important in situations where there is a high degree of dependence on someone else—precisely the situation when a client hires a professional for advice or buys a complex product or service from him. Trust between a client and a professional is both a necessity and an important asset for both parties: if there is mutual trust, everything works better, faster, and more smoothly. When a client trusts her professional adviser, a number of positive things happen:

- When you suggest additional work to your client, she believes you are proposing the work because you honestly believe it will help her, not because you need more business.
- Your client will be willing to buy services from you that extend beyond your core expertise. Trust allows you to increase the depth and breadth of the relationship.
- If you make an honest mistake or slip up in some way, your client will most likely forgive you and won't hold it against you.
- You will be able to work with your client on a more informal basis, leading to a more relaxed and creative process. There will be a decreased need to carefully document and check everything you do.
- When you make recommendations, they will have more impact. Your client will believe that your words are backed with integrity and that your only agenda is to help solve her problem.

Trust, in other words, is a professional's most powerful ally. Trust is worth a fortune (it is, literally, if we're talking about keeping a client for life), yet you can't purchase it, a fact noted by J. P. Morgan when he testified before Congress in 1912. What is trust, exactly? We know it's missing in many aspects of our society, and we know how powerful it can be when it's present, but it's easier to articulate the *feeling* of trust than the elements that actually create it. Trust is complex: in some situations, it means "I believe you are competent to perform this service"; in others, "I know you will act in my interests, not yours." Author Robert Shaw proposes a general definition of trust: "A belief that those on whom we depend will meet our expectations of them."[4]

Harry Hopkins: Franklin Roosevelt's Most Trusted Adviser

Harry Hopkins, who served as an adviser to Franklin Roosevelt from 1936 to 1945, was one of the most remarkable political advisers in U.S. history. Much of his success was based on a relationship of extraordinary trust that he developed not just with the U.S. president but with other world leaders at the time, such as Winston Churchill and Joseph Stalin. Hopkins, who had almost no formal position in the White House during World War II, was influential in both the success of the New Deal and the effective conduct of the war. The trust he engendered, added to his native abilities, enabled him to play a highly unusual role in both increasing Roosevelt's effectiveness as president and in facilitating a highly productive relationship among the Allied war leaders. Secretary of the Army George Marshall, who was not prone to hyperbole, said that Hopkins "rendered a service to this country which will never even vaguely be appreciated."

A professional social worker by training, Hopkins as a young man showed little hint of the greatness he would achieve as the most important adviser to a famous U.S. president. He headed the Federal Emergency Relief Administration and the Works Progress Administration during the mid-1930s and was secretary of commerce from 1938 to 1940. Ironically, it was when Hopkins abandoned any personal political aspirations that his power increased exponentially. He had a bout with cancer, then was diagnosed with a chronic, wasting intestinal ailment that doctors believed would be fatal. Because of his health, he gracefully stepped down as commerce secretary in 1940, but soon after Roosevelt was re-elected, he asked Hopkins to move into the White House and become his informal adviser. It was during the war years, when he held no major post, that Hopkins established a unique relationship with Roosevelt.

Living in a guestroom at the White House, Hopkins joined Roosevelt for virtually all his meals and attended every important meeting with him. Roosevelt got to know Hopkins intimately, reinforcing their personal chemistry and a sense that they shared many of the same values. Based on Roosevelt's deep trust in Hopkins, he sent him as his personal emissary to London in January 1941, to meet with Churchill (Roosevelt and Churchill did not yet know each other personally, although they had met once years earlier). Hopkins and Churchill spent two weeks together, including three weekends in the countryside at Chequers, the prime minister's country estate, where they talked, drank, and relaxed together. The relationship Hopkins established with Churchill during this trip built a foundation of trust that allowed Hopkins to create an unusual link between the two leaders.

Moreover, as Hopkins's biographer, Robert Sherwood, notes, "there was by now an intimacy between the two men which developed to such a degree that it is no exaggeration to say that Churchill reposed the same confidence in Hopkins that Roosevelt did." After yet a second visit with Churchill, Sherwood tells us, "there was started at this time correspondence without precedent: an informal, off-the-record but none the less official correspondence between the heads of two governments through a third party, Hopkins, in whose *discretion and judgment each had complete confidence.* Time and time again, when the Prime Minister wanted to sound out the President's views on some new move, he would address a private cable to Hopkins . . . [italics added]."[5]

Hopkins exercised impeccable discretion. Despite being privy to virtually every state secret and private conversation of the president, he never, ever—not even once—betrayed the confidences placed in him. He never leaked news or used his information for personal gain. In July 1941, shortly after the Germans had invaded Russia, Roosevelt sent Hopkins to meet with Stalin in Moscow to assess the situation. It was a historic set of meetings, the first between Stalin and a direct representative of the U.S. president. Very little was reported in the newspapers, however. During the press conferences he held afterward, Hopkins revealed virtually nothing about the substance of their talks, even though to do so would have enhanced his prestige and highlighted the powerful and unprecedented role he was playing. Roosevelt knew that Hopkins was as silent as a tomb, and it magnified his ability to trust him.

Hopkins's reliability and consistency further reinforced Roosevelt's belief in his integrity. He never overstepped his bounds; if Roosevelt sent him on a mission to meet with a foreign leader, he knew that Hopkins would assiduously adhere to the agenda and limits that had been set for him. After every meeting, Hopkins would carefully draw up a detailed memo for the president that succinctly laid out the key points and issues to consider.

Hopkins didn't believe in political patronage, and he was incorruptible. When he administered relief funds for Roosevelt as head of the Federal Emergency Relief Administration, he did it strictly by the book, favoring no particular state or constituency. A few times, Roosevelt had to intervene to satisfy some political ally whom Hopkins had treated too impartially. Hopkins never profited from his position of enormous influence; when he died in 1945, his estate was worth only a few hundred dollars. Yet this had been a man who had personally overseen the disbursement of $9 billion in aid during the Depression and who had been a director of the lend-lease program during World War II, which allocated over $50 billion in military spending.

In *Roosevelt and Hopkins,* Robert Sherwood sums up Hopkins the adviser: "Hopkins did not originate policy and then convince Roosevelt it was right. He had too much intelligence as well as respect for his Chief to attempt the role of mastermind. He made it his job to provide a sounding board for discussions of the best means of attaining the goals that the President set for himself. Roosevelt liked to think out loud, but his greatest difficulty was finding a listener who was both understanding and entirely trustworthy. That was Hopkins."[6] Because he had set aside his own personal ambitions for formal office, Hopkins's agenda was Roosevelt's agenda. This, together with his unwavering integrity, made it easy for Roosevelt to trust him.

If we look at Harry Hopkins and his relationship with Roosevelt—indeed, if we examine any business relationship with a high degree of trust—several factors stand out that uniquely affect the level of trust that a client has in you. The first major quality that underpins trust is integrity. The discretion, consistency, and reliability that you demonstrate, and your sense of right and wrong—these will influence, more than just about anything else, the degree of trust people place in you. Hopkins exhibited these qualities to Roosevelt on a daily basis, always coming through for the president, never forgetting a commitment, as incorruptible on the last day of his tenure as on the first.

Hopkins's strong performance at every task Roosevelt gave him illustrates an additional factor that builds trust: competence. In a business setting, a client's trust will naturally be influenced by whether or not he thinks you're competent to do the job you've promised. The risk of trusting someone is a final consideration, and that perceived risk will raise or lower the total amount of trust that a client has in you.

These three factors—integrity, competence, and risk—can be combined into a trust formula:

$$\text{Trust} = \frac{\text{Integrity} \times \text{Competence}}{\text{Risk}}$$

Your clients' perception of each factor in the equation will raise or lower the trust they place in you.

INTEGRITY: THE BACKBONE OF TRUST

Integrity is a state of wholeness in which you act in accordance with a set of coherent values or principles. In other words, you know what's right, you're clear about what you believe in, and you consistently follow your beliefs.

Integrity has several main dimensions to it. The first, according to Yale law professor Stephen Carter, is discernment between right and wrong.[7] Just acting consistently with your beliefs is not enough; you have to have beliefs that are ethical and moral. Adolf Hitler, for example, passed many of the tests of integrity—he acted on his beliefs quite consistently—but he had evil, wrong beliefs. There was no discernment.

In Dante's *Inferno,* which is the first part of his *Divine Comedy,* the "false counselors" are found in the eighth circle of hell, one of the lowest, just below common thieves. These false counselors are spiritual thieves, who advised others to commit fraud. They used their intellect to rob people of their integrity, and as a result must walk for eternity enveloped in painful flames. Using one's intellectual powers to deceive and encourage wrongdoing was, for Dante, an especially egregious crime. *Honesty* is an important manifestation of discernment.

The Importance of Discretion

Discretion is a second dimension of integrity that is of particular importance to clients. Asked to describe the important characteristics of great professionals, many corporate leaders that we interviewed first mentioned *discretion.* Big-picture thinking skills and good judgment were high on their lists, but often not as high as discretion. Perhaps their responses are not so surprising if we consider that people in positions of responsibility and authority look for advisers who can keep confidential information to themselves.

Indiscretion has been a constant source of shame, humiliation, and legal difficulties for both individuals and corporations. The public condemnation of Linda Tripp over her alleged betrayal of confidences while acting as a personal adviser to White House intern Monica Lewinsky demonstrates a near universal abhorrence of indiscretion. And this reaction extends as well to corporations and professional firms, where an indiscretion can result in major losses.

Not long ago, a major investment bank inadvertently released the news of a pending merger between two large corporations. This confidential information was made public to a nationwide network of stockbrokers during a routine morning conference call. Once the news hit the airwaves, the merger collapsed, costing one of the companies over $1 billion in market value. One client, remarking on the lack of discretion shown by advisers he had used in the past, commented to us that "If I'm considering an acquisition, I bring in outside bankers and lawyers as *late in the process as possible.* There's too high a risk that what we're doing will get leaked."

Often, the need for discretion creates serious dilemmas for the adviser. Consultant James Kelly recounts this story:

> I was advising the CEO of a $4 billion company on how to revitalize his strategy and organization. I conducted numerous interviews with his executive team—discussions that I prefaced with the usual assurances of confidentiality, which is a prerequisite to free, honest discussion. One by one, the managers recounted how the CEO's dysfunctional, overly critical personal style was sinking the company. The CEO would attack people openly in meetings and berate them mercilessly. Morale was terrible, and many of the general managers were thinking of leaving. The issue is how do you handle this? The best thing for the company is to get the CEO to change his behavior. Do you go right to the CEO and report what his executives have said, hoping he'll respond positively but violating your interviewees' confidences and also risking your client's wrath? Whose interests come first here?
>
> In fact, I did confront the CEO with his behavior. I couched it in terms of my own personal observations of how he handled his executives, however, not in terms of anything that had been said to me by his direct reports. I

pointed out some of the dysfunctional behavior I had witnessed and made suggestions for better ways of managing. He was actually grateful for the feedback and slowly began to change for the better.

Many professionals, however, can't seem to resist the temptation to exploit confidential information for their own benefit. In some cases they use confidential information to enhance personal standing, power, and prestige in the eyes of clients, others in the organization, or even friends at social gatherings. Insecure and perhaps even lonely, they divulge confidential information in hopes of bringing others into their personal circle. Some professionals are disrespectful or condescending to their clients, leading them to treat lightly the information that's been shared with them.

Consistency and Reliability

A client has to feel that when you say you'll do something, you'll follow through—always. Think about how you feel when a busy colleague says, "I'll get that name and address for you," and the next day he has left a voice mail or sent a fax with the needed information. You sense immediately that you can depend on that person—he's reliable and he does what he says he'll do. Multiply this by one hundred or one thousand, over many months or years, and you can see how absolute dependability greatly reinforces people's belief in your integrity. In contrast, recall the times people have promised you things that they never followed through on. "Flakey" and "unreliable" are words that come to mind to describe them.

Consistency makes you predictable to your client, and it reinforces the feeling that you have integrity, that you don't change your beliefs or principles on a situation-by-situation basis, but rather consistently apply them. Consistency has several dimensions. It means that:

- You remain true to your beliefs and views, no matter whom you are talking with.
- Your habits are consistent. You don't do a great job on one piece of work, and deliver it on time, and then the next time around do a sloppy job that's late.
- You treat people consistently, regardless of rank or position. A warning sign to any perceptive client is a professional who is courteous and attentive to top executives but treats everyone else like a lackey.

When you are inconsistent, your clarity about who you are and what you stand for is diminished. As nineteenth-century novelist Nathaniel Hawthorne put it, "No man can for any considerable time wear one face to himself and another to the multitude without finally getting bewildered as to which is the true one."

A final aspect of integrity that is proposed by Yale's Professor Stephen Carter is that you are willing to act on your beliefs. In other words, it's not enough to have good intentions—you have to be prepared to put them into action and potentially suffer losses. If there is no risk of loss, he tells us, there cannot be much integrity.[8] It doesn't take integrity, for example, to turn down a client who you know will be unprofitable—there's no cost to your action. Refusing a highly lucrative engagement for ethical reasons, however, does demonstrate integrity.

COMPETENCE

Competence is the third term in the trust equation. A client has to feel not only that you've got integrity but that you have the skills and knowledge to do the job right.

Sometimes, a quiet skepticism about your competency can be behind a lack of trust. A consultant who had done a great job in one division of a large company, for example, was asked by the CEO to do a similar project for a different division based several thousand miles away. To facilitate the work, he asked another partner from his firm, who lived near the second division, to be part of the team. They jointly attended several initial meetings with the division head, then developed a proposal to do a major profit improvement project. The client kept postponing a decision about the project, however, and eventually asked his controller to work directly with the two consultants to "provide more detail" in the proposal document. The controller's demands kept growing; after insisting on multiple revisions of the proposal, he then asked for a *daily* schedule of their planned activities for the entire six-month duration of the work. Frustrated, the original partner called up the division chief and informed him that if they weren't happy with the proposal as it stood, they probably couldn't work together. The manager immediately agreed, and the proposal died.

Some time later, the partner asked the CEO, who had encouraged the original opportunity with the new division, why things had been so difficult. "It's simple," the CEO explained. "They thought your partner was a lightweight. They didn't trust him to do the job." Had the consultant understood this earlier, perhaps by opening up a more frank dialogue with the client, the situation might have been salvaged.

RISK

A client's trust will vary depending on the perception of the risk of trusting you. You might trust your favorite babysitter to take care of your children for an evening, for example, but not to take them on a three-day camping trip. Similarly, a client may trust you with a small project that has little downside, but not with a large one whose failure could jeopardize the viability of the whole company. Perceived risk can be based on many factors—belief in your competence, the absolute importance of the task, and a client's past experience with your integrity (how discreet, reliable, and consistent have you been?). High perceived risk reduces trust; conversely, professionals can increase trust by decreasing the amount of risk for the client.

Building Trust in a Low-Trust World

For some, the word "stockbroker" evokes images of cold-calling and account churning rather than trust. Ron Moeller of A. G. Edwards, however, is for his clients a paragon of trustworthiness. One of A. G. Edwards's top-performing brokers in the country, with twenty-five years in the business, Moeller has a composed, serene demeanor that reflects his long-term approach to both investing and client relationships. "Perhaps we should talk after the market has closed," we suggest to him, "when things are calmer for you." No, Ron wants to talk in the middle of the morning.

"I'm not on the telephone all day as you might think," he explains to us. "I make regular, in-person appointments with my clients to review their portfolios and reassess their overall financial and personal situations. It's not in my clients' best interest to be trading their accounts day in and day out." Moeller learned early on that intimacy facilitates trust. Back in the 1970s, his firm sponsored free financial planning seminars. "The key was getting them to subsequently come visit me in the office in person. A one-on-one meeting is critical to really assessing their needs and for them to get to know me."

No client is too big or small for Moeller. He is consistent: he has always agreed to take on small, mom-and-pop accounts, often ignored by other brokers, as well as the accounts of millionaires. He demonstrates his competency through a prudent, conservative investing philosophy, and he is clear about the limits of his competence: he frequently refers clients to a lawyer, an accountant, or other professionals in order to complete the total management of their financial affairs.

Moeller reinforces the trust his clients put in him by constantly emphasizing that the only agenda is the client's agenda, and he never convinces himself that actions taken in his own interest are actually good for the client. "I do lots of things that earn me very low commissions—I have to, because it's in the best interest of my clients. I put their money into CDs and Treasuries when it's appropriate. I 'buy and hold' many investments because again, even though the commissions are small, it makes sense to do it."

He also manages their expectations—a critical step in maintaining trust. "I am very careful to educate my clients about the expected returns for different types of investments. We've seen major increases in stock prices over the last five or six years, for example, but the average annual return over the long term is 11 percent. If you lead people to believe you can consistently deliver 15 percent or 20 percent a year on their investments, eventually you'll lose their confidence, because you won't be able to achieve that year in and year out."

Ron Moeller: a stockbroker who is a trusted adviser to his clients. Nothing fancy here—no tricks. He develops a personal relationship with each individual. He demonstrates integrity by being reliable, maintaining consistency, and always putting his clients' agendas first. He carefully sets and manages expectations. He applies a low-key approach to investing and building wealth. He believes everyone who needs his services, rich or not, should have access to them. It works— precisely because there are no tricks.[9]

PROFESSIONAL AND PERSONAL ETHICS: WHAT GUIDES YOU?

When we're confronted with an ethical or moral dilemma, most of us do what "feels right" to us. Implicitly, our sense of integrity guides us to make what we feel is intuitively a good decision. Not surprisingly, great minds have pondered the issue of ethical decision making for thousands of years. John Stuart Mill, for example, the great nineteenth-century philosopher, developed a "universal principle" for resolving ethical and moral issues. He believed that you should take whatever action brings the greatest happiness to the greatest number of people. For a modern professional, this prescription is certainly powerful in theory, but so general that it is almost impossible to interpret and implement.

Two of the extraordinary advisers we have profiled in previous chapters—Aristotle and Machiavelli—had a lot to say about ethics as well, and it's worth considering their thinking. Aristotle, who as you recall tutored Alexander the Great, wrote the *Nicomachean Ethics,* a set of notes for his lectures on ethics. Aristotle sets out the following criteria for arriving at sound ethical decisions:[10]

- You have to develop your character and become a sound, thoughtful, mature individual;
- You have to develop your ethical instinct—this embraces common sense, logic, and attention to ethical principles;
- You should draw on important ethical, moral, and social practices in the culture where you live;
- You have to understand the relevant facts about the situation.

Niccolò Machiavelli, as we know, had a very different approach to ethics. His concern was how to acquire, maintain, and use princely power, and he believed that whatever means were required to accomplish this were justified. Machiavelli was not an immoral man; he believed that it was good to be ethical and moral, but that it was slightly more important to be expedient, bold, and clever if the stability of the regime was at stake. "How one lives," he wrote, "is so far distant from how one ought to live . . . for a man who wishes to act entirely up to his professions of virtue soon meets with what destroys him among so much that is evil." In other words, it's hard to be good in a bad world. Today, of course, our world is very different from Machiavelli's sixteenth-century Italy, and we have to be careful to interpret Machiavelli for *our* times.

So where does this leave the modern professional? Ethics professor Joseph Badaracco of Harvard Business

School recommends, in his book *Defining Moments,* that you ask yourself four questions to help determine your response to an ethical dilemma.[11] These questions very nicely weave together some of the best historical thinking on ethics with the modern, individualistic need for each of us to find our own way:

- How do my feelings and instincts define the dilemma?
- Which of the responsibilities and values in conflict have the deepest roots in my life and in communities I care about?
- Looking to the future, what is *my* way?
- How can expediency and shrewdness, along with imagination and boldness, move me toward the goals I care about most strongly?

Remember that while we're talking here about dilemmas you encounter professionally, there should be little or no distinction between how you handle your personal life and your professional life. A number of clients that we interviewed made this specific point: a professional's values and character are an important part of the equation that defines whether or not a long-lasting professional relationship will develop.

Wes Cantrell, CEO of Lanier Worldwide, commented to us that "an adviser's personal conduct is very relevant to me. For example, if a man can't be loyal to his wife, will he be loyal to me?" Personal standards of fidelity and marital conduct, of course, will vary from person to person and between cultures. While some professionals might feel uncomfortable about having their private conduct judged by a client, this is inevitable. Clients assess you as a total person, just as you, in turn, evaluate a client's integrity based on a variety of inputs, some of which may derive from experiences outside of work. The point is that you will be a more integrated professional if similar principles guide both your professional and personal behavior.

HOW YOU CAN BUILD TRUST

Trust is like a fine Oriental rug that is carefully woven over many months or even years, rather than an edifice that is erected overnight. Lots of small things go into building trust. Here are some areas to consider:

Face Time with Clients

"One of my few client relationships that went badly," Spencer Stuart's Andrea de Cholnoky tells us, "was due to lack of face time. The client told me that he just hadn't seen enough of me, that it didn't seem like I had the energy in the assignment. I immediately called up every single one of my other clients and took them out to lunch! You've got to invest, continually, in face-to-face time with clients."

There is simply no substitute for meeting with a client and allowing time so that the two of you can come to know each other personally. The purpose is not to make the client like you—we're not talking about "schmoozing." And there's no guarantee that if you spend time together the trust will increase. If, however, there is personal chemistry, as well as shared values and interests, personal time together will bring this out, and it will subtly facilitate the development of trust. Face time provides an opportunity for your client to see your sterling qualities firsthand. It amplifies your competence and integrity.

Setting and Reviewing Expectations

We said early on that a client's satisfaction is a function of expectations versus actual (or perceived) performance. Trust works the same way: you may very well fulfill your commitments on time, but if you and your client don't agree on what a particular commitment was in the first place, your *perceived* integrity will suffer and trust will diminish.

Carefully Making Promises

The worst kind of professional is someone who constantly promises things and never delivers. This kind of credibility gap, once established, is almost insuperable. Lewis Smedes, an ordained minister, beautifully sums up the meaning of a promise in a sermon entitled "The Power of Promises": "When a person makes a promise, he stretches himself out into circumstances that no one can control and controls at least one thing: he will be there no matter what the circumstances turn out to be."[12]

Here are some suggestions for how to keep commitments:

- Don't be cavalier with promises. Don't say, "Let's have lunch" or "I'll call so-and-so for you" unless you really mean it. Being known as a person of your word is a powerful thing. Don't dilute your integrity with thoughtless commitments.
- If necessary, make conditional agreements. If an event or occurrence could get in the way of a promise, state it clearly up front. This way there will be no surprises.
- If you can't keep a promise, let the other person know as early as possible. The longer you wait to reveal the bad news, the worse things get. If you have built up trust by keeping your previous commitments, then that client will probably understand.
- Learn to say no. Busy, successful people are the ones who are always asked to do things. Be selective about what you commit to.

Demonstrating Loyalty

Loyalty means having an allegiance to your client and putting her agenda before your own. When clients experience a sense of loyalty from you, it reinforces their perception of your integrity and strengthens their ability to trust you. Someone who feels third or fourth on your list of priorities, who gets the impression that she's just one of dozens or hundreds of clients, is never going to trust you very deeply. Think about how you feel when a doctor barely recognizes you and has to visibly reorient himself as he walks into the examining room. Everyone wants to feel special—your clients are no different.

It's also important never to criticize anyone who is not present. You win the trust of the people you're with by showing loyalty to those who aren't there. If someone is indiscreet and tells you a piece of gossip or confidential information, it becomes difficult to trust that individual. If he or she is always criticizing other people, it makes you wonder, What will this person say about me to others?[13]

Nurturing Trust on a Daily Basis

There is no doubt that one dramatic event can establish a great deal of trust. For example, when George Washington voluntarily relinquished the presidency after his second term had expired, he instilled a deep public trust both in himself and in the new American government. Few if any major heads of state before him had ever stepped down of their own free will. What really cements and develops a sense of trust, however, is the *daily* nurturing of your relationships. Stephen Covey's metaphor for this reservoir of trust is the emotional bank account. When an action reinforces trust, you have made a deposit; when you do something to undermine trust, such as letting someone down, you make a withdrawal. You have to make lots of deposits, regularly, to sustain trust.

There Are No "Minor" Commitments

At Beth Israel Hospital in Boston, legendary chief of surgery Dr. William Silen tells his residents, "I don't know what the difference is between 'major' and 'minor' surgery. I just know that no one performs 'minor' surgery on *me!*" In a similar vein, there is no such thing as a minor commitment. Each promise you make, large or small, should be treated with the same seriousness. "Character is made in the small moments of our lives," offered nineteenth-century clergyman Phillips Brooks. It's all the little things that you do—often when no one is looking—that constitute your character and define your integrity.

Knowing What You Stand For

By definition, integrity is a wholeness or completeness that is underpinned and bounded by a set of beliefs and values. What are your principles? What do you stand for? What guides your professional and personal life? Where do you draw the line when your beliefs are challenged or threatened? The previous chapter sets out some of the questions you need to ask yourself in order to clarify what you stand for and believe.

Law professor and best-selling author Alan Dershowitz told us this story about clarity of principles and integrity: "Several years ago I helped a large law firm win a very important case. To celebrate, the partners took me out to dinner to a private club. I learned that the club did not allow women inside the door, however, a practice that violated one of my basic beliefs about equality between the sexes and non-discrimination. When I refused to go to the club, they said 'but there's no other good place to eat.' I insisted, and we ended up holding the victory dinner at McDonalds."

Being Prepared to Talk on TV

All professionals are faced with ethical and moral dilemmas just about every week of their lives. Some are relatively minor. Should I fly first class or economy? Should I put hotel laundry on my expense report? Some are major. Should I agree to an accounting practice that I feel is wrong? There are no simple rules for how to conduct yourself. Hemingway's quip that "I only know that moral is what you feel good after and immoral is what you feel bad after"[14] can take you only so far. One good principle to follow as a professional is what we call the "light-of-day" test. Whatever action you take, be it staying in a certain class of hotel or meeting with a client's competitor, would you be comfortable discussing it with your client the next morning in the full light of day? What if you were interviewed on television and asked about something you did? Would you feel comfortable explaining it?

"Anything related to issues of integrity, trust, and ethics are fatal flaws"[15] commented Rebecca Guerra, the vice president for human resources at eBay, the online auction house. Speaking to *The New York Times,* she emphasized that while failure in one's past was OK, questions about character were unacceptable to her company.

Another way of looking at this is that you shouldn't have any secrets. By secrets we don't mean confidential client information, which you are duty-bound to protect. Rather, you should have nothing to hide; you should be comfortable sharing details of your professional conduct with a client, without embarrassment or defensiveness.

Reducing Your Client's Risk

Recall that the amount of trust a client has in you will go up or down depending on the risk he perceives. You can do several things to reduce this risk. First of all, you have to demonstrate consistency and reliability right from the start, even for the smallest of things. Showing integrity itself, in other words, reduces risk.

Second, you can either implicitly or explicitly guarantee your work. A guarantee doesn't have to take the form of a certificate that your clients mail in to you. More likely, it will be an understanding between you and your client. You want your clients to feel that if they are not satisfied at any time with your work, you will rectify it as best you can—period. The words "we'll work on this until you're satisfied" can be the occasional reminder of the fact that you'll stand behind your work and strive to address any issues they may have with your performance.

WHEN TRUST IS LOST

Sometimes, even though you feel you have demonstrated a high level of integrity and competence, trust is lost. Here are some principles to remember about losing trust:

Clients don't inform you when they stop trusting you. Trust can vanish rapidly and mysteriously, and you're always the last to know. Because the symptoms of a loss of trust can be so varied, and because some of them can also signify other problems or issues, it's always hard to pinpoint when your client stops trusting you. Perhaps you lose a follow-on assignment that you were sure you would win; or suddenly the client throws your business open for a competitive bid. Often, a client can't even articulate that she's lost trust in you. She feels a vague dissatisfaction, and she stops sharing information with you and turning to you for advice. You have to watch and listen very carefully.

As we suggested in chapter 3 on empathy, it's useful to hold a frank and open discussion with your client when the engagement ends, something that is easier to do if you set the expectation, right up front, that you'll be having this discussion three or six months down the road. Unfortunately, by the time you discover that the trust has dried up, it may be too late to do anything about it.

Clients don't care why you let them down. Unless a catastrophe has occurred—an earthquake or a death in the family—clients, like most people, don't particularly care what the reason was that caused you not to deliver on a commitment. You may believe you had perfectly good reason to let them down, and the excuses are myriad: you caught a cold, the work took longer than you had planned, another client had an emergency, your computer crashed, you forgot to write it down in your agenda, you wrote it down in the wrong agenda, your secretary forgot to tell you about it, and so on. But your client doesn't really care, and trying to explain it won't help. It's better to say, "I let you down, I'm sorry, and it won't happen again." If you have built up a reservoir of trust with your client, he may let it pass.

Sometimes, repairing a lapse in trust can enhance your relationship. If you let a client down, you may be able to recover her confidence. How you react to the incident and the way in which you go about remediating it are critically important. Several years ago, a management consultant conducting an assignment for a large West Coast company carelessly left a draft copy of his report on a BART train in San Francisco. An unscrupulous passenger found it, contacted the client, and demanded $50,000 in ransom for the return of the document. All hell broke loose: the company threatened not just to terminate its relationship with the consultants, but to file a major lawsuit as well. The consulting firm went into action immediately. Its president flew out to California the next day and met with the CEO of the client company. He apologized for the incident, offering no excuses. He informed the CEO that the consultant had been disciplined and that the firm was assigning a task force of partners to develop new policies and procedures to minimize the possibility that such an incident could reoccur. Then he offered to conduct a major study for the client, free of charge, on a key issue the company faced. The client accepted, and the relationship continued successfully for another four years.

This anecdote illustrates some cardinal rules for dealing with a breach of trust:

- Admit that you've made a mistake. Own up to the lapse.
- Don't make excuses—no one wants to hear them.

Have You Developed Trust with Your Clients?

✔ Sometimes, you conduct assignments based on a minimum of documentation. Once you and your client have agreed on the objectives and deliverables, your client trusts you to follow through.

✔ Clients may remind you of something you're supposed to do, but they rarely "check up" on you.

✔ Clients ask you to tackle issues that are of major importance to them.

✔ If on a rare occasion you slip up and miss a commitment, your clients are very forgiving.

✔ There is a quality of openness to your client relationships. Both you and your clients feel free to bring up touchy or awkward subjects with each other.

✔ Your clients have become familiar with your particular skills as well as your values and beliefs. They can predict how you will react to a particular situation or dilemma.

✔ Clients' trust in you extends beyond their belief that you will do good work; it is a deeper, broader trust based on both professional competence and personal integrity.

- Provide value-added compensation to the client. Some clients might value having the fee reduced; for others, such as the client in the example above, a free piece of work can be appropriate.
- Learn from the incident, and let your client know that you are learning from it. Tell them what you're going to do to make sure it doesn't happen again.

There may be situations where you feel that you are 100 percent in the right and that the client is absolutely in the wrong. Even in these cases, keep in mind that the client perceives that you have let him down. You may have to walk away from the relationship, but be careful about how you deal with it; you don't want to leave burned bridges behind you. If there has been good communication between you and the client, however, and expectations have been set, you should be able to avoid this kind of confrontation.

DEEP PERSONAL and professional trust, which boils down to a client's belief in your integrity and your competence, is a hallmark of the long-term relationships that great professionals are able to develop. Clients expect and will forgive occasional errors of judgment, but lapses of integrity are a red flag to everyone around you. As the fifth-century religious leader St. Augustine wrote in his essay *On Lying*. "When regard for the truth has been broken down or even slightly weakened, all things will remain doubtful." Set high standards of conduct for yourself. Tirelessly develop your reputation for integrity and honesty, and it will become one of your biggest assets as a professional.

NINE

PITFALLS AND DILEMMAS
Avoiding the Land Mines
in Client Relationships

Princes like to be helped, but not surpassed. When you counsel someone, you should appear to be reminding him of something he had forgotten, not the light he was unable to see.

BALTASAR GRACIÁN,
seventeenth-century Jesuit priest and adviser

B Y THE MIDDLE of the sixth century B.C., King Croesus of Lydia had become an extraordinarily wealthy man. His kingdom—in what is today western Turkey—was the first in the ancient world to issue and use metal currency, and the accompanying economic boom filled his coffers with gold. He had a dilemma, however: the Persians, his neighbors, were constantly threatening his empire. Croesus wondered if he should take the offensive and preemptively invade Persia. Pondering this question, he resolved in 555 to send envoys to Delphi in Greece to ask the famed oracle for advice. He knew he would receive sage counsel from the oracle. After all, generations of leaders in the ancient world had regularly made the pilgrimage to consult with the resident priestess at Delphi.

After a journey over sea and land of nearly a month, Croesus's envoys arrived at the mountainous sanctuary of Delphi. Early one morning, accompanied by an entourage of   217 priests and guards, they made their way into the temple of Apollo where the priestess gave her consultations. They paused upon entering to read the inscription etched over the entrance: KNOW THYSELF. First, they bought sacred cakes and offered them at the altar near the entrance. Next, they sacrificed a goat on the hearth of the inner room. Finally, they were led into the inner sanctuary where they waited in silence for the priestess to speak.

Sitting on a small seat suspended within a large tripod and concealed behind a curtain, she had been inhaling the vapors from a cauldron of laurel leaves for several hours and was by now in a state of complete delirium from the hallucinogenic effects of the medicinal plant. She began mumbling incoherently. The envoys listened in rapt attention, although her words were incomprehensible. The chief interpreter, who stood in front of the curtain, was responsible for translating what the priestess had said. He turned to them and spoke:

> *I know the number of the sands, and the measure of the sea. I understand the dumb and hear him who does not speak. If you attack Persia, you will destroy a great empire.*[1]

When word was brought back to Croesus, he was elated. The oracle had spoken—victory would be his! He and his advisers began plotting a military campaign against the Persians in which Lydia would form alliances with Babylon, Egypt, and Sparta. He would crush the Persian emperor, Cyrus the Great.

The oracle was, of course, correct: if Croesus attacked the Persians, a great empire would indeed be destroyed. Croesus had forgotten to ask, however, *which* empire would fall. His Persian campaign was a disaster. After a failed invasion attempt, Cyrus pursued Croesus to Sardis with a superior army, caught him by surprise, and demolished his forces.

MANAGING CLIENT RELATIONSHIPS IS NEVER EASY

Soothsaying, prior to the scientific revolution, was a major source of advice. Wealthy ancients made the trip to Delphi, and less affluent ones looked for signs about the future in animal offal. The Chinese used to read the cracks in heated tortoise shells. To the twenty-first-century mind, the story of the oracle at Delphi may seem vaguely humorous, yet who is to say that her predictions were any less good than those of many modern prognosticators? The Croesus episode does, however, hint at several of the pitfalls faced by modern advisers and their clients.

Providing services and advice to demanding clients has never been easy. Lawyers, consultants, accountants, and others are frequently the target of mean, condescending humor, yet in reality their work is very difficult. Extensive travel, long hours, and demanding clients are just the start of it. Many of the services that professionals offer—consulting and advertising, for example—are discretionary, and a client can decide to drop them at any time.

Often, clients feel that they have their own expertise in your field, and they constantly challenge your views. This can be healthy, but it can also diminish respect for your knowledge and experience as a professional. Linda Srere, chief client officer for advertising giant Young & Rubicam, tells this story about client "expertise":

> I was attending a conference at a hotel, and early one morning I went to the spa. While I was waiting for my treatment, the man in front of me struck up a conversation. When he learned I worked in advertising, he asked if I was familiar with a certain ad campaign, which I was. He then told me that he was the chairman of the company that made the product. And did I know who created this award-winning campaign? "That little lady over there," he said. "My wife. It was all her idea."

The idea may in fact have been his wife's, but the

point is that everyone thinks he knows something about our business. Clients hire us for our expertise and knowledge, but then they don't recognize it.

Even the best professionals occasionally find themselves in awkward situations with no easy way out, or at the beck and call of difficult clients they wish would go away. Based on our discussions with many extraordinary professionals and demanding clients, as well as on our own experiences as advisers, we've identified the most important pitfalls for professionals. The first set of pitfalls relates to the seven attributes we've described in this book. The second set concerns either difficult situations or types of advisers and clients that should be avoided.

WHEN THE SEVEN ATTRIBUTES
ARE OUT OF BALANCE

The talents, skills, and attitudes of great professionals neatly combine into a powerful whole when they are expressed with balance and moderation. When individual attributes are taken to either negative or positive extremes, however, the result is dysfunctional and even neurotic behavior. The trick is to achieve equilibrium. Let's examine each attribute in turn:

Selfless independence is by definition a delicate balance between client dedication and detachment. When this balance is not achieved, professionals veer toward one extreme or the other. If you are too selfless, you become subservient to your clients and can be exploited by them. If you are overly independent, you become aloof and detached and never develop the collaborative aspects of the relationship. You go back to being a mere purveyor of expertise rather than a broad-based adviser.

When *empathy* is in balance you are able to tune into your client's feelings, thoughts, and context. You have an attitude of healthy humility; you demonstrate strong self-awareness and self-control; and you benefit from well-honed listening skills. When you have too much empathy, you overly identify with your client. Your judgment gets clouded because you're worried about hurting your client's feelings, or upsetting him. You lose your objectivity. If you have too little empathy, on the other hand, you become insensitive, and you stop learning.

A *deep generalist* in balance is a professional with a passion for learning, who has great expertise in one subject but also deep knowledge about his clients, the industries he works in, and the business functions that influence his work. He engages in extensive exploratory learning and uses multiple learning methods to deepen and broaden his knowledge base.

When learning becomes superficial or overly broad, however, there is imbalance. You become a dilettante, someone who has a superficial knowledge of many things with no deep expertise. You are full of clever management sound bites, such as "underpromise and overdeliver," "empowerment is critical," and "cash is king," but there is no depth of understanding behind the concepts. At the opposite extreme, you can become overly specialized and never break out of the prison that is your narrow expertise.

A good *big-picture thinker* has strong powers of analysis *and* synthesis. She identifies critical issues, sees the whole picture, and then uses a variety of tools for synthesis such as analogies, frameworks, multiple perspectives, and pattern recognition. She regularly engages in practices that aid synthesis—suspension of judgment, solitary reflection, whole-brain thinking, and so on.

If you have a positive imbalance of *synthesis*—too much big-picture thinking—you develop a generalized understanding of the problem with no appreciation of the details. You tend to issue-sweeping platitudes rather than specific recommendations. Clients feel you're "up at 35,000 feet" when they need a close-up view as well. You tell your client, for example, that he's got to "leverage key resources," and he walks around for days wondering exactly what that means and how to do it. If you undertake too little synthesis, you'll remain forever at the level of analysis. You'll never see the forest for the trees.

When a professional has balanced *judgment,* he carefully blends facts, experience, and personal values to arrive at sound decisions. He avoids the many traps, such as overconfidence and groupthink, which can cloud the judgment of both professional and client. He neither shoots from the hip nor overanalyzes the situation. When judgment is out of balance, the tendency is either to become paralyzed or to rush to judgment too quickly. Professionals and clients whose judgment is paralyzed typically want to analyze everything to death. They insist on having all the facts before they feel comfortable making a decision. At the other extreme are the advisers who have an opinion on everything and make rapid-fire but flawed judgments. They're cocky and overconfident.

Strong, genuine *conviction* that is balanced drives extraordinary performance. It is rooted in deeply held beliefs and values and an accompanying sense of mission. Conviction is reinforced by empathy for your audience, communications skills, and personal energy. It's bounded by your integrity— you have conviction for the things you truly believe are right, rather than what's expedient at that moment. Too much conviction results in closed-mindedness, dogma, and overconfidence. Clients also call it "bull." It's the professional who is, in the words of Jim Robinson, former CEO of American Express, "100 percent sure but only 70 percent right." Unbalanced, radical conviction, which is characteristic of religious and political fanatics, can turn into dangerous obsession. An imbalance can also occur when you have too little conviction. This results in insecurity and an inability to communicate and persuade.

When *trust* is in balance in a relationship, there is openness between professional and client. The professional demonstrates solid integrity—based on discretion, reliability, consistency, and a clear understanding of right and wrong— as well as competence. He works to reduce the client's risk of trusting him.

An imbalance in trust can occur in several ways. One party may blindly trust the other, for example, without reciprocity, resulting in disillusionment and disappointment. Integrity can also be taken to extremes. An exaggerated sense of integrity can make you uncompromising and lead to a confusion between standards and principles. It's the difference between an unwillingness to lie (a principle, which is part of your integrity) and insisting that your client always show up on time for meetings (a standard). A professional might quit a client engagement with great flourish, for example, claiming that she won't "compromise her integrity," when in reality it was her expectations or standards that were not precisely met. Too little integrity—subtly cutting corners, convincing yourself of untruths, putting your needs first, engaging in secretiveness—is the other extreme to avoid.

The table "When the Seven Attributes Are Out of Balance" summarizes how each attribute gets transformed—or better put, transmogrified—when it's out of balance.

Every professional, of course, will possess a unique blend of these attributes. Each of us will tend to develop certain ones more than others, and while in theory there will be an

When the Seven Attributes Are Out of Balance		
Attribute	**Out of Balance Becomes**	
	Too Little	Too Much
Selfless independence	Subservience	*Aloofness*
Empathy	Insensitivity	*Overidentification*
Knowledge depth/breadth	Overspecialization	*Superficiality*
Synthesis	Narrowness	*Generic advice*
Judgment	Paralysis	*Hip-shooting*
Conviction	Insecurity	*Overconfidence*
Integrity	Dishonesty	*Rigidity*

ideal point of balance, in practice there is a range of healthy expression for each one.

TRAPS TO AVOID

In addition to errors of imbalance that professionals can make as they develop and practice the seven attributes, there are frequent pitfalls and dilemmas in client relationships. The first group of these represents what we call "traps," and even the best professionals and clients fall into them:

The Wrong Client

The right client is the individual who owns the problem at hand, can act on your recommendations, and can authorize your fees or payments. Sometimes, several or more individuals fulfill these various roles; especially in a large organization, there may be no single executive who can do all these things.

Often, professionals end up with the wrong client during the sales process. A group of management consultants, for example, pitched a major restructuring project to a large retailing chain. They invested over $200,000 in preparing the proposal, visiting stores, doing financial analysis, and holding meetings with various vice presidents and even the president. The chairman, who was a major shareholder, decided to go to the final presentation. Until then, however, he had been out of the picture entirely. All of the executives had assured the consultants that the project was "in their bailiwick," and that the chairman was not operationally involved in the company. At the end of the session, which the consultants hoped would be the kick-off meeting for the multimillion-dollar project they had proposed, the chairman suddenly stood up and said, "There's no way we're doing this. I want my own organization to figure out a way to do this work without recourse to expensive outsiders." The consultants glumly filed out. They hadn't been working with the right client.

The Wrong Problem

In the early 1990s, the Greyhound Bus Company, in an effort to revitalize its operations, decided it needed to revamp all of its information systems and create an electronic reservations system. Advised by outside accountants and consultants, it spent millions of dollars and several years implementing the new systems. Once in place, however, not only was the system full of glitches, but it turned out that most of the company's passengers didn't need or want the system. They typically rode only one trip segment at a time and had no need for advance reservations for connecting buses. The real problem had to do with poor scheduling, dirty buses, and ineffective target marketing, not technology.

The great client advisers we've studied constantly ask themselves: Am I working on the right problem? Have I defined the problem correctly?

The Wrong Adviser

Smart, well-educated professionals feel that they ought to have something intelligent to say about everything. The really smart ones, though, know when *not* to give advice, and they admit when there is a mismatch between their expertise and experience and the client's problem. When we interviewed clients about their roles as advisers (many are directors of other corporations and, as experienced executives, are sought after for advice by a variety of people), most of them said that they refuse to give opinions on subjects they know little about and wished their professional advisers would do the same!

One accounting firm, for example, which was short-staffed, sent a partner whose expertise was in the shipping industry to lead a turnaround effort for a distribution company. The company was in bankruptcy, losing almost $100 million a year. At the end of nine months, however, the accounting team had identified only about $10 million in cost cuts. Because of the perceived failure of the engagement, the client sued. The partner whom the firm sent didn't have the experience and sense of urgency required to manage the turnaround. He was the wrong adviser.

One of the best ways to earn respect and trust from a client is to be honest about your capabilities and to recommend other qualified professionals if you're not the right person for the job. If you're asked for advice on a subject, and you don't feel you can give a meaningful response, say so. By replying, "I need to think about that one," or "I know where I can get a good answer—let me get back to you," you increase, not diminish, your client's confidence in you.

Vicariously Exercising Power or Expertise

Professionals sometimes invoke the name and authority of their client to obtain respect and support in the organization. At other times the client executive himself may use the expertise and opinion of the professional adviser to shore up his own position. When done excessively, this practice undermines both client and adviser. President Richard Nixon and Secretary of State Henry Kissinger, for example, both encountered this pitfall. Nixon would tell people, "Henry thinks that. . . ," or "Henry strongly believes such-and-such," mentioning the name of his brilliant adviser in order to add weight to his own words. Kissinger, in turn, would try to bolster his own power by saying, "the president is fully behind this" and "this comes directly from the president." A professional's authority in a client organization has to be based on respect for his knowledge and integrity, not awe or fear of his relationship with a senior executive. Similarly, if a client repeatedly leans too heavily on your expert opinion in public forums, it will eventually undermine—not reinforce—your prestige in the company.

Too Much Bad News

Strategy adviser C. K. Prahalad points out that clients have a limited "bandwidth for bad news." He tells us, "Very few executives have the stamina and ability to constantly push, year after year, the way General Electric CEO Jack Welch does—he's unique in this regard. At the CEO level, most players have one great performance in them. When they get toward the end of that performance, their bandwidth for bad news diminishes substantially. It's at the beginning, when they are receptive and open, that you can have the most impact."

In fact, virtually any client who is just starting out in a new position—not just a CEO—is more open to constructive criticism, new ideas, and suggestions than she will be at the end of her tenure. You have to be able to gauge, therefore, where your client is in her overall career and how open she will be to your counsel. Another way of putting this is that you have to choose your battles carefully. You can't take on your client over every issue, else you risk winning the battle but losing the war. A client will put up only so long with a professional who does nothing but criticize and point out what's wrong.

President Franklin Roosevelt, for example, was far more receptive to his advisers' suggestions during his first term than during his second. As his knowledge of the job grew, and his victories accumulated, he became less open to hearing about what was wrong with the country and his administration. His advisers had to pick their battles with increasing care in order to remain effective.

Staying in a Bad Marriage

Sometimes the personal chemistry between professional and client is just plain lousy. You may have conflicting values, or your personalities may just be so different that you clash on even the smallest issues. Clients are like the rest of us—

you will occasionally find some who are nasty. One professional described a situation where the client engaged in routine verbal abuse:

> I was in my mid-twenties, and we had undertaken a small assignment for a large professional association. They wanted to know where the industry was headed and what changes their members should consider in training and in the management of their individual companies. The client, who ran his own firm in addition to heading the association, was a tyrant. At first, it just seemed like he was a particularly exacting, demanding executive. About a month into the study, however, I met with him to review a memo I had written, and he found a typo on the second page. He became hostile and began yelling at me, berating me for shoddy, substandard work. It was the worst professional experience I have ever had. I was young, and the project was on my shoulders; so I just slinked out of his office feeling terrible instead of confronting him. Today, I would never put up with that kind of mean, disrespectful behavior, and I probably shouldn't have back then, either.

If you find yourself in a bad relationship with a client, try to ascertain whether it's fixable—perhaps there is a misunderstanding that can be cleared up—or whether you are just incompatible. If it's the latter, develop a plan to move on or replace yourself as the lead professional on the assignment.

Accepting Opinions and Judgments at Face Value

Whenever a company collapses into bankruptcy, the finger-pointing quickly reaches a frenzied pace. No matter how obvious it appears in hindsight that facts were misrepresented, losses concealed, and illicit practices condoned, no one—the company directors, the chairman, the CEO, the CFO, the controller, and their outside advisers (accountants, lawyers, bankers, and so on)—ever seems to know anything about what is really going on. Behind this is often the facile acceptance of other people's opinions, judgments, and representations of the facts.

Great professionals constantly challenge what they see and hear. They accept very little at face value, especially when it comes to people's character and competency. Nancy Peretsman, who heads the media group for investment bankers Allen & Company, puts it this way: "You always have to check the facts yourself—you can't put too much trust in what others tell you. This is especially true regarding character issues. You can make business mistakes, and this is natural—there's always risk in business decision making. But you don't want to misjudge people. You've got to invest the time to form your own opinion about people—their character and competency."

Losing the Support of the Broader Organization

Throughout history, advisers to kings have always walked a thin line between the security and power that derived from their relationship with the leader, and the weakness and unpopularity that resulted from the enmity of the king's subordinates—the nobles and the population at large. Cardinal Wolsey, who was lord chancellor before Thomas More, was the son of a butcher. Because of his background, politics, and strong influence over the king, the English nobles hated him. In another case, an adviser to a sixteenth-century German monarch was assassinated by a group of nobles when he advised the king to raise taxes. Harry Hopkins was vilified by Roosevelt's opponents (and some of his allies, as well) because of the intimate relationship he enjoyed with the president.

The fact is, the closer you become to a particular executive you work with, the harder it is to also be effective with the broader organization. It's not just a question of envy. As you develop a close personal relationship with your client, the relationship changes in ways that make it hard to advise his subordinates as well. You become a trusted confidant of that individual, privy to highly confidential information. Others may now hesitate to open up to you for fear that what they say may get passed on to their boss. Or they may ask you for advice, which poses a different dilemma: How much of what you know, in terms of confidential information your client has shared with you, do you bring to bear in the giving of that counsel? Suppose, for example, you know that the manager seeking advice from you is slated to be fired? There are other dangers, as well. For example, if you don't have broad support in the organization, it will be harder to get your ideas implemented, even if you have a strong, energetic client. And if your client leaves, so most certainly will you.

There is no easy answer here. If you work with organizations, you have to weigh your close personal and professional relationship with one client against the need to have multiple relationships. It means that at all times you have to strive to be an independent, honest broker who keeps confidences. The worst thing you can do is try to vicariously project authority based on the relationship you have with your client. This will only confirm people's worst suspicions, and you'll quickly be isolated.

SIX TYPES OF INEFFECTIVE PROFESSIONALS

So far, we've been talking about awkward or difficult situations that professionals can find themselves in—traps you should avoid. Based on their many years of experience in hiring advisers, the clients we interviewed identified various types of ineffective professionals. Here are the ones they cited most frequently:

Agenda Pushers

These are professionals who are focused on what they want and need rather than on the client's agenda. Carlos

Palomares, a senior executive of Citigroup, describes how this feels from the client's perspective: "We had a group of consultants analyze our credit card business, which is an important contributor to corporate profits. They did a very good job during the course of the project, but the final presentation was awkward. After describing their findings, they dedicated the last forty-five minutes of the meeting to telling us how important it was for them to help us with implementation. It was embarrassing, and we felt pressured. A slide or two on the subject would have been OK, but they went on and on. Everyone in the audience was uncomfortable. It had the opposite effect of what was intended—it made us want to use them *less*, not more."

Many historical advisers diminished their stature and effectiveness by pushing an agenda of personal power and influence. Cardinal Richelieu, for example, although brilliant as an adviser and statesman, was very manipulative toward his main client, the French King Louis XIII.

One Size Fits All

"Where you sit is where you stand" goes the old adage, and it is certainly true of many professionals. Ray Smith of Bell Atlantic talks about this type of client adviser: "Many professionals find one good solution and then apply it to every client, to every situation. By way of illustration—I had a friend who got a job as a printer's helper in college, and then started his own printing business. He's a very bright, engaging guy. But for him, the solution to everything is a brochure. If you tell him you've got problems with your computer, he'll enthusiastically say to you, 'Let's put together a pamphlet.' I avoid these one-size-fits-all advisers—they grab on to one solution that works one place then try to sell it everywhere."

Another client concurred: "I'm not looking for the pet solution. Unfortunately, most professional firms are like this—I can just about tell you in advance what solution they will propose. Firm A will always have Solution X; Firm B, Solution Y; and so on."

Gurus

"Guru" is a term that today carries connotations of both respect and disparagement. As described by the business leaders we have spoken to, gurus are professionals with a set of acclaimed, "hot" ideas that they market from coast to coast in speeches and seminars. These gurus can unquestionably be very helpful; they can act as a catalyst for a client, and they can offer important new ideas. But many leaders felt that they are ineffective as valued client advisers and can even mislead an organization. Reginald Jones, the former chairman of General Electric, commented to us that "I have never really fallen for the gurus. At GE we avoided them entirely. They come in with all the slogans and the buzzwords, they give a spellbinding lecture, and they disappear. Two days later, you can't remember anything they said that you can really use in the organization. The outstanding professionals, in contrast, offer advice and insights that are more specific and practical. They address your context."

Crowd Pleasers

These are the advisers who tell their clients exactly what they want to hear. They lack integrity, conviction, and independence. They are like one of the protagonists in the joke about the wildlife biologist who goes to a small town in the Rockies to study mountain lions. In the general store, he asks the clerk if he's ever seen any mountain lions around the town. "Absolutely not," the clerk replies, seeking to reassure the stranger.

"That's too bad," says the biologist. "I've come out here from Boston to study them and was hoping to stay awhile."

"Actually," the clerk tells him, hoping he'll stay, "I saw a big one just last night near my house."

George Fisher, chairman and CEO of Kodak, reflected on his experiences in buying professional services and advice: "The effective professionals focus on doing a great job on the project at hand, rather than spending their time paving the way for the next assignment. They are willing to work as part of a team, and they bring to bear value-added facts. The really ineffective ones, though, just tell you what you want to hear and feed back to you what you've already told them."

Crowd Followers

Jim Robbins, CEO of Cox Communications, says that "a good outside adviser is someone who is really thinking on the edge, who will challenge the status quo and be willing to go against the crowd." Out of insecurity, lack of imagination, or just plain conservatism, however, some professionals always advise their clients to go with the crowd, and they stick to preconceived notions about the right solution. Political advisers are notorious for this. Based on the most recent poll results, they will push their clients to espouse positions that maximize their popularity at that moment in time.

During the 1970s and 1980s, many large corporations became enamored of the burgeoning computer business and felt they just had to be a part of it. Following the crowd, companies as diverse as AT&T, Xerox, and Exxon all made ill-fated, expensive forays into computers and related high-technology products that they have since abandoned.

Recyclers

Clients want services tailored to their particular situation, not recycled, boilerplate advice. Polonius, who advises the king and queen in Shakespeare's *Hamlet,* is a classic example of the adviser who offers stale, clichéd counsel. Spouting platitudes to his son Laertes, such as "Neither a borrower nor a lender be" and "Above all, to thine own self be true," he exposes his own shallowness and lack of insight (his theory about Hamlet's madness is wrong). Polonius recycles the same silly advice over and over.

Several years ago, *The Wall Street Journal* chronicled an extraordinarily embarrassing incident of recycling by a large human resources consulting firm. The company had been asked by a dozen different clients to study their affirmative action and diversity policies and make recommendations. Two of the clients happened to compare the reports they were given, only to find them virtually identical, down to the specific recommendations, which were supposed to be tailored for each client. A reporter's subsequent investigation surfaced the fact that all of the reports were essentially the same. The clients were furious.

INEFFECTIVE CLIENTS

Just as clients recognize types of ineffective advisers, many of the extraordinary professionals with whom we've spoken pointed out several kinds of ineffective clients, who should also be avoided. This is not a new subject: Machiavelli alluded to at least one type of ineffective client five hundred years ago in *The Prince:* "Here is an infallible rule: a prince who is not himself wise cannot be well advised."

Do the following attitudes sound familiar?

"I don't really want to change"

Some clients go through the motions of hiring outside professionals, listen carefully to their recommendations, but never act on the advice they're given. These same clients then complain about the stacks of "theoretical reports" gathering dust on their bookshelves. Nothing, of course, is more demoralizing for a professional than to do good work that is ignored and unimplemented.

Peter Drucker tells an amusing story about his relationship with Alfred Sloan, who headed General Motors when

Drucker wrote his seminal book *The Concept of the Corporation* (1946). He says, "For the next twenty years he would . . . ask me once or twice a year to have lunch alone with him in his New York apartment. . . . Above all, he wanted to talk about *My Years with General Motors,* on which he had been working for many years. He asked for my opinions and carefully listened—and he never once took my advice."[2]

While we can't judge for sure how difficult or easy Sloan was as a client, the story is striking. We'd assume that anyone who had the chance to meet regularly with Drucker would heed at least some of his advice!

"I'm not listening"

There are those clients, it seems, who just never listen. They have a retort for everything you say, usually something like "We tried that ten years ago, and it didn't work," or "Our company's culture is unique—that doesn't make sense for us." What we can rarely determine, however, is whether our advice does indeed have a subtle effect on our clients' thinking, or if their views are absolutely fixed and they really aren't listening. Sometimes, a client is so carried away by his current success that he becomes impenetrable and feels he has no need to listen to anyone else.

"My judgment is infallible"

Bill Leigh of the Leigh Bureau, a leading speakers bureau and literary agency, describes how bad judgment on the part of an individual client can make life difficult for the professional: "An important part of my job is to help my clients manage and develop their careers as speakers and authors. But if a client constantly demonstrates bad judgment, it becomes impossible to advise them. One person, against my advice, accepted an absurdly high advance for a book. The book flopped, and he's having to start his career over again. Another client left us to go with another bureau, feeling—despite my well-argued counsel—that he'd make more money with our competitor. After a year he was disillusioned and unhappy and approached me about coming back. Unfortunately, this was the second time he had done this. At that point there wasn't a lot I could do to help him. If someone makes one poor career judgment, I don't mind—he or she becomes motivated, and your advice can have high leverage. But if they make the same mistake twice—two similar blunders—then you have to question whether it makes sense to keep them as a client."

"Please confirm my opinion"

Most people want confirmation, not advice. So goes the old adage, and there is some truth to it. Clients always have opinions about how to proceed, and some of them are looking—sometimes subconsciously—for an outsider to support the direction they've chosen. When a client calls in a professional firm simply to confirm what he or she wants to do, however—to rubber-stamp a decision with the firm's brand name—the ground gets slippery. If you honestly reach the same conclusion as your client, then you can feel comfortable about your advice. Using "rubber-stamp" engagements to fill up billable hours, however, will do nothing to enhance your reputation or motivate your professional staff.

"Professionals are like pencils"

Some clients don't want a broad-based relationship. By dint of personality and outlook, they're not comfortable with the deep advisory relationships we're talking about in this book. They want a professional to deliver a service for a fixed price and then leave. There is nothing wrong with this; in fact, all of us will invariably have some assignments that fall into this category. Some clients go beyond this, however, and they treat educated professionals like pencils, a commodity to be bargained for and bought from the cheapest supplier.

There are two issues to consider here. The first is balance. If *all* your clients have this "professionals are just commodities" mindset, then you'll never stop being an expert for hire who works on a transaction basis (and you'll be run ragged after a few years). The second issue is trying to turn a client who wants an expert—who thinks he's just buying a commodity such as pencils—into someone he isn't. One executive told us about a consulting engagement that went wrong for this very reason. His metaphor seems very apt: "I had leaks and wanted a plumber. Instead, I got a general contractor who kept pushing me to renovate the whole house. After they left I still had the leaks." He was not happy.

If a client isn't interested in a long-term relationship, you won't convince him to have one with you. The best you can shoot for is a lifetime recommendation from that person based on doing a great job at what he asked you to do. Clients reach out to a professional—just as we would—and draw that person in. They choose us as trusted advisers; we don't choose them.

"The best advice is free advice"

Clients do, from time to time, exploit the professionals they work with. Usually, exploitation happens subtly; most clients don't consciously plot to make you work for free. What usually takes place is they undervalue your time and ideas. Bankers who work on a success-fee basis, for example—who get paid when a transaction occurs—are sometimes asked by clients to provide advice and do research outside of the normal course of a deal. Some clients feel that the banker should just put in time for free, proffering the bait, "We'll retain you to do a deal if one materializes."

This dilemma brings us back to the concept of *selfless independence:* you need to be dedicated to your client and willing to go the extra mile on a day-to-day basis, but you also have to manage the overall profitability of the relationship. You should always be prepared to give some free advice—to provide, even, some services without charge—but be careful. Know the person with whom you are dealing. A professional who works to add extra value in an effort to exceed client expectations can also become exploited.

GREAT PROFESSIONALS don't just cultivate the seven attributes that are the focus of this book. They consciously avoid the pitfalls and actively manage the dilemmas that even the

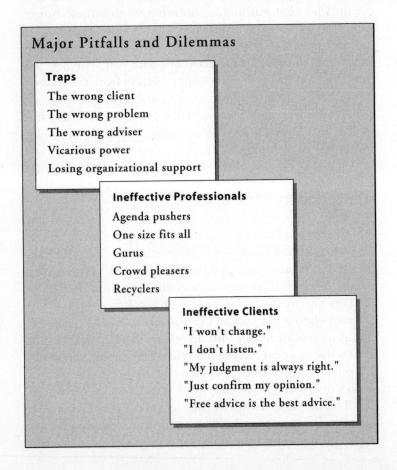

Major Pitfalls and Dilemmas

Traps
The wrong client
The wrong problem
The wrong adviser
Vicarious power
Losing organizational support

Ineffective Professionals
Agenda pushers
One size fits all
Gurus
Crowd pleasers
Recyclers

Ineffective Clients
"I won't change."
"I don't listen."
"My judgment is always right."
"Just confirm my opinion."
"Free advice is the best advice."

most talented client advisers face. These are summarized in the table "Major Pitfalls and Dilemmas."

Some of these pitfalls are specific traps that can happen to anyone, whereas others concern particular types of ineffective professionals and difficult clients. Every so often, assess your engagements and the clients you're working with to see if you recognize any of them. Make sure you're not about to step on a land mine.

You will, of course, make some mistakes. The question will be how much you learn from the experience: Do you become cynical and bitter, or are you able to channel the incident into a greater sense of personal conviction and independence? If you allow the former to occur, remember that trust begets trust, and cynicism can provoke a vicious circle: if you become suspicious and mistrustful, it will bring out these very same qualities in your clients.

TEN

THE SOUL OF
THE GREAT PROFESSIONAL

This is the true joy of life, the being used by a purpose recognized by yourself as a mighty one; the being thoroughly worn out before you are thrown on the scrap heap; the being a force of nature instead of a feverish, selfish little clod of ailments and grievances complaining that the world will not devote itself to making you happy.

GEORGE BERNARD SHAW, *Man and Superman*

REAT PROFESSIONALS become extraordinary client advisers by developing the seven attributes that are the centerpiece of this book. These attributes encompass the important talents, skills, and attitudes that enable professionals in any field to build and sustain long-term, broad-gauge client relationships on a consistent basis.

The great advisers we've studied also possess certain outlooks that frame and inform their work. We call these outlooks the *soul* of the great professional. They are not so much personal characteristics as they are ways of looking at the world. If you cultivate them, your ability to add value will be enhanced, and you'll become a more appealing person to your clients—someone they will both respect and enjoy spending time with. In addition, you'll be better able to shape and manage your own career. These outlooks—the elements of this *soul*—can be discerned in virtually all of the

240

professionals we have studied who command strong client loyalty.

Great Professionals Have an Abundance Mentality

An abundance mentality allows you to see the possibilities and opportunities inherent in every situation.[1] The opposite is a *scarcity* mentality, which focuses on limitations and risks.

Professionals with an abundance mentality:

- Always look for opportunities, growth, and expansion
- Constantly generate new ideas
- Are positive and upbeat in their demeanor
- Feel that there are rewards enough to go around for everyone—they know that a "rising tide" lifts all boats
- Are willing to invest time and money in the short term in order to earn more later

Professionals with a scarcity mentality, in contrast, have very different attitudes. They:

- Are primarily concerned with what might go wrong and what won't work
- Focus on the risks of new proposals rather than the potential rewards
- Believe that life is a zero-sum game, with a limited amount of opportunity to go around
- Are concerned with "getting their fair share" at all times
- Won't make investments that don't show an immediate return

If you were a client, whom would you rather spend time with? There's no contest here: all of us would prefer a positive, energizing individual to someone who always sees the dark side of things. Some situations, such as a tax audit, may benefit from the scarcity mentality we've described. But in general, clients prefer and benefit from the expansive thinking of the professional who sees abundance, not scarcity.

Don't confuse an abundance mentality with laxness, laziness, or imprudence. The professionals who perceive abundance often have a healthy dissatisfaction with the way things are done today. They know there's often a better solution. Like strong organizational leaders, they push and stretch for new ideas and innovations; they don't wait for them to float down from the sky. That's why clients like having them around so much: these professionals constantly energize, motivate, and inspire others.

The sources of your fundamental outlook on life—abundance versus scarcity—are varied and complex. Your early childhood experiences and upbringing clearly have a strong influence on this dimension of your personality. Someone who suffers physical or emotional deprivation as a child, for example, may always harbor a deep-seated sense of scarcity. A lack of love and affection damages self-esteem, making it hard to have an abundance outlook. There is no doubt an element of personal "constitution" involved—some individuals just seem to be born with more resilience against the vicissitudes of life—but family and parental role models are also an important influence on your adult attitudes of either abundance or scarcity.

We believe that the education you receive plays a critical role as well. Economics and engineering, which are typical backgrounds of many professionals in business, are founded on principles of scarcity. Both disciplines are concerned with the optimal use of scarce resources. They focus on the *trade-offs* that have to be made—for example, "guns versus butter," a graph recognizable to many readers, which is found in many introductory economics textbooks. The liberal arts, in contrast, are premised on abundance. The liberal arts perspective sees a world of nearly infinite ideas and resources, a world where trade-offs are not always necessary. It also raises important philosophical questions.

Rajat Gupta, McKinsey's worldwide managing director, says that he reads poetry at the end of each partners' meet-

ing: "At first, that took people by surprise. But over time, poetry has affected what we're doing. Poetry helps us reflect on
the important questions: What is the purpose of our business? What are our values?"[2]

The European Renaissance, which was a time of enormous scientific as well as artistic ferment and innovation, exemplifies the power of the liberal arts perspective. The
concept of *humanism,* which fueled the Renaissance, was
based on a belief in the potential of human beings and their
ability to reach self-fulfillment without recourse to higher
powers or supernatural means. The most accomplished and
inventive figures of the period, from Niccolò Machiavelli to
Leonardo da Vinci, were consummate liberal arts scholars,
equally at home with art, science, mathematics, philosophy,
history, and literature.

Does this mean you have to study liberal arts to become
an accomplished professional and develop lifelong clients?
Yes and no. What we have found is that the best client advisers, regardless of what they majored in at college or studied
in graduate school, become *deep generalists* like the ones we
described in chapter 4. They read widely, take an interest in a
variety of subjects and disciplines, and cultivate personal interests as well as professional expertise. Recall Peter Drucker,
for example, who has a passion for Japanese art, or David
Ogilvy, who had a deep interest in French culture (he eventually went to live in France). The risk of burrowing too deeply
into one discipline like economics, engineering, or accounting is that you will begin to adopt a scarcity mentality. Broad
knowledge and learning, in contrast, open the way for an outlook of abundance.

Great Professionals Have a Mission Orientation

The individuals who have had a significant impact on
history—figures such as Jesus, Buddha, Joan of Arc, Gandhi,
and Abraham Lincoln—had clear missions that led them to
perform at extraordinary levels. The great advisers we've

looked at in this book also had well-developed personal missions. For Thomas More, it was fulfilling God's work in this life; for Niccolò Machiavelli, it was creating a stable, unified Italian state; for J. P. Morgan, it was establishing an orderly financial system in the absence of regulatory agencies. Gertrude Bell's mission was to promulgate an understanding of the Arab world among Westerners and ensure peaceful cohabitation of the Iraqis and the British. Early on, General George Marshall was driven by a desire to create a professional, respected U.S. Army founded on principles of excellence, efficiency, compassion, and hard work; later, his mission became no less than ensuring that the United States kept the world safe for democracy.

For most of us, our personal missions are perhaps more down-to-earth but no less sincere, sacred, and important to us. When you ask great professionals what drives them in their careers, you will hear phrases such as "making a difference to my clients' business"; "enriching management practice through my ideas"; "being a teacher—teaching and explaining the importance of people's rights"; "educating managers so they lead more successful, effective lives"; or simply "practicing excellence in everything I do."

Fred Brown, who descends from the famed Brown Brothers Harriman banking family, is an example of an extraordinary adviser who has a clear mission that drives his daily behavior. A highly successful personal financial consultant, Brown has authored several books on financial management. He writes a weekly newspaper column entitled "Money and Spirit," and he has a waiting list of clients. He could well afford a trophy house and late-model luxury cars, but his relatively modest home in the Southwest and his utilitarian Subaru suit him just fine—he prefers to live his values of moderation and balance rather than flaunt his achievements through flashy possessions. Using a powerful, unique approach to financial management that blends cutting-edge financial expertise with a deep understanding of each client's personal, familial, professional, and spiritual life, Brown has developed an intensely loyal following of individuals and families who come back to him year after year.

Brown charges an hourly rate that is a fraction of what the market could bear, but this is a conscious choice he has made that is consistent with his mission of helping people lead better lives through improved financial management. "By charging what I do," Brown tells us, "I am able to serve a very broad clientele—I get the millionaires but also people who are scraping by and desperately need help just to survive."

The opposite of a mission orientation is the strictly material orientation. Your main focus becomes money, title, promotion, or publicity. When a professional has no sense of mission, he or she risks becoming a mercenary—someone that Machiavelli cautioned against five hundred years ago when he wrote, "Mercenaries are disunited, thirsty for power, undisciplined, and disloyal."[3] Machiavelli urged the creation of national militias—citizens' armies with an overriding purpose and an intense loyalty to their home state—a revolutionary concept at the time but now the accepted norm.

The author Victor Frankl, who survived the Nazi concentration camp at Auschwitz during World War II, wrote that "Nothing is more likely to help a person overcome or endure troubles than the consciousness of having a task in life."[4] A mission orientation not only helps you overcome difficulties, but it will give you great strength in practicing the seven attributes. It will be easier for you to be an empathetic listener; your conviction will intensify; your integrity will be strengthened; and it will be far easier to practice selfless independence.

Great Professionals Channel Adversity into Wisdom and Confidence

The extraordinary client advisers we've profiled have all gone through difficult experiences. They've made mistakes, suffered reversals of fortune, and even been humiliated. Whereas many people become embittered, cynical, or distrustful as a result of these setbacks, the really great professionals get stronger. They become wiser, more confident, and humble. Their comfort zones expand, enabling them to tackle an ever-broader variety of situations and client assignments.

Laura Herring's story illustrates how extraordinary setbacks can create resolve and determination. In less than ten years, Herring's firm, The IMPACT Group, has grown to 120 professionals who deliver a variety of relocation support services, from counseling to résumé preparation. It had an inauspicious beginning, however. The concept got its start when Herring, originally a family therapist, pointed out to a Fortune 500 executive that relocation was one of the toughest personal issues facing his employees. Challenged to develop a solution, Herring invested $360,000 and months of time to create a program called Momentum. Just after the company placed a major order for her services, however, its relocation manager vetoed the idea, leaving Herring with no business. "I had double-mortgaged my house," she tells us, "and sold some real estate my husband and I owned. I was deeply in debt, with no cash flow. Panic set in." She goes on to say:

> I was unable to go home and tell my husband what had happened. So I went to the phone book, and began looking through the Yellow Pages for other companies that I could sell the program to. I called the vice president of marketing at United Van Lines and told him I thought he should have the first shot at buying our services. He agreed to meet the next day. He loved the materials so much that he immediately placed an order for 10,000 tapes, books, and related services—it was a $1 million sale. I was ecstatic. Two days later, however, he called me back with terrible news. "We've decided to develop this internally," he told me. "We can't go forward with the order." Unfortunately, I didn't have a signed contract.

Shortly afterward, Herring flew to a relocation conference being held in Florida—her last hope—but after arriving, she learned she couldn't actively market to any of the participants. There, after three fruitless days walking the floors of the conference hall, she finally met a top Johnson & Johnson executive who was literally walking out the door. Intrigued with her new (but still untested) service, he invited Herring to come to his office to make a presentation. "Gary Gorran," Herring concludes, "was the J&J executive. He became our first client, and thirteen years later he is still one of our best and largest clients."

When asked about how this and other difficult experiences affected her, Herring replies: "The other day I took my young niece to a club I belong to in St. Louis. When we walked in, a lot of people came over and greeted me. My niece was a bit shocked—she said to me, 'Everyone knows you—do you ever marvel at how far you've come? And I told her that I know what it's like to be *invisible,* and therefore I never take the end result for granted—you've got to earn it. There's always someone out there who is better and smarter than you are. There's always someone's uncle who *knows more.* You just have to keep driving toward your goals. I believe that failure is not a possibility."

Herring's account, and how it steeled rather than diminished her resolve and determination, is typical of great professionals. Consultant James Kelly tells another story of early-career trauma:

> When I finished business school, Professor Dick Vancil hired me with the idea of building a faculty-based consulting firm [which under Kelly's leadership became the MAC Group, a $125 million strategy consulting business]. The second year we did so well that we extended employment offers to a dozen top MBA graduates from around the country. But suddenly our backlog of business just died. It was early summer, and we were going to go bankrupt if we took on all these new hires. I had to call each one of them up, tell them what had happened, and rescind the offers. It was one of the worst days of my professional life.

Although it may seem that Kelly (who was twenty-six at the time) exercised poor judgment in hiring so many new people, he learned from the episode. He could have become gun-shy, retrenched, and never made a bold hiring move again. Instead, he assimilated the experience in a balanced, constructive way. His subsequent careful management of revenues, backlog, and professional staffing at the MAC Group resulted in twenty-five years of continual growth and profitability under his leadership—a far better record than most consulting firms can show.

Great Professionals Always View Old Clients As New Clients

A marriage requires constant work and investment—just ask any couple that has successfully been together for fifteen or twenty years. When a couple divorces, the partners will often look back and describe a long period of mutual neglect prior to the eruption of real acrimony. If one spouse is working in a demanding occupation, for example, it may seem as if his or her job gets all the time and attention, leaving little energy for the other person.

The bases for successful marriages and successful long-term client relationships are similar. When you've been working with a client for many years, the tendency is to take each other for granted. If you're like the vast majority of professionals, most of your marketing and promotional resources go to new, prospective clients rather than to your existing clients. As benign neglect sets in, your long-term client may become intrigued by other professionals in your field—competitors whose ideas seem newer and fresher, who are courting him aggressively. Just as in a marriage, the antidote to wandering clients is constant reinvestment that revitalizes the relationship.

When we look at professionals who have long-term, broad-based client relationships, who inspire great client loyalty, they all have a similar approach: they treat each assignment as if it were the first one for that client. They bring the same energy, creativity, and drive to their long-term clients as they do to the new client they are trying to impress. They communicate constantly, and the flow of ideas never stops. Even if they aren't working on an assignment for the client at that moment, they are in touch at least two or three times a year. The courtship, so to speak, never stops.

Great Professionals Engage in Continual Self-renewal

Most professionals focus on their income statement—their annual tally of expenses and revenues, leading to a figure that represents their total income for that year. This is true whether you work for a large firm or on your own. If you invested a lot in a client proposal that fell through, your year-end bonus may be reduced. If you sold a large piece of follow-on business, your bonus may be larger than usual. The focus is this year's sacrifices and rewards.

If you earnestly develop the attributes and outlooks we've been discussing, however, you will naturally build your balance sheet assets. *Deep generalists,* for example, make investments in learning and acquiring knowledge that may have no immediate payback but bring rewards two or three years down the road.

Your personal capital—the sum of your talents, skills, experiences, and knowledge—can be developed in many ways. This personal development can but doesn't have to occur through dramatic actions, such as taking a formal sabbatical or making a career change. Often, professionals embed it in their daily routines, indulging in leisurely reading, self-study, and the gradual cultivation of new areas of interest.

Harvard Law School professor Alan Dershowitz, for example, after writing a series of very successful nonfiction books, recently published his first novel. Renowned management consultant Ram Charan just followed up several years of work on how effective corporate boards function with a book on growth strategies. Although part of the pre-Internet generation, financial consultant Fred Brown is going up a steep learning curve and setting up an interactive Web site, which may not yield significant results for a year or two, to extend the reach of his innovative financial counseling.

How do you know when it's time to push into new areas? Peter Drucker counsels that it's time for a change "When the harder you work, the less you seem to accomplish—or when you're sure that you know all the answers, and you've stopped asking, 'What are the right questions?' "[5]

Just as successful professionals take a long-term view of client relationships, they also have a multiyear perspective on their own personal and professional development. They follow Thomas More's injunction to "live as if you are to die tomorrow, study as if you were to live forever." When you focus on building your balance sheet—on self-renewal—remember that your income statement may take some hits. This is why it's so important to cultivate qualities such as independence and conviction. Without them it will be difficult to navigate the inevitable squalls that are part of asset building.

Great professionals successfully develop and integrate the seven core attributes into a powerful whole, and then in-

The Ingredients for Breakthrough Relationships

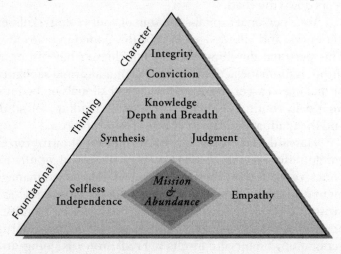

fuse everything they do with their soul of abundance, mission, and self-renewal. This combination of attributes and outlooks, summarized in the accompanying illustration, enables professionals to create broad-based, abiding client relationships that engender collaboration and insight.

SEIZING BREAKTHROUGH OPPORTUNITIES

So where do you start? What immediate steps can you take to develop more of the deep, enduring relationships we've been talking about? To begin with, it's helpful to examine each of your client relationships through the lens of the seven attributes that we've set out. If you critically assess your performance with respect to each of the attributes, you will probably discover that there are a number of actions you can take to enhance and strengthen both the client relationship and your ability to add insight. Ask yourself tough questions about each of your engagements. Has your work been long on analysis but short on synthesis? Have you met with your client recently to listen deeply and empathetically to his concerns, hopes, and objectives? Have you taken a stand on an issue and presented your views with great conviction? Are you acting selflessly and focusing on your client's agenda rather than your own? Does your work reflect a deeply felt sense of independence as a professional?

It's also important to determine what role you're currently playing with each of your clients—expert for hire, steady supplier, or trusted adviser. At each stage, there are some specific strategies to consider that will help your relationship evolve. For example, as an expert for hire your main task is to differentiate yourself from all the other experts out there. Some professionals accomplish this by doing unusually high-quality work on their first assignment; others by surprising their clients, right off the bat, with real insight as opposed to just expertise.

If you're in a steady supplier relationship, you've got to

develop high levels of interpersonal trust and confidence and become deeply knowledgeable about your client—at all levels—to move to the next stage.

As a trusted adviser, the challenge is to create and sustain a true intellectual partnership between you and your client. The professionals who succeed at this level collaborate with their clients in the development of solutions and share the same goals and aspirations for the business. You're an outsider, but your client considers you part of his team.

Regardless of what stage you've reached, you need to look for and seize what we call *breakthrough opportunities* in your relationships. In examining the careers of great professionals, we have found that there are always notable moments when they perform in extraordinary ways. The result is a major increase in their stature and in the respect and trust that clients place in them. These distinguishing moments are enormously important: they can separate you from the rest of the pack and propel you toward the breakthrough relationships that we've been discussing in this book.

The extraordinary historical advisers we've profiled all had moments when they forcefully demonstrated qualities such as great conviction, perceptive big-picture thinking, and independence, or when they simply acted rapidly and decisively on their client's behalf. These instances illustrate how great professionals distinguish themselves from ordinary ones.

George Marshall: A Junior Officer Stands Up to the Legendary General Pershing

In October 1917, George Marshall was a young colonel serving under Major General William L. Silbert at the front lines of battle in France. During a field inspection, the commander of the U.S. forces in Europe, General "Black Jack" Pershing, publicly chastised Marshall's commanding officer for having conducted sloppy field maneuvers. Without hesitating, the young Marshall spoke up and vigorously defended Silbert, telling Pershing that his criticisms were unfair and his staff didn't know what they were doing. When Pershing tried to defend himself, saying that he had had some difficulties in his headquarters organization, Marshall retorted, "Yes, General, but we have them every day and they have to be solved at night." Instead of becoming angry, Pershing was immensely impressed with Marshall's loyalty, conviction, and honesty in the face of authority, and he asked him to become his aide-de-camp after the war. Pershing, who was a legendary war hero, became a mentor to Marshall and greatly aided Marshall's subsequent career in the army.

Harry Hopkins: A Social Worker Breaks Through

During Franklin Roosevelt's first one hundred days in office as president, he asked Harry Hopkins, whose training was as a social worker, to head the Federal Emergency Relief Administration, which had been created to provide direct financial relief to regions of the country that had been impoverished by the Great Depression. Told by the president that his job was to "get relief to people who needed it," Hopkins, whose new office didn't even have a desk, immediately sent telegrams flying all over the country, and in his first few hours on the job he had already distributed millions in aid. Knowing that he was ruffling the feathers of various politicians, Hopkins said to a colleague, "I'm not going to last six months around here, so I'll do as I please." A newspaper article the next day began, "The half-billion dollars for direct relief of States won't last a month if Harry L. Hopkins, new relief administrator, maintains the pace he set yesterday in disbursing more than $5 million during his first two hours in office."[6] Roosevelt instantly recognized that Hopkins, who viewed his job as identifying the president's objectives and getting them accomplished as soon as possible, was no ordinary White House adviser. From that day onward, he began increasingly to draw Hopkins into his most important initiatives.

Henry Kissinger: From Academic to Presidential Adviser

As President John F. Kennedy's helicopter waited on the lawn of the White House, an aide ran to the door with a small folder. Inside was a memo written by Henry Kissinger, who at the time was merely an informal foreign policy adviser to several of Kennedy's staffers. As Kennedy leafed through Kissinger's note, he realized that he now had the right conceptual framework for dealing with Soviet aggression. It became the centerpiece of a major foreign policy speech on Berlin—where the wall was about to go up—the very next night.

At issue was how the United States should react to Russian threats in Berlin and other parts of the world. Was there any option between doing nothing and engaging in all-out nuclear war? The only viewpoint that Kennedy had was the all-or-nothing, black-and-white one that had been prepared by Secretary of State Dean Acheson. But he needed something more workable. Toiling feverishly the day before the speech, Kissinger poured out a five-page memo that advocated a "flexible response"—for example, the limited use of tactical nuclear weapons—to Russian moves. "We intend to have a wider choice," the president subsequently said in his speech, "than humiliation or all-out nuclear action." While it would be seven more years before Kissinger formally entered the White House, the incident greatly raised his personal capital in Washington and enhanced his reputation for flexible, big-picture thinking.

Later, in another breakthrough incident, Kissinger was asked by Nelson Rockefeller to advise him during his 1968 presidential bid. When told he would report through one of Rockefeller's staff aides, Kissinger refused. "I must report directly to Nelson," he replied dryly, and Rockefeller assented. It was a risky move, but one that set Kissinger apart from all the other advisers hovering around Rockefeller's presidential bid. Kissinger wanted to be able to influence leadership directly, and he was willing to walk away from the job if his conditions were not met.

"I HOLD in the utmost contempt," writes Tom Peters, "a 'thoroughly professional job' . . . that does not meet the striking demands of the times."[7] It's not enough simply to do *good work* for your clients; you have to act boldly and decisively on their behalf. To stand out—to be seen as an extraordinary professional—you need to demonstrate a strong sense of purpose and mission and allow the attributes we've been discussing to infuse your words and actions.

Look around at your client relationships and ask yourself: How and where can I truly distinguish myself? Try to identify and capitalize on breakthrough opportunities where you can dramatically demonstrate the seven attributes, display a rare sense of urgency, and show that you are unusually capable of helping to accomplish your clients' objectives. If you do this, they will always remember you. They will call on you again and again for your sound, wise advice.

THE HISTORICAL ADVISERS
IN CLIENTS FOR LIFE

The Oracle at Delphi (about 600 B.C.–362 A.D.)

For nearly 1,000 years, leaders from throughout the ancient world journeyed to Delphi, Greece, to consult with the oracle in the temple of Apollo. According to tradition, the god Apollo responded to advice seekers through the Pythia (the oracle), a local priestess who was more than fifty years old and who had led a "blameless life." There were other oracles in Greece, but Delphi was the most famous.

Aristotle (384–322 B.C.)

Aristotle was not only a great scholar and philosopher but also an adviser to influential Greeks and Macedonians. His range was extraordinary: Aristotle wrote over fifty books, with titles such as *On the Soul, On Pleasure, On the Sciences, On Magnets,* and *Proverbs.* His most famous student and advisee was Alexander the Great, whom Aristotle tutored for three years while he was an adolescent. According to some accounts, Aristotle accompanied Alexander on his great campaign as far as Egypt, but as Alexander listened to him less and less, he withdrew back to Greece.

Merlin (450–536 A.D.)

Some historians believe Merlin was a real person, although the Arthurian legends are unquestionably a blend of both fact and fantasy. A Welsh religious figure, Merlin counseled not just King

Arthur but his father, Uther, and several other monarchs as well. It was reputedly Merlin who advised Uther to establish the Knights of the Round Table, and he foretold that Uther's true heir would be revealed by a test that involved drawing a sword from a stone. As an infant, legend holds that Arthur was taken by Merlin into the forest, where he reared and carefully educated the young prince to prepare him for his role as king.

Niccolò Machiavelli (1469–1527)

Machiavelli's enormous influence as an adviser has been through his writings rather than an active career as a counselor to leaders. A fairly good diplomat, a brilliant thinker, and a superb writer, Machiavelli has to some extent been unfairly pilloried over the centuries for advocating amoral, unethical leadership practices in *The Prince*. This view is too narrow, and in fact there has recently been a resurgence of interest in his philosophies and a raft of new books exploring his thinking in a modern context.

Thomas More (1478–1535)

Thomas More, Henry VIII's chief adviser, was immortalized twice: first by the Catholic Church, which bestowed sainthood on him, and second by Robert Bolt's play *A Man for All Seasons*, which chronicled his rise and fall and was made into a major motion picture. Considered one of the most brilliant legal minds in history, More had Solomon-like judgment and was one of the most erudite figures of his age. Peter Ackroyd's 1999 biography of More, *The Life of Thomas More*, is a stunning work.

Armand-Jean du Plessis Richelieu (Cardinal) (1585–1642)

Cardinal Richelieu is not profiled in depth in this book, but in many respects he belongs in the pantheon of great historical advisers. He had enormous powers of persuasion, keen and decisive judgment, and a grasp of the big picture that enabled him to conceptualize France's strategy as a nation during the tumult of the seventeenth century. Born into a family of modest means, Richelieu rose to become a cardinal and Louis XIII's "first minister." Known as the "éminence rouge" (red eminence) because of his red cardinal's cap, his own assistant, Bishop Joseph, was called the "éminence grise" (gray eminence). The king's mother, Marie de Medicis, felt Richelieu was usurping her influence, and in a famous showdown in 1630 Louis chose his adviser over his mother, fearing her maternal domination. She fled the country.

Baltasar Gracián (1601–1658)
Born in Aragon, Spain, Gracián became a Jesuit priest, church administrator, and confessor to many famous Spaniards. He was known for his clever aphorisms, and he wrote a number of books including *The Hero*, about the ideal leader, and *The Oracle*, a book of wise sayings on various subjects. The latter is now in print as *The Art of Worldly Wisdom—A Pocket Oracle*. Throughout their history, the Jesuits have exercised enormous influence as advisers to business and political leaders in whatever country they lived.

John Pierpont Morgan (1837–1913)
A shy man, Morgan was driven by an intense need for order and stability more than power, money, or even the desire to run a large bank. Business and political leaders of all stripes sought him out for advice, and he relished the role. Despite his commanding presence, he was an excellent listener and would often let others go on for hours before interjecting his opinion or trying to steer the outcome a certain way. *The House of Morgan* by Ron Chernow and *Morgan: American Financier* by Jean Strouse are both engrossing works about J. P. Morgan and his bank.

Gertrude Bell (1868–1926)
Some figures in history are so ahead of their time that they belong in a different era—Bell was one of these. She had an uncanny knack for being quickly accepted by the various Middle East cultures of her day, and her keen intelligence, objectivity, and great listening skills made her a sought-after adviser by both Western and Arab leaders. She devoted the last three years of her life to establishing an archaeological museum in Baghdad,

insisting that antiquities excavated should stay in the country of their origin. *Desert Queen,* by Janet Wallach, is a fascinating account of Bell's colorful life.

George Marshall (1880–1959)

Even some of the best advisers we have profiled were not perfect. The great Sir Thomas More hunted down and burned heretics in his day, and more than a few times the brilliant Henry Kissinger's ego got in the way of his presidential counsels. Marshall was viceless and selfless, however. After leading the Allied armies to victory in World War II, he designed and implemented the Marshall Plan to rebuild Europe. A key adviser to both Roosevelt and Truman, he became Truman's secretary of state in 1947 and secretary of defense in 1950. Marshall was awarded the Nobel Peace Prize in 1953.

Harry Hopkins (1890–1946)

Trained as a social worker, Hopkins became President Franklin Roosevelt's most trusted adviser. Other world leaders also developed great confidence in Hopkins, and they respected his capacity to translate Roosevelt's objectives into realizable plans and specific actions. His trip to visit Churchill during the blitz was instrumental in convincing Roosevelt—and eventually the whole country—that Britain desperately needed U.S. support against Hitler. Hopkins had a wasting, fatal intestinal ailment that put a stop to his political ambitions, enhancing, ironically, his influence and power as an adviser.

Peter Drucker (1909–)

Drucker is still alive and actively writing and advising leaders, but he certainly goes under the category of "historic" in the sense that he is already a major figure in the history of modern management philosophy and practice. Often referring to himself as an "insultant" rather than a consultant—a reference to the difficult, prickly questions he asks his clients—he now plays a major role advising leaders in the nonprofit sector.

David Ogilvy (1911–1999)

Like some other great client advisers such as Peter Drucker, Ogilvy practiced a number of trades—apprentice chef, stove salesman, farmer, and British intelligence agent—before settling in to become one of the greatest advertising geniuses of all time. He worked with the famous pollster George Gallup for a time in the United States, an experience he later said underpinned his success in advertising. Author of several witty, clever books (such as *Ogilvy on Advertising*), Ogilvy is best remembered for his establishment of the importance of branding.

Henry Kissinger (1923–)

Like Drucker, Kissinger still actively advises business and political leaders, and his place in history is assured by the bold role he played as adviser to two U.S. presidents, Richard Nixon and Gerald Ford, during the Vietnam and cold war eras. His incisive, far-reaching advice has always been sought after, although while in the White House Kissinger was sometimes torn between bolstering the power of his presidential clients and enhancing his own prestige. Walter Issacson's biography, *Kissinger,* is a great read that chronicles the often strange relationship between Kissinger and Nixon.

NOTES

Introduction

1. See, for example, Frederick F. Reichheld, "Learning from Customer Defections," in *The Quest for Loyalty*, ed. Frederick F. Reichheld (Boston: Harvard Business Review Books, 1996).

one: WHAT CLIENTS WANT

1. Robert E. Sherwood, *Roosevelt and Hopkins: An Intimate History* (New York: Harper & Brothers, 1948), p. 3.
2. Quoted in Patricia Sellers, "The 50 Most Powerful Women in American Business," *Fortune*, October 25, 1999, p. 115.
3. *Eminence grise* refers to Father Joseph (1577–1638), a capuchin monk who became the personal secretary and influential behind-the-scenes adviser to Cardinal Richelieu—himself called the "éminence rouge"—who was King Louis XIII's first minister. *Mentor* comes from the *Odyssey:* it was the name of an Ithacan nobleman whose form the goddess Athena assumed in order to advise Telemachus and encourage him to go search for his father, Odysseus; a later French play emphasized Mentor's role in the story, solidifying the word's meaning of *sage counselor. Machiavellian* means crafty or deceitful, deriving from popular interpretation of the philosophy that Niccolò Machiavelli, the Florentine statesman and diplomat, set out in his book *The Prince.*
4. Professional services add up to over $500 billion in annual revenue in the United States alone. Some selected data on these markets:

—Management consulting: $113 billion (Global estimate for 2000; most is in the U.S. Source: Kennedy Information Research Group).
—Accounting: $59.3 billion (1997, U.S. only. Source: Statistical Abstract of the United States, 1998).
—Advertising: $34.2 billion (1997, U.S. only. Source: Statistical Abstract of the United States, 1998).
—Legal Services: $132.8 billion (1997, U.S. only. Source: Statistical Abstract of the United States, 1998).
—Stockbrokers: $85.5 billion (1999 estimate, U.S. only. Total securities industry revenue for 1999 is estimated at $175.9 billion; conservatively 50 percent of this can be attributed to individual and corporate transactions

where advice is given; there are 620,000 stockbrokers in the U.S. alone. Source: Securities Industry Association).

—Corporate/Investment Banking: $80.1 billion (1998, U.S. only. Total banking revenue for 1998 was $400.3 billion. We have estimated that 20 percent of this revenue is associated with corporate or private banking clients. Source: *Business Week,* 1/12/99, p. 132).

—Executive Search: $8.3 billion (2000 estimate. Source: *Business Week,* 5/17/99).

5. *The New York Times,* May 15, 1999, reported that doctors' median incomes have declined 1.4 percent a year since 1993.
6. Ron Chernow, *The House of Morgan* (New York: Simon & Schuster, 1990), p. 49.

two: SELFLESS INDEPENDENCE

1. Peter Ackroyd, *The Life of Thomas More* (New York: Doubleday, 1999), p. 82.
2. Ackroyd, p. 146.
3. Sarah Barlett, "Who Can You Trust?" *Business Week,* October 5, 1998, p. 150.
4. Tom Peters, *The Professional Service Firm 50* (Alfred A. Knopf, 1999), pp. 26–28.

three: HIDDEN CUES

1. This scene is described in Janet Wallach, *Desert Queen* (New York: Nan A. Talese, 1996), p. 326.
2. Peter Drucker, *Adventures of a Bystander* (New York: John Wiley and Sons, 1997), p. 24.
3. Jack Beatty, *The World According to Peter Drucker* (New York: Broadway Books, 1999), p. 182.
4. Hendrie Weisinger, *Emotional Intelligence at Work* (San Francisco: Jossey-Bass, 1998), p. 4.
5. Drawn from the authors' interview with Laura Herring and also from Thomas Petzinger, Jr., "The Front Lines," *The Wall Street Journal,* July 17, 1999.
6. For example, see Madelyn Burley-Allen, *The Lost Art of Listening* (John Wiley and Sons, 1995), p. 14.
7. Stephen R. Covey, *The 7 Habits of Highly Effective People* (New York: Simon & Schuster, 1989), p. 245.

four: DEEP GENERALISTS

1. David Ogilvy, *Ogilvy on Advertising* (New York: Vintage Books, 1985), p. 21.
2. Jack Beatty, *The World According to Peter Drucker* (New York: Broadway Books, 1999), p. 21.
3. Shunryu Suzuki, *Zen Mind, Beginner's Mind* (New York: Weatherill, 1994), p. 21.
4. Leslie Kaufman, "My Transforming Moments," *The New York Times,* October 6, 1999, p. C12.
5. The young Einstein's mind is described in *Creating Minds* by Howard Gardner (New York: Basic Books, 1993), p. 88.

6. Paolo Novaresio, *The Explorers* (New York: Stewart, Tabori & Chang, 1996), p. 9.

7. Ellen J. Langer, *The Power of Mindful Learning* (Reading, Mass.: Perseus Books, 1998), p. 4.

8. Beatty, p. 14.

9. Beatty, p. 182.

10. Peter Drucker, "The Next Information Revolution," *Forbes,* August 24, 1998, p. 47.

11. Beatty, p. 182.

12. Lucy McCauley, "The State of the New Economy," *Fast Company,* September 19, 1999, p. 120.

13. Ron Chernow, *The House of Morgan,* (New York: Simon & Schuster, 1990), p. 21.

14. "DLJ Hiring Spree of Merger Bankers from Rivals Pays Off," *The Wall Street Journal,* April 6, 1999, p. C24.

15. Hara Estroff Marano, "The Power of Play," *Psychology Today,* July/August 1999, pp. 38–40.

16. Vincent Ryan Ruggiero, *The Art of Thinking* (Reading: Addison-Wesley, 1998), p. 101.

17. Peter Schwartz, *The Art of the Long View* (New York: Doubleday, 1991), p. 62.

18. Baltasar Gracián, *The Art of Worldly Wisdom* (New York: Doubleday, 1991), p. 152.

five: THE BIG PICTURE

1. Henry Mintzberg, "The Rise and Fall of Strategic Planning," *Harvard Business Review,* November/December 1995, p. 108.

2. Harvard Business School case study no. 9-393-066, "McKinsey & Company (A): 1956," Harvard Business School, 1992, p. 3.

3. Keshavan Nair, *A Higher Standard of Leadership* (San Francisco: Berrett-Koehler, 1994), p. 110.

4. See Carl Shapiro and Hal R. Varian, "Versioning: The Smart Way to Sell Information," *Harvard Business Review,* November/December 1998, p. 106.

5. Jack Beatty, *The World According to Peter Drucker* (New York: Broadway Books, 1999), p. 30.

6. Walter Issacson, *Kissinger* (New York: Simon & Schuster, 1992), p. 760.

7. Cited in Guy Kawasaki, *Rules for Revolutionaries* (New York: HarperBusiness, 1999), p. 40.

8. Cited in Howard Gardner, *Creating Minds* (New York: Basic Books, 1993), p. 103.

9. Tony Schwartz, "Going Postal," *New York Times Magazine,* July 19, 1999, p. 35.

10. Peter Ackroyd, *The Life of Thomas More* (New York: Doubleday, 1999), p. 254.

11. John Fauvel, Raymond Hood, Michael Shorthand, and Robin Wilson, eds., *Let Newton Be!* (New York: Oxford University Press, 1992), p. 15.

12. Hara Estroff Marano, "The Power of Play," *Psychology Today,* July/August 1999, p. 60.

13. Michael Gelb, *How to Think Like Leonardo da Vinci* (New York: Delacorte Press, 1998), p. 166.

14. Printing presses were used before the Renaissance, but they were inferior predecessors to Johann Gutenberg's invention. Gutenberg actually developed

four innovations that together revolutionized book printing: a stamping mold to produce consistent metal type; metal type made out of a special alloy of lead, tin, and antinomy; a new type of printing press, which exerted more pressure and produced clearer print; and a special printing ink with an oil base.
15. Cited in Alan Riding, "Where Are the Beret Factories of Yesteryear?" *The New York Times Book Review*, August 1, 1999, reviewing *France on the Brink* by Jonathon Fenby.

six: AN EYE FOR WINNERS

1. Kara Swisher, "When Bill Met Steve," *The Wall Street Journal*, June 22, 1998, p. B7.
2. Ron Chernow, *The House of Morgan* (New York: Simon & Schuster, 1990), p. 79.
3. Chernow, p. 32.
4. Robert Sobel, *When Giants Stumble* (Prentice Hall, 1999), p. 328.
5. Robert B. Cialdini, *Influence: The Psychology of Persuasion* (New York: William Morrow, 1984), p. 72.
6. Irving Janis, *Groupthink* (New York: Houghton Mifflin, 1982).
7. Bill Gammage, *The Broken Years: Australian Soldiers in the Great War* (Canberra: Australian National University Press, 1974).
8. Adapted from *Webster's New World College Dictionary* (USA: Macmillan, 1998), p. 731.
9. J. Edward Russo and Paul J. H. Shoemaker, *Decision Traps* (New York: Simon & Schuster, 1989), p. 115.
10. Gary Klein, *Sources of Power: How People Make Decisions* (Cambridge, Mass.: MIT Press, 1998), p. 32.
11. This particular framework for understanding intuition is adapted from Klein's book, *Sources of Power*.
12. Scott Plous, *The Psychology of Judgment and Decision-making* (New York: McGraw-Hill, 1993), p. 20.
13. Plous, p. 103. This concept of "disconfirming questions" has been suggested by several researchers, including Russo and Shoemaker.
14. Vincent Ryan Ruggiero, *The Art of Thinking* (London: Longman, 1998), p. 5.

seven: THE POWERS OF CONVICTION

1. Mark A. Stoler, *George C. Marshall* (Boston: Twayne Publishers, 1989), p. 65.
2. James Grant, "A Real Constitutional Expert," *The Wall Street Journal*, December 22, 1998, p. A16.
3. Alasdair MacIntyre, *After Virtue* (Notre Dame, Ind.: University of Notre Dame Press, 1984), p. 114.
4. Joseph L. Badaracco, *Defining Moments* (Boston: Harvard Business School Press, 1997), p. 73.
5. Phillip L. Berman, ed., *The Courage of Conviction* (New York: Ballantine Books, 1985), p. 204.
6. Debra Benton, *Secrets of a CEO Coach* (New York: McGraw-Hill, 1999).

eight: WHAT MONEY CANNOT BUY

1. Ron Chernow, *The House of Morgan* (New York: Simon & Schuster, 1990), p. 154.
2. Francis Fukuyama, *Trust* (New York: Free Press, 1995), p. 310.
3. Fukuyama, p. 311.
4. Robert Bruce Shaw, *Trust in the Balance* (San Francisco: Jossey-Bass, 1997), p. 21.
5. Robert E. Sherwood, *Roosevelt and Hopkins: An Intimate History* (New York: Harper & Brothers, 1948), p. 269.
6. Sherwood, p. 212.
7. Stephen L. Carter, *Integrity* (New York: HarperPerennial, 1997), p. 7.
8. Carter, p. 7.
9. Several authors have discussed the idea that there are no "tricks" for developing trust. For example, see Gerald M. Weinberg, *The Secrets of Consulting* (New York: Dorset House, 1985), p. 198.
10. Joseph L. Badaracco summarizes these points from Aristotle in *Defining Moments*, p. 52.
11. Badaracco, p. 82.
12. Carter, p. 33.
13. Stephen R. Covey, *The 7 Habits of Highly Effective People* (New York: Simon & Schuster, 1989), p. 196.
14. Ernest Hemingway, *Death in the Afternoon* (New York: Simon & Schuster, 1996), p. 4.
15. Leslie Kaufman, "Failed at Your Last Job? Wonderful! You're Hired," *The New York Times*, October 6, 1999, p. C12.

nine: DILEMMAS AND PITFALLS

1. James Hangar, *The Atlas of Sacred Places: Meeting Points of Heaven and Earth* (New York: Henry Holt, 1993), p. 194.
2. Alfred P. Sloan, Jr., *My Years with General Motors* (New York: Doubleday, 1990), p. vi.

ten: THE SOUL OF THE GREAT PROFESSIONAL

1. Several authors have treated this subject at length, including Stephen Covey (e.g., see *The 7 Habits of Highly Effective People*, p. 219) and Wayne Dyer.
2. Lucy McCauley, "The State of the New Economy," *Fast Company*, September 19, 1999, p. 120.
3. Niccolò Machiavelli, *The Prince* (London: Penguin Books, 1995), p. 39.
4. Cited in Wayne W. Dyer, *Real Magic* (New York: HarperCollins, 1992), p. 7.
5. McCauley, p. 111.
6. Robert E. Sherwood, *Roosevelt and Hopkins: An Intimate History* (New York: Harper & Brothers, 1948), p. 44.
7. Tom Peters, *The Professional Service Firm 50* (Alfred A. Knopf, 1999), p. 67.

ACKNOWLEDGMENTS

THIS BOOK BEGAN five years ago as a small, undeveloped idea fueled mainly by the authors' enthusiasm. We had the basis for a concept, but the detailed findings came later after several years of hard work. You especially tend to remember those who got excited along with you at the beginning—the early converts, so to speak—and foremost among them was James Kelly, a renowned consultant and best-selling author in his own right. James not only encouraged this project from the start but, even more usefully, challenged our ideas and critiqued our progress along the way.

Helen Rees, our agent, also believed in the book early on but, more important, she continually pushed us to sharpen and develop our ideas. A good exemplar of *selfless independence*, Helen was devoted to the cause but always told us what she thought, and she was usually right. Pat Wright helped us put our writing and ideas in shape from book proposal through to final copy, and like a good adviser provided not just editorial expertise but solid ideas and big-picture thinking. Michael Shnayerson, an accomplished author and friend, gave us guidance and encouragement from the beginning as well.

Fred Hills of Simon & Schuster, a truly wise editor, provided insight, encouragement, and tough love as we shaped the manuscript. Dr. Raymond Sobel, emeritus professor of psychiatry at Dartmouth Medical School, and father of coauthor Andrew Sobel, was a constant sounding board during the project, contributing ideas but generally trying just to listen without giving too much advice, showing that wisdom does indeed increase with age.

We're very grateful to the many client executives, professional advisers, and others who took their valuable time to speak with us and share their insights and perspectives. It would be unfair to single out any one of them; most are listed at the end of this section. They all made important contributions, and many are quoted in the text.

Top-flight research support was provided by Hugh Elliot, for whom no information request was too obscure; and Elizabeth Eaton artfully turned our charts into first-rate illustrations. Thanks, finally, to the group of individuals who reviewed various stages of the manuscript and made substantive, helpful suggestions: Salvatore Amato, Warren Bennis, Fred Brown, Barbara Hendra, Anne Johnson, James Kelly, Paul Naumann, Andy Sinauer, Mary Jane Sobel, Ben Strickland, and Siva Wilde.

SPECIAL THANKS TO:*

DUANE ACKERMAN	Chief Executive, BellSouth
SALVATORE AMATO	Vice President, A. T. Kearney
PAUL BASZUCKI	Chief Executive, Norstan
WARREN BENNIS	Distinguished Professor of Business Administration, University of Southern California
WIN BISCHOFF	Chairman, Schroders
MEL BLAKE	Chief of Staff, FleetBoston Financial
KENNETH BLANCHARD	Coauthor, *The One Minute Manager*
DAVID BLUMENTHAL	Jay and Leslie Cohen Professor of Judaic Studies, Emory University
JOSEPH BOWER	Donald K. David Professor of Business Administration, Harvard Business School
WAYNE G. BROEHL, JR.	Benjamin Ames Kimball Professor of the Science of Management (emeritus), Amos Tuck School of Business
FRED BROWN	Financial Consultant
WES CANTRELL	Chief Executive, Lanier Worldwide
SCOTT CUNNINGHAM	Managing Director, Cos Cob Associates
A. W. "BILL" DAHLBERG	Chief Executive, Southern Company
ANDREA DE CHOLNOKY	Senior Director, Spencer Stuart
STEFANO DELLA PIETRA	Chief Executive, CIT Group
ALAN DERSHOWITZ	Felix Frankfurter Professor of Law, Harvard Law School
BENJAMIN EDWARDS, III	Chief Executive, A. G. Edwards
GEORGE FISHER	Chief Executive, Kodak
EILEEN FRIARS	President, Bank of America Card Services
ORIT GADIESH	Chief Executive, Bain & Company
TOM GAGE	President, Marconi Pacific

Title or position at time of interview.

BOB GALVIN	Chairman of the Executive Committee, Motorola
VITO GAMBERALE	Chairman, Telecom Italia Mobile
MICHAEL GORMLEY	Physician
GENERAL ALFRED GRAY	Commandant (ret.), U.S. Marine Corps
JAMES HEFFERNAN	Frederick Sessions Beebe '35 Professor in the Art of Writing, Dartmouth College
LAURA HERRING	President, The IMPACT Group
ANNE JOHNSON	Principal, IBM Global Services
REGINALD JONES	Chief Executive (ret.), General Electric
GENERAL GEORGE JOULWAN	U.S. Supreme Army Commander (ret.), Europe
JAMES KELLY	Cofounder, the MAC Group and former Chairman, Gemini Consulting
STEVE KERR	Vice President of Corporate Leadership and Development and Chief Learning Officer, General Electric
EDWARD KNAPP	Director (ret.), National Science Foundation
DAVID LAGOMARSINO	Associate Professor of History, Dartmouth College
FRED LAWRENCE	Chief Executive, Adaptive Broadband
BILL LEIGH	President, The Leigh Bureau
CHARLES M. LILLIS	Chief Executive, MediaOne
GIANNI LORENZONI	Professor of Management, University of Bologna
PAUL MANOD	Professor of History, Middlebury College
ANN MEDLOCK	Founder and Director, the Giraffe Project
RON MOELLER	Senior Vice President–Investments, A. G. Edwards
PAUL NAUMANN	Managing Director, Deutsche Banc Alex. Brown
CARLOS PALOMARES	Chairman, Citibank International
NANCY PERETSMAN	Executive Vice President and Managing Director, Allen & Company
BRIAN PITMAN	Chairman, Lloyds TSB Group
C. K. PRAHALAD	Harvey C. Fruehauf Professor of Business Administration, University of Michigan Business School

J. Brian Quinn	William and Josephine Buchanan Professor of Management (emeritus), Amos Tuck School of Business
Jim Robbins	Chief Executive, Cox Communications
James Robinson	Chief Executive (ret.), American Express
Eric Silverman	Managing Partner, Milbank Tweed
Andrew Sinauer	President, Sinauer Associates
Ray Smith	Chairman, Bell Atlantic
Raymond Sobel	Professor of Psychiatry (emeritus), Dartmouth Medical School
Linda Srere	Chief Client Officer and Chief Executive, Young & Rubicam New York
Ben Strickland	Chairman, Iron Cross Insurance
Randall Tobias	Chief Executive, Eli Lilly
Siva Wilde	Psychotherapist
Walter Wriston	Chief Executive (ret.), Citibank

ABOUT THE AUTHORS

THE AUTHORS have collectively spent over fifty years consulting to and advising senior management in several hundred organizations around the world. Jagdish Sheth, Ph.D., is the Charles H. Kellstadt Professor of Marketing at the Goizueta Business School, Emory University. A distinguished educator, author, speaker, and senior management adviser, Dr. Sheth has been rated as one of the top business professors in the country. He is internationally known for his intellectual insight in the areas of market strategies, global competition, strategic thinking, and customer relationship management, and he has published over 200 articles and research papers and 12 books in different areas of marketing and business strategy. He is the founder of the Center for Telecommunications Management at the University of Southern California and the Center for Relationship Marketing at Emory University. He has won many awards, including the Viktor Mataja Medal from the Austrian Research Society, the Outstanding Marketing Educator Award from several organizations, and the American Marketing Association's Converse Award. Dr. Sheth is a Fellow of the American Psychological Association, and a Distinguished Fellow of the Academy of Marketing Science and the International Engineering Consortium. His corporate clients have included AT&T, Ford, General Motors, Motorola, Nortel, Texas Instruments, Whirlpool, Young & Rubicam, and dozens of other major organizations. Dr. Sheth serves as corporate director of Norstan, PacWest, and Wipro.

Andrew Sobel has spent twenty years as an adviser to senior executives in over thirty countries around the world, helping both service firms and high-technology companies create winning strategies, renew their organizations, and develop client- and customer-focused cultures. His clients have included companies such as American Express, Citigroup, Cox Communications, Hewitt Associates, Lanier Worldwide, Lloyds Bank, Pacific Bell, and Telecom Italia. He was a senior vice president of one of the world's largest management consulting firms and co-founded its international practice, helping it to grow from four to 800 professionals and $300 million in revenue. He served as an office head, country managing director, and member of the European Management Committee. During this time he led many large, complex client engagements in both strategy development and implementation and was responsible for successfully hiring and training hundreds of high-performance professionals. He is a graduate of Middlebury College and earned his MBA from the Amos Tuck School of Business at Dartmouth. He lived and worked abroad for thirteen years and speaks four languages. Andrew currently heads his own strategy consulting firm and speaks frequently to corporate audiences around the world about how to develop breakthrough client relationships.

Please contact the authors with comments or queries: *jag@jagsheth.com* or *andrew@andrewsobel.com,* whose site contains additional material and downloadable articles on developing clients for life.